ANECDOTE BIOGRAPHIES

OF

THACKERAY AND DICKENS

Bric-a-Brac Series

ANECDOTE BIOGRAPHIES

OF

THACKERAY AND DICKENS

EDITED BY

RICHARD HENRY STODDARD

NEW YORK
SCRIBNER, ARMSTRONG, AND COMPANY
1874

RIVERSIDE, CAMBRIDGE:
STEREOTYPED AND PRINTED BY
H. O. HOUGHTON AND COMPANY.

CONTENTS.

PREFACE.

IF we could analyze carefully the various elements contained in a good biography, and decide which interested us most in the reading, and which we remembered longest after the reading, I think we would discover that it was the element of Anecdote. The chief facts in a biography — the general drift of the life of its subject — may impress themselves upon the memory for a time, but that which remains permanently, and which refuses to be forgotten, is something different from these, — some incident or incidents in the life in question — a smart saying, a humorous jest, a rapier thrust of wit, — it may be anything that is salient. We remember somewhat, perhaps, of the life of Lamb, for example: how he went to Christ's Hospital with Coleridge; how he was a clerk in the India House; how he wrote "Elia," and so on; what we certainly remember, if we have any feeling, is his going across the fields with his sister Mary to the mad-house, in which it was necessary that she should be confined, and weeping with her, as he went; what we can never forget, if we have any sense of humor, are his humorous sayings.

Apart from their works, we remember different authors for different reasons, but generally for what their biographers would consider trifles; but which are not trifles in that they make us forget the biographers. As a rule we have too much of the biographer in the biography. What we want is the man whose life he purports to narrate, not as he sees him, but as he was, — dressed in his habit as he lived, in his dressing-gown and slippers, if need be. The average biographer objects to this, as he generally objects to telling the whole truth — when it would injure the character of his hero. As if all men, the greatest and best, were not compounded of the same poor clay as the rest of us! The wine they drink is made of grapes; their headaches are as veritable, and perhaps a trifle more frequent, than ours.

Most biographers start with preconceived ideas regarding the characters they are to depict, and with the mistaken notion that these characters, when depicted, should be rounded and harmonious. They also mistake the nature of their office, which is not that of a special pleader, either for good or evil. They should take their men, as they were, not as they would have them: should state what they did, not what they might have done:

> "Nothing extenuate,
> Nor set aught down in malice:"

and, their work being finished, they should leave it, as Bacon left his tarnished fame and memory, "to men's charitable speeches, to foreign nations, and the next ages." They may throw dust in the eyes of their contemporaries, but the vision of Posterity will be clear. Posterity will judge their work, and, likely enough, will judge it by apparent trifles, — trifles which are omitted, but which Posterity will recover, and upon which it will set an inestimable value. Such priceless trifles may take the form of anecdotes, which frequently reveal what the biographers have concealed, and which are surer indications of character than the most labored biographies. Fuller's description of the "wit combats" between Shakespeare and Ben Jonson is the liveliest and most graphic presentation extant of the two men.

The two great men to whom this little volume is devoted will pass, we may be sure, under the sharp scrutiny of Posterity. They divided in their life-time the suffrages of all who speak and read the English tongue; but they cannot be said to have divided it equally, for one sprang into popularity, — a popularity which he retained to the day of his death, while the other labored long before he was recognized; his reputation was wrung from the world. They had their adherents, as Jonson and Shakespeare had theirs, and battles were fought about them, they remaining the while, let us hope, indifferent, but amused, spectators of the fight. The biography of one has been written; the biography of the other has not. There will be no biography of Thackeray, if his wishes and the wishes of his daughters are respected.

This being the case, it seems to me that a collection of the best papers that have been written concerning him, — the best, I mean, in an anecdotal sense, — will be acceptable to his admirers. I have accordingly made the collection which follows, and which contains, I believe, everything that is worthy of preservation in the shape of personal reminiscence of this great writer and great and good man. It contains at least everything that has come within my own observation, with the exception of a lively sketch in Mr. James T. Fields's "Yesterdays with Authors," which I cannot accept as a faithful portrait of Thackeray, although it may, perhaps, reflect one side of his nature with tolerable accuracy. The writer obtrudes himself too much, and his tone, if I am not mistaken, is one of condescension towards the robust-minded gentleman who honored him with his friendship.

A few words in regard to the Thackerayana here, may not be without interest. The opening paper — "Haud Immemor. — Thackeray in America," was written by Mr. William B. Reed, of this city, formerly of Philadelphia, and at one time, United States Minister in China. Mr. Reed printed a private edition of this charming Monograph, which was written in May, 1864, — a copy of which found its way across the ocean, and was reprinted in "Blackwood" for June, 1872. It is reprinted here by his permission. The brother of Mr. Reed to whom reference is made on page 7, Mr. Henry Reed, was one of the most thoughtful scholars of English Literature that America has yet produced. Born in Philadelphia in 1808 he entered the Sophomore Class at the University of Pennsylvania in 1822, and was graduated as Bachelor of Arts in 1825. He began the study of law, and four years later was admitted to the bar. In 1831 he relinquished his practice and was elected Assistant Professor of English Literature in the University. In 1835, his twenty-seventh year, he was elected Professor of Rhetoric and English Literature. In 1854 he visited England, where he was warmly received by a host of friends, beginning with Wordsworth, with whom he had long corresponded, and whose reputation he had enhanced in America, and ending with Thackeray, — a bead-roll of illustrious names, including the Southeys, Coleridges, and Arnolds, Lord Mahon, Aubrey de Vere, and Mr. — now Sir, — Henry Taylor. It was while returning from this visit, on the 27th of September, 1854, almost in sight of his native land, that the *Arctic*, the ship upon which he had taken passage, sank, with nearly every soul on board. His literary remains were edited by Mr.

William B. Reed. They are "Lectures on English Literature, from Chaucer to Tennyson" (Phila. 1855); and "Lectures on the British Poets" (Phila. 1857). The loss of Mr. Henry Reed was a loss to American scholarship.

To continue with our Thackerayana: — "Thackeray's Literary Career" is reprinted by permission of Messrs. J. R. Osgood & Co. from the second series of "Spare Hours," by Dr. John Brown, of Edinburgh, who remarks in a note that the larger and better part of this paper is by his young and accomplished friend, Henry H. Lancaster, Advocate. "Some Recollections of Thackeray," "A Friend of my Childhood," and "A Child's Glimpse of Thackeray," are reprinted, by permission, from the pages of "Lippincott's Magazine." "Hodder's Recollections of Thackeray" are taken from a volume of "Memories," the exact title of which escapes me. The eight short papers that follow, — anecdotes, let us say, — are taken, with one exception, from "Thackeray, the Humorist, and the Man of Letters," by Theodore Taylor, *Membre de la Société des Gens de Lettres* (London, 1864), a collection of Thackerayana, made shortly after Thackeray's death. The exception, "Personal Appearance of Thackeray," is extracted from Mr. Blanchard Jerrold's "Best of all Good Company." Mr. Shirley Brooks's paper appeared in the "London Illustrated News;" Mr. James Hannay's in the "Edinburgh Courant," of which he was the editor; and Mr. Dickens's "In Memoriam" in the "Cornhill Magazine." The "Obituary Poems" are from several sources. The first appeared in "Punch;" the second in "Fun;" and the third, which was written by Lord Houghton, in the "Cornhill." The fourth was written by Dr. Thomas W. Parsons, of Boston; the last was written by myself.

A number of Thackeray anecdotes have fallen in

my way while this volume has been passing through the press. Here is one which was related by the late Charles Sumner: "When Thackeray was in this city (Washington), we visited, among the earlier places, the capitol rotunda. Thackeray was an artist by birthright, and his judgment was beyond chance or question. He took a quiet turn around the rotunda, and in a few words gave each picture its perfectly correct rank and art valuation. 'Trumbull is your painter;' he said, 'never neglect Trumbull.' Other places of interest were then seen, after which we started homeward. He had not yet been at my house, and my chief anxiety was to coach him safely past that Jackson statue. The conversation hung persistently upon art matters, which made it certain that I was to have trouble when we should come in view of that particular excrescence. We turned the dreaded corner at last, when, to my astonishment, Mr. Thackeray held straight past the hideous figure, moving his head neither to the right nor left, and chatting as airily as though we were strolling through an English park. Now I know that the instant we came in sight of poor Jackson's caricature he saw it, realized its accumulated terrors at a glance, and in the charity of his great heart took all pains to avoid having a word said about it. Ah, but he was a man of rare consideration."

Here is a cluster of little anecdotes: "Thackeray was not a humorist, in the sense that Dickens was, nor a wit, in the sense that Jerrold was, but he now and then said a good thing in a quiet way. He was pestered on one occasion, while in this country, by a young gentleman of an inquiring turn of mind, as to what was thought of this person and that person in England. 'Mr. Thackeray,' he asked, 'what do they think of Tupper?' 'They don't think of Tupper,' was the reply. Another man of letters was mentioned, and it transpired that he was addicted to beer drinking. 'Yes,' said Thackeray, 'take him for half and half he was a man.' His connection with 'Fraser's Magazine' was the subject of conversation, and the right of an editor to change the 'copy' of his contributors was discussed. Thackeray maintained that no such right existed, except as regarded errors of grammar, and declared that the only person who could make alterations for the better was the author himself; as a rule, editorial changes were blunders. 'I told an editor so once and he did not like it. "I have no objection to your putting your hoofs on my paragraphs," I remarked, "but I decidedly object to your sticking your ears through them."' 'He never forgave you, of course.' 'I never thought to ask.' Thackeray and Jerrold used to sit near each other at the 'Punch' dinners, and Jerrold was inclined to wrangle, if everthing was not to his liking; but Thackeray *would* keep the peace. 'There's no use in our quarreling,' he said, 'for we *must* meet again next week.'"

The last poem that we shall probably have from the pen of Thackeray was lately found among his papers. It sees the light in the June number of the "Cornhill."

KING FRITZ.

King Fritz at his palace of Berlin
 I saw at a royal carouse,
In a periwig powdered and curling
 He sat with his hat on his brows.
The handsome young princes were present,
 Uncovered they stood in the hall;
And oh! it was wholesome and pleasant
 To see how he treated them all!

Reclined on the softest of cushions
 His Majesty sits to his meats,

The princes, like loyal young Prussians,
  Have never a back to their seats.
Off salmon and venison and pheasants
  He dines like a monarch august:
His sons, if they eat in his presence,
  Put up with a bone or a crust.

He quaffs his bold bumpers of Rhenish,
  It can't be too good or too dear,
His princes are made to replenish
  Their cups with the smallest of beer.
If ever, by words or grimaces,
  Their highnesses dare to complain,
The King flings a dish in their faces,
  Or batters their bones with his cane.

'T is thus that the chief of our nation
  The minds of his children improves,
And teaches polite education
  By boxing the ears that he loves.
I warrant they vex him but seldom,
  And so if we dealt with our sons,
If we up with our cudgels and felled 'em,
  We 'd teach 'em good manners at once.

Thackeray was sensitive, satirist though he was, and cannot be acquitted of techyness, in regard to what was written concerning himself, and his private affairs. When it came to large things, — to his work and his life, — he was supremely indifferent. He left his Work to the world, as Shakespeare did : his Life was of no importance. He left no record of it, and he would not have it related. It was otherwise with Dickens, as we cannot but feel after reading Mr. Forster's Life of him. He was from the beginning conscious that he was a man of genius, and conscious that the world would one day want to know all about him. He never forgot himself in his work, though he loved his work because it was a part of himself. There was an intellectual selfishness in him from which the larger and stronger nature of Thackeray was free. It is not my intention, however, to draw comparisons between the two men ; and, if it were, this is not the place to do it.

It is to be regretted that the Life of Thackeray has not been written. It is also to be regretted that the Life of Dickens has been written, — at least by Mr. Forster. Mr. Forster has long been credited with qualities which go to the making of a good biographer. His Life of Goldsmith was a good one, of its kind. His Life of Landor, whatever its kind, was not good. It was not so much a Life of Landor, as a series of long and rather dull criticisms upon his writings ; altogether it was a tedious book. His Life of Dickens is not tedious — it could not well be that — but it is constructed, I venture to think, upon an erroneous plan, and it is narrow, in that it presents Dickens only as he was seen by Mr. Forster. A voluminous letter-writer all his life, Dickens must have written letters to other persons than Mr. Forster, — letters that are as worthy of preservation as those that he has preserved, and are as worthy of a place in his Memoir as those that were written to him. He had, he could have, no exclusive right to knowledge of Dickens, despite his life-long intimacy with him and his friendship for him. Dickens was known to many besides Mr. Forster, and known differently to them than to him. He does not appear to think so, and the result is his narrow and unsatisfactory Life of Dickens. It is an interesting, an instructive, and a painful book.

It has been completed so recently, and has been so widely read, that any extracts from it would be out of place here. I have indicated what seems to me some of its defects: I have not named one which is prominent — the absence of anecdotes. Mr. Forster's ideal of Biography is graver than suits most readers. He does not unbend, nor let his hero unbend enough. The gossip concerning Dickens which was called forth by his death, — the recollections of those who were acquainted with him at the beginning of his literary career, — these are naught to Mr. Foster. They possess — they could not but possess — interest, springing as they did spontaneously from the memories of their writers, to whom the sudden taking off Dickens was like the loss of a personal friend. They possess, at any rate, a freshness which is not imparted by Mr. Forster to any of the facts, or incidents, to which they refer, or which they embody.

The greater portion of the anecdotes about Dickens in this volume are derived from "Charles Dickens, the Story of his Life." It was published in London not long after his death, and is the work of Mr. Theodore Taylor, whom I have already mentioned, and who was a diligent collector of Dickens *ana*. I have not a very high idea of the class of writers to which he belongs, but they are not without their uses, as Mr. John Timbs, the head of the class, has shown. They preserve many things which would perish but for them; occasionally a jewel may be found among their paste. Mr. Blanchard Jerrold's paper is taken from his "Best of all Good Company;" the paper by Sir Arthur Helps from "Macmillan's Magazine," and "Reminiscences of Dickens" from the "Englishwoman's Magazine." The first of the obituary poems, "Charles Dickens," appeared in "Punch." "Dickens at Gad's Hill" was written by Mr. Charles Kent, and published, I believe, in the "Athenæum." "Dickens in Camp" was written by Mr. Bret Harte; "At Gad's Hill" was written by myself.

The anecdote in relation to "Oliver Twist," on page 211, has been the subject of a controversy, which was begun with bitterness by Mr. Foster, and continued with pertinacity by Mr. Cruikshank. Mr. Forster reprints it in his "Life of Dickens" (vol i. page 155), and stigmatizes it as "a wonderful story originally promulgated in America with a minute conscientiousness and particularity of detail that might have raised the reputation of Sir Benjamin Backbite himself. Whether all Sir Benjamin's laurels, however, should fall to the original teller of the tale, or whether any part of them is the property of the alleged authority from which he says that he received it, is unfortunately not quite clear. There would hardly have been a doubt, if the fable had been confined to the other side of the Atlantic; but it has been reproduced and widely circulated on this side also; and the distinguished artist whom it calumniates by fathering its invention upon him, either not conscious of it or not caring to defend himself, has been left undefended from the slander." That the distinguished artist did care to defend himself, and could do so, Mr. Forster discovered when he read the following letter in the column, of the "London Times."

"*To the Editor of 'The Times.'*

"SIR, — As my name is mentioned in the second notice of Mr. John Forster's 'Life of Charles Dickens,' in your paper of the 26th inst., in connection with a statement made by an American gentleman (Dr. Sheldon Mackenzie) respecting the origin of 'Oliver Twist,' I shall be obliged if you will allow me to give some explanation upon this subject. For some time past I have been preparing a work for publication, in which I intend to give an account of the origin of 'Oliver Twist,' and I now not only deeply regret the sudden and unexpected decease of Mr. Charles Dickens, but regret also that my proposed work was not published during his life-time. I should not now have brought this matter forward, but as Dr. Mackenzie states that he got the information from me, and as Mr. Forster declares his statement to be a falsehood, to which, in fact, he could apply a word of three letters, I feel called upon, not only to defend the doctor, but myself also from such a gross imputation. Dr. Mackenzie has confused some circumstances with respect to Mr. Dickens looking over some drawings and sketches in my studio, but there is no doubt whatever that I did tell this gentleman that I was the originator of the story of 'Oliver Twist,' as I have told very many others who may have spoken to me on the subject, and which facts I now beg permission to repeat in the columns of 'The Times' for the information of Mr. Forster and the public generally.

"When 'Bentley's Miscellany' was first started, it was arranged that Mr. Charles Dickens should write a serial in it, and which was to be illustrated by me; and in a conversation with him as to what the subject should be for the first serial, I suggested to Mr. Dickens that he should write the life of a London boy, and strongly advised him to do this, assuring him that I would furnish him with the subject and supply him with all the characters, which my large experience of London life would enable me to do. My idea was to raise a boy from a most humble position up to a high and respectable one — in fact, to illustrate one of those cases of common occurrence, where men of humble origin by natural ability, industry, honest and honorable conduct, raise themselves to first-class positions in society. And as I wished particularly to bring the habits and manners of the thieves of London before the public (and this for a most important purpose, which I shall explain one of these days), I suggested that the poor boy should fall among thieves, but that his honesty and natural good disposition should enable him to pass through this ordeal without contamination, and after I had fully described the full-grown thieves (the 'Bill Sykes') and their female companions, also the young thieves (the 'Artful Dodgers') and the receivers of stolen goods, Mr. Dickens agreed to act upon my suggestion, and the work was commenced, but we differed as to what sort of boy the hero should be. Mr. Dickens wanted rather a queer kind of chap, and although this was contrary to my original idea, I complied with his request, feeling that it would not be right to dictate too much to the writer of the story, and then appeared 'Oliver asking for more;' but it so happened, just about this time, that an inquiry was being made in the parish of St. James, Westminster, as to the cause of the death of some of the work-house children who had been 'farmed out,' and in which inquiry my late friend Joseph Pettigrew (surgeon to the Dukes of Kent and Sussex) came forward on the part of the poor children, and by his interference was mainly the cause of saving the lives of many of these poor little creatures. I called the attention of Mr. Dickens to this inquiry, and said if he took up this matter his doing so might help to save many a poor child from injury and death, and I earnestly begged of him to let me make Oliver a nice pretty little boy, and if we so represented him, the public — and particularly the ladies — would be sure to take a greater interest in him, and the work would then be a certain success. Mr. Dickens agreed to that request, and I need not add here that my prophecy was fulfilled; and if any one will take the trouble to look at my representations of 'Oliver' they will see that the appearance of the boy is altered after the two first illustrations, and by a reference to the records of St. James's parish, and to the date of the publication of the 'Miscellany,' they will see that both the dates tally, and therefore support my statement. I had a long time previously to this directed Mr. Dickens's attention to 'Field Lane,' Holborn Hill, wherein resided many thieves and receivers of stolen goods, and it was suggested that one of these receivers, a Jew, should be introduced into the story; and upon one occasion Mr. Dickens and Mr. Harrison Ainsworth called upon me at my house in Myddleton Terrace, Pentonville, and in course of conversation I then and there described and performed the character of one of these Jew receivers, who I had long had my eye upon; and this was the origin of 'Fagan.' Some time after this Mr. Ainsworth said to me one day, 'I was so much struck with your description of that Jew to Mr. Dickens, that I think you and I could do something together,' which notion of Mr. Ainsworth's, as most people are aware, was afterwards carried out in various works. Long before 'Oliver Twist' was ever thought of, I had, by permission of the city authorities, made a sketch of one of the condemned cells in Newgate prison; and as I had a great object in letting the public see what sort of places these cells were, and how they were furnished, and also to show a wretched condemned criminal therein, I thought it desirable to introduce such a subject into this work; but I had the greatest difficulty to get Mr. Dickens to allow me to carry out my wishes in this respect, but I said I must have either what is called a Christian, or what is called a Jew in a condemned cell, and therefore it must be 'Bill Sykes' or 'Fagan;' at length he allowed me to exhibit the latter.

"Without going further into particulars, I think it will be allowed from what I have stated that I am the originator of 'Oliver Twist,' and that all the principal characters are mine; but I was much disappointed by Mr. Dickens not fully carrying out my first suggestion.

"I must here mention that nearly all the designs were made from conversation and mutual suggestion upon each subject, and that I never saw any manuscript of Mr. Dickens until the work was nearly finished, and the letter of Mr. Dickens, which Mr. Forster mentions, only refers to the last etching — done in great haste — no proper time being allowed, and of a subject without any interest; in fact, there was not anything in the latter part of the manuscript that would suggest an illustration; but to oblige Mr. Dickens I did my best to produce another etching, working hard day and night, but when done, what is it? Why, merely a lady and a boy standing inside of a church looking at a stone wall!

"Mr. Dickens named all the characters in this work himself, but before he had commenced writing the story he told me that he had heard an omnibus conductor mention some one as Oliver Twist, which name, he said, he would give the boy, as he thought it would answer his purpose. I wanted the boy to have a very different name, such as Frank Foundling or Frank Steadfast; but I think the word Twist proves to a certain extent that the boy he was going to employ for his purpose was a very different sort of boy from the one introduced and recommended to him by, Sir, your obedient servant,

GEORGE CRUIKSHANK.

"HAMPSTEAD ROAD, *Dec.* 29, 1871."

Mr. Forster refers to this letter in the corrections to the first volume of his "Life of Dickens," and says in regard to "the foregoing fable" that "Mr. Cruikshank is to be congratulated on the prudence of his rigid silence respecting it so long as Mr. Dickens lived." As Mr. Forster had seen, while he was writing his first volume, the "Life of Dickens" by Dr. R. Shelton Mackenzie, in which it is stated that Mr. Cruikshank laid claim to "Oliver Twist" as far back as 1847, twenty-three years before the death of Dickens, Mr. Forster is to be congratulated for — what?

But Mr. Cruikshank made other claims than the one in regard to "Oliver Twist," for in a published letter written, over a year earlier than the letter to the "Times," he wrote, "I was the first artist to illustrate any of Mr. Dickens's writings, and the earliest of them was the first volume of 'Sketches by Boz' (January, 1836), and the next was the second volume under this title, the greater part of which was written from my hints and suggestions." He continues, in the same letter, "I am preparing to publish an explanation of the reason why I did not illustrate the *whole* of Mr. Dickens's writings, and this explanation will not at all redound to his credit." That Mr. Cruikshank believed then, and believes now, that Dickens was largely indebted to him, is evident from a speech delivered by him on the 20th of April of the present year. The following paragraph in relation to it appeared in the "London Globe" of April 21st: "Mr. George Cruikshank delivered an address yesterday on intemperance, at Manchester. In supporting a vote of thanks to the veteran artist the Mayor referred to Mr. Cruikshank's illustration of Charles Dickens's works. Mr. Cruikshank, in responding, said the only work of Dickens which he had illustrated was 'The Sketches by Boz.' Then came the question why he had not illustrated the others. The Mayor: You forget 'Oliver Twist.' — Mr. Cruikshank: That came out of my own brain. I wanted Dickens to write me a work, but he did not do it in the way I wanted. I assure you I went and made a sketch of the condemned cell many years before that work was published. I wanted a scene a few hours before the strangulation, and Dickens said he did not like it, and I said he must have a Jew or a Christian in the cell. Dickens said, 'Do as you like,' and I put Fagan, the Jew, into the cell. Dickens behaved in an extraordinary way to me, and I believe it had a little effect on his mind. He was a most powerful opponent to teetotalism, and he described us as 'old hogs.' "

That something has had a little effect upon the mind of Mr. Cruikshank is evident from his language, which must be characterized as rather intemperate in the mouth of a veteran teetotaler. It is not in this *rôle*, however, nor as the originator of "Oliver Twist," that he will be known to posterity, but as an artist of peculiar and great power, who in the latter part of his long and active life created materials for a chapter which has yet to be written in the "Curiosities of Literature," and which should be christened "The Delusions of an Artist."

R. H. S.

WILLIAM MAKEPEACE THACKERAY.

Haud Immemor. — Thackeray in America.

R. THACKERAY (who that has heard him with sweetness of voice unequaled, speak of Mr. Joseph Addison, and Mr. Congreve, and Mr. Fielding, and Mr. Atterbury; who that has read "Henry Esmond," or "The Virginians," — will find fault with me for so describing him?) came to Philadelphia on his first visit to America in the month of January, 1853. My impression is that he brought very few letters of personal introduction, and was rather careless of what may be called "social success," though anxious about the work he had in hand, — his course of lectures on the English Humorists, — and, as he used to say, "the dollars he wished to make, not for himself, but for his little girls at home." With or without letters, he soon made friends, on the hearts of whom the news of his death has struck a sharp pang. As one of them, I venture to jot down a few memories of him who is gone.

The lectures were very successful. There are two classes of people in every American microcosm — those who run after celebrities, and those, resolute not to be pleased, who run as it were against them. All were won or conquered by his simple naturalness; and, as I have said, the lectures were a great success.

My personal relations to him happened to become very intimate. He seemed to take a fancy to me and mine, and I naturally loved him dearly. He used to come to my house, not the abode of wealth or luxury, almost every day, and often more than once a day. He talked with my little children, and told them odd fairy tales; and I now see him (this was on his second visit) one day in Walnut Street walking slowly along with my little girl by the hand — the tall, gray-haired, spectacled man with an effort accommodating himself to the toddling child by his side; and then he would bring her home: and one day when we were to have a great dinner at the club given to him, and my wife was ill, and my household disarranged, and the bell rang, and I said to him, "I must go and carve the boiled mutton for the children, and take for granted you do not care to come;" and he got up, and with a cheery voice, said, "I love boiled mutton, and children too, and I will dine with them," and we did; and he was happy, and the children were happy, and our appetite for the club dinner was damaged. Such was Thackeray in my home.

I met him once at the house of a friend, and there happened to be an odd collocation at the table. There was a guest, a man of brilliant talent, of mature age, and high education, measured at least by our American standard, who was marked by two peculiarities — his remarkable physical resemblance to Thackeray, and the fact that, although upwards of fifty years of age, born and bred in Kentucky, he had never before crossed the Alleghanies, and never until that very day seen a ship, or any square-rigged vessel. They — the bright backwoodsman, who had never looked upon the ocean, and the veteran Londoner, who had made a voyage from India before the days of steam, and had seen a fat man in white clothes and a big straw hat at St. Helena called "Buonaparte" — were a charming contrast. The year 1863 carried both to their graves — one in Kensal Green, and the other on the banks of the Ohio.

It was a bright moonlight night on which we (Thackeray and I) walked home from that dinner: and I remember well the walk and the place, for I seem to localize all my associations with him, and I asked him what, perhaps, he might have thought the absurd question, "What do you honestly think of my country? or rather, what has most struck you in America? Tell me candidly, for I shall not be at all angry or hurt if it be unfavorable, or much elated if it be not." And then his answer, as he stopped (we were walking along Penn Square), and, turning round to me, said: "You know what a virtue-proud people we English are. We think we have got it all to ourselves. Now that which most impresses me here is, that I find homes as pure as ours, firesides like ours, domestic virtues as gentle; the English language, though the accent be a little different, with its home-like melody; and the Common Prayer Book in your families. I am more struck by pleasant resemblances than by anything else." And so I sincerely believe he was.

There was a great deal of dining out while "the great satirist," as we used to address him, was here; but although always genial, I do not think, according to my recollection, he was a brilliant conversationist. Those who expected much were often disappointed. It was in close private intercourse he was delightful. Once — it was in New York — he gave a dinner, at which I was a guest, to what are called "literary men," — authors and lawyers, and actors (two very accomplished ones, and most estimable gentlemen — one still living), and editors and magazine men. Then he made what seemed to be an effort. He talked for the table. He sang some odd post-prandial songs; one in a strange sort of a "recitative" about Doctor Martin Luther. But, as I have said, it was an effort, and I liked him better at home and alone. It was on this occasion, or rather on our return journey to Philadelphia, that, on board the steamboat (here again am I localizing), he spoke to me of domestic sorrows and anxieties too sacred to be recorded here.[1] And yet it was this man whom vulgar-

[1] He referred to a friend whose wife had been deranged for many years, hopelessly so; and never shall I forget the look, the manner, the voice with which he said to me: "It is an awful thing for her to continue so to live. It is an awful thing for her

minded people called heartless! As he thus talked to me, I thought of lines of tenderness, often quoted, which no one but he could have written: —

> "Ah me! how quick the days are flitting!
> I mind me of a time that 's gone,
> When here I 'd sit, as now I 'm sitting,
> In this same place, but not alone.
> A fair young form was nestled near me,
> A dear, dear face looked fondly up,
> And sweetly spoke and smiled to cheer me, —
> There 's no one now to share my cup."

It is no part of this little Memorial to refer to what may be called his public relations, and his success as a lecturer. I merely record my recollection of the peculiar voice and cadence; the exquisite manner of reading poetry; the elocution, matchless in its simplicity; his tranquil attitude — the only movement of his hands being when he wiped his glasses as he began and turned over the leaves of his manuscript; his gentle intonations. There was sweet music in his way of repeating the most hackneyed lines, which freshened them anew. I seem still to hear him say, —

> "And nightly to the listening earth
> Repeats the story of her birth."

Or, in his lecture on Pope, —

> "Lo! thy dread empire, chaos, is restored;
> Light dies before thy uncreating word.
> Thy hand, great Anarch! lets the curtain fall,
> And universal darkness buries all!"

But to resume my personal recollections. He was too sincere a man to talk for effect, or to pay compliments; and on his first visit to America, he seemed so happy, and so much pleased with all he met, that I fancied he might be tempted to come, and for a time live amongst us. The British Consulate in Philadelphia became vacant, the incumbent, Mr. William Peter, dying suddenly; and it seems from the following note,

so to die. But has it never occurred to you, how awful the recovery of lost reason must be, without the consciousness of the loss of time? She finds the lover of her youth a gray-haired old man, and her infants young men and women. Is it not sad to think of this?"

written at Washington, that I urged him to take the place if he could get it. I give the note exactly as it was written, venturing even to retain the names of those whom he kindly remembered; and Philadelphians of the old school will smile at the misspelling of the name of the founder of the Wistar parties of our ancient days.

"MR. ANDERSON'S MUSIC STORE, PENNS AVENUE (1853),
Friday.

"MY DEAR REED, — (I withdraw the Mr. as wasteful and ridiculous excess, and gilding of refined gold), and thank you for the famous autograph and the kind letter inclosing it, and the good wishes you form for me. There are half a dozen houses I already know in Philadelphia where I could find very pleasant friends and company; and that good old library would give me plenty of acquaintances more. But, home among my parents there, and some few friends I have made in the last twenty-five years, and a tolerably fair prospect of an honest livelihood on the familiar London flagstones, and the library at the Athenæum, and the ride in the Park, and the pleasant society afterwards; and a trip to Paris now and again, and to Switzerland and Italy in the summer — these are little temptations which make me not discontented with my lot, about which I grumble only for pastime, and because it is an Englishman's privilege. Own now that all these recreations here enumerated have a pleasant sound. I hope I shall live to enjoy them yet a little while before I go to '*nox et domus exilis Plutonia,*' whither poor, kind old Peter has vanished. So that Saturday I was to have dined with him, and Mrs. Peter wrote, saying he was ill with influenza: he was in bed with his last illness, and there were to be no more Whister parties for him. Will Whister himself, hospitable, pigtailed shade, welcome him to Hades? And will they sit down — no, stand up — to a ghostly supper, devouring the ιφθιμους ψυχας of oysters and all sorts of birds? I never feel pity for a man dying, only for survivors, if there be such passionately deploring him. You see the pleasures the undersigned proposes to himself here in future years — a sight of the Alps, a holiday on the Rhine, a ride in the Park, a colloquy with pleasant friends of an evening. If it is death to part with these delights (and pleasures they are and no mistake) sure the mind can conceive others afterwards; and I know one small philosopher who is quite ready to give up these pleasures; quite content (after a pang or two of separation from dear friends here) to put his hand into that of the summoning angel, and say, 'Lead on, O messenger of God our Father to the next place whither the divine goodness calls us!' We must be blindfolded before we can pass, I know; but I have no fear about what is to come, any more than my children need fear that the love of *their* father should fail them. I thought myself a dead man once, and protest the notion gave me no disquiet about myself — at least, the philosophy is more comfortable than that which is tinctured with brimstone.

"The Baltimoreans flock to the stale old lectures as numerously as you of Philadelphia. Here the audiences are more polite than numerous, but the people who do come are very well pleased with their entertainment. I have had many dinners. Mr. Everett, Mr. Fish — our minister, ever so often — the most hospital of envoys. I have seen no one at all in Baltimore, for it is impossible to *do* the two towns together; and from this I go to Richmond and Charlestown, not to New Orleans, which is too far; and I hope you will make out your visit to Washington, and that we shall make out a meeting more satisfactory than that dinner at New York, which did not come off. The combination failed which I wanted to bring about. Have you heard Miss Furness of Philadelphia sing? She is the best ballad-singer I ever heard. And will you please remember me to Mrs. Reed and your brother, and Wharton, and Lewis and his pretty young daughter; and believe me ever faithfully yours, dear Reed,

"W. M. THACKERAY."

The "famous autograph" was, if my memory does not mislead me, a letter of Washington, for which he had expressed a wish, and which I gladly gave him; and the plan of coming to America, as will be seen, though at first rejected, seems to have taken root in his mind.

Thackeray left us in the winter of 1853, and in the summer of the year was on the Continent with his daughters. In the last chapter of "The Newcomes," published in 1855, he says: "Two years ago, walking with my children in some pleasant fields near to Berne, in Switzerland, I strayed from them into a little wood; and coming out of it presently told them how the story had been revealed to me somehow, which for three-and-twenty months the reader has been pleased to follow." It was on this Swiss tour that he wrote me the following characteristic letter, filled with kindly recollections of convivial hours in Philadelphia, of headaches which he had contributed to administer, and of friends whose society he cherished. On the back of this note is a pen-and-ink caricature of which he was not conscious when he began to write. It is what he alludes to as "the rubbishing picture which I did n't see." The sketch is very spirited, and, as a friend to whom I have shown it reminds me, evidently is the original of one of the illustrations of his grotesque fairy tale of "The Rose and the Ring," written, so he told a member of my family years afterwards, while he was watching and nursing his children, who were ill during this vacation ramble.

NEUFCHATEL, SWITZERLAND, *July* 21, 1853.

"MY DEAR REED, — Though I am rather slow in paying the tailor, I always pay him: and as with tailors, so with men; I pay my debts to my friends, only at rather a long day. Thank you for writing to me so kindly, you who have so much to do. I have only begun to work ten days since, and now in consequence have a little leisure. Before, since my return from the West, it was flying from London to Paris, and *vice versa*, dinners right and left, parties every night. If I had been in Philadelphia, I could scarcely have been more feasted. Oh, you unhappy Reed! I see you (after that little supper with McMichael) on Sunday, at your own table, when we had that good Sherry-Madeira, turning aside from the wine-cup with your pale face! That cup has gone down this well so often (meaning my own private cavity), that I wonder the cup is n't broken, and the well as well as it is.

"Three weeks of London were more than enough for me, and I feel as if I had had enough of it and pleasure. Then I remained a month with my parents; then I brought my girls on a little pleasuring tour, and it has really been a pleasuring tour. We spent ten days at Baden, when I set intrepidly to work again; and have been five days in Switzerland now; not bent on going up mountains, but on taking things easily. How beautiful it is! How pleasant! How great and affable, too, the landscape is! It 's delightful to be in the midst of such scenes — the ideas get generous reflections from them. I don't mean to say my thoughts grow mountainous and enormous like the Alpine chain yonder; but, in fine, it is good to be in the presence of this noble nature. It is keeping good company: keeping away mean thoughts. I see in the papers now and again accounts of fine parties in London. *Bon Dieu!* is it possible any one ever wanted to go to fine London parties, and are there now people sweating in Mayfair routs? The European continent swarms with your people. They are not all as polished as Chesterfield. I wish some of them spoke French a little better. I saw five of them at supper at Basle the other night with their knives down their throats. It was awful! My daughter saw it, and I was obliged to say, 'My dear, your great-great-grandmother, one of the finest ladies of the old school I ever saw, always applied cold steel to her wittles. It 's no *crime* to eat with a knife,' which is all very well: but I wish five of 'em at a time would n't.

"Will you please beg McMichael, when Mrs. Glyn, the English tragic actress, comes to read Shakespeare in your city, to call on her, do the act of kindness to her, and help her with his valuable editorial aid? I wish we were to have another night soon, and that I was going this very evening to set you up with a headache to-morrow morning. By Jove!

how kind you all were to me! How I like people, and want to see 'em again! You are more tender-hearted, romantic, sentimental than we are. I keep on telling this to our fine people here, and have so belabored your [Here the paper was turned and revealed the sketch. At the top is written: 'Pardon this rubbishing picture; but I did n't see and can't afford to write page 3 over again.'] country with praise in private that I sometimes think I go too far. I keep back some of the truth, but the great point to try and ding into the ears of the great stupid virtue-proud English public is, that there are folks as good as they in America. That 's where Mrs. Stowe's book has done harm, by inflaming us with an idea of our own superior virtue in freeing our blacks, whereas you keep yours. Comparisons are always odorous, Mrs. Malaprop says.

"I am about a new story, but don't know as yet if it will be any good. It seems to me I am too old for story-telling; but I want money, and shall get 20,000 dollars for this, of which (D. V.) I 'll keep fifteen. I wish this rubbish (the sketch) were away; I might put written rubbish in its stead. Not that I have anything to say, but that I always remember you and yours, and honest Mac, and Wharton, and Lewis, and kind fellows who have been kind to me. and I hope will be kind to me again. Good-by, my dear Reed, and believe me ever sincerely yours, W. M. THACKERAY."

The next year, 1854, was a year of sorrow to me and mine. But for the sympathy which, in that overpowering grief, I had from my friend, I should not allude to it. My only surviving brother, Mr. Henry Reed, in company with his wife's sister, visited Europe, saw, and were kindly treated by, Mr. Thackeray; and on their return voyage, on the 24th September, perished in the shipwreck of the *Arctic.* Thackeray had known my brother in this country, and duly estimated what I may be pardoned for describing as his gentle virtues and refined and scholar-like tastes. He measured, too, the anguish which, even at this lapse of time — now nearly ten years — freshens when I think of it, and which then bowed a whole family to the earth. It was in reply to my letter announcing that all hope of rescue or escape was over, and that "a vast and wandering grave was theirs," that in November he wrote to me the following. It is an interesting letter, too, in this, that it mentions what may not be known on the other side of the Atlantic — that he had had some transient diplomatic visions.

"ONSLOW SQUARE BROMPTON, *November* 8.

"MY DEAR REED, — I received your melancholy letter this morning. It gives me an opportunity of writing about a subject on which, of course, I felt very strongly for you and for your poor brother's family. I have kept back writing, knowing the powerlessness of consolation, and having I don't know what vague hopes that your brother and Miss Bronson might have been spared. That ghastly struggle over, who would pity any man that departs? It is the survivors one commiserates of such a good, pious, tender-hearted man as he seemed whom God Almighty has just called back to Himself. He seemed to me to have all the sweet domestic virtues which make the pang of parting only the more cruel to those who are left behind. But that loss, what a gain to him! A just man summoned by God, — for what purpose can he go but to meet the divine love and goodness? I never think about deploring such; and as you and I send for our children, meaning them only love and kindness, how much more Pater Noster? So we say, and weep the beloved ones whom we lose all the same with the natural selfish sorrow; as you, I dare say, will have a heavy heart when your daughter marries and leaves you. *You* will lose her, though her new home is ever so happy. I remember quite well my visit to your brother — the pictures in his room, which made me see which way his thoughts lay; his sweet, gentle, melancholy, pious manner. That day I saw him here in Dover Street, I don't know whether I told them, but I felt at the time that to hear their very accents affected me somehow. They were just enough American to be national; and where shall I ever hear voices in the world that have spoken more kindly to me? It was like being in your grave, calm, kind old Philadelphia over again; and behold: now they are to be heard no more. I only saw your brother once in London. When he first called I was abroad ill, and went to see him immediately I got your letter, which he brought and kept back, I think. We talked about the tour which he had been making, and about churches in this country — which I knew interested him — and Canterbury especially, where he had been at the opening of a missionary college. He was going to Scotland, I think, and to leave London instantly, for he and Miss B. refused hospitality, etc.; and we talked about the memoir of Hester Reed which I had found, I did n't know how, on my study-table, and about the people whom he had met at Lord Mahon's — and I believe I said I should like to be going with him in the *Arctic.* And we parted with a great deal of kindness, please God, and friendly talk of a future meeting. May it happen one day! for I feel sure he was a just man. I wanted to get a copy of 'Esmond' to send by him (the first edition, which is the good one); but I did not know where to light on one, having none myself, and a month since bought a couple of copies at a circulating library for *7s. 6d.* apiece.

"I am to-day just out of bed after another, about the dozenth, severe fit of spasms which I have this year. My book would have been written but for them, and the lectures begun, with which I hope to make a few thousand more dollars for those young ladies. But who knows whether I shall be well enough to deliver them, or what is in store for next year? The secretaryship of our Legation at Washington was vacant the other day, and I instantly asked for it; but in the very kindest letter Lord Clarendon showed how the petition was impossible. First, the place was given away: next, it would not be fair to appoint out of the service. But the first was an excellent reason, not a doubt of it. So if ever I come, as I hope and trust to do this time next year, it must be in my own coat, and not the Queen's. Good-by, my dear Reed, and believe that I have the utmost sympathy in your misfortune, and am most sincerely yours,

"W. M. THACKERAY."

The copy of "Esmond" was for my wife, who had expressed her liking for it beyond all his works. It came the next year thus inscribed:

"With the grateful regards of

W. M. THACKERAY.

LONDON, *October* 1855."

And is now among the most cherished volumes in our library.

In the winter of 1855, Mr. Thackeray made his second and last visit to this country, and gave us the first-fruits of his new lecture experiment, "The Georges." I met him in New York and heard his "George IV." — to my mind the least agreeable of the course — delivered before a literary society in Brooklyn. He thence came to Philadelphia, and renewed his old intimacies and associations. His friends were glad to see him, and he them. The impression we all had was that two years had oldened him more than they should have done; but there was no change in other respects. "The Georges" were, if possible, a greater success than "The Humorists;" though I confess I had, and have, a lurking preference for the genial communion with Steele and Fielding (his great favorites), and Swift and Sterne (his aversions), to the dissection of the tainted remains of the Hanoverian kings. But there was in one of these lectures a passage familiar to every listener and every hearer which I reproduce here, not merely from an association presently to be referred to, but because it seems to me in transcribing it that I have the dead again before me, and hear a sweet voice in the very printed words: —

"What preacher need moralize on this story; what words save the simplest are requisite to tell it? It is too terrible for tears. The thought of such a misery smites me down in submission before the Ruler of kings and men, the Monarch supreme over empires and republics, the inscrutable Disposer of life, death, happiness, victory. O brothers! speaking the same dear mother tongue. O comrades! enemies no more, let us take a mournful hand together, as we stand by this royal corpse and call a truce to battle! Low he lies to whom the proudest used to kneel once, and who was cast lower than the poorest: dead, whom millions prayed for in vain. Driven off his throne; buffeted by rude hands; with his children in revolt; the darling of his old age killed before him untimely; our Lear hangs over her breathless lips and cries, 'Cordelia, Cordelia, stay a little!'

'Vex not his ghost! — Oh let him pass —
He hates him
That would upon the rack of this rough world
Stretch him out longer!'

Hush! strife and quarrel, over the solemn grave! Sound, trumpets, a mournful march! Fall, dark curtain, upon his pageant, his pride, his grief, his awful tragedy!"

Was it this, or was it the other passage about the Princess Amelia and the old King praying for returning reason, which Thackeray referred to in the following note, written to me from Baltimore, in answer to one sending an adverse criticism in a small newspaper of Philadelphia?

"BALTIMORE, *January* 16, 1856.

"MY DEAR REED, — Your letter of the 9th, with one from Boston of the 8th, was given to me last night when I came home. In what possible snow-drift have they been lying torpid? One hundred thanks for your goodness in the lecture, and all other matters; and if I can find the face to read those printed lectures over again, I'll remember your good advice. That splendid crowd on the last lecture night I knew would make our critical friend angry. I have not seen the last article, of course, and don't intend to look for it. And as I was reading the George III. lecture here on Monday night, could not help asking myself, 'What can the man mean by saying that I am uncharitable, unkindly — that I sneer at virtue?' and so forth. My own conscience being pretty clear, I can receive the 'Bulletin's' displeasure with calmness — remembering how I used to lay about me in my own youthful days, and how I generally took a good tall mark to hit at.

"Wicked weather, and an opera company which performed on the two first lecture nights here, made the audiences rather thin; but they fetched up at the third lecture, and to-night is the last; after which I go to Richmond, then to go further south, from Charleston to Havannah and New Orleans; perhaps to turn back and try westward, where I know there is a great crop of dollars to be reaped. But to be snow-bound in my infirm condition! I might never get out of the snow alive.

"I go to Washington to-morrow for a night. I was there and dined with Crampton on Saturday. He was in good force and spirits, and I saw no signs of packing-up or portmanteaus in the hall.

"I send my best regards to Mrs. Reed and your sister-in-law, and Lewis and his kind folks, and to Mac's whisky-punch, which gave *me* no headache; I'm very sorry it treated you so unkindly. Always yours, dear Reed.

"W. M. THACKERAY."

The allusion in this letter to the printed lectures recalls a little incident which was very illustrative of his generous temper, and is not unlike "the pill-box with the guineas," which I have seen lately in some literary notices. It was this: On his return to Philadelphia, in the spring of 1856, from the south and west, a number of his friends — I as much as any one — urged him, unwisely as it turned out, to repeat his lectures on "The Humorists." He was very loath to do it, but finally yielded, being, I doubt not, somewhat influenced by the pecuniary inducements accidentally held out to him. A young bookseller of this city offered him a round sum — not very large, but, under the circumstances, quite liberal for the course — which he accepted. The experiment was a failure. It was late in the season with long days and shortening nights, and the course *was* a stale one, and the lectures had been printed, and the audiences were thin, and the bargain was disastrous, not to him, but to the young gentleman who had ventured it. We were all disappointed and mortified; but Thackeray took it good-humoredly; the only thing that seemed to disturb him being his sympathy with the man of business. "I don't mind the empty benches, but I cannot bear to see that sad, pale-faced young man as I come out, who is losing money on my account." This he used to say at my house when he came home to a frugal and not very cheerful supper after the lecture. Still the bargain had been fairly made, and was honorably complied with; and the money was paid and remitted, through my agency, to him at New York. I received no acknowledgment of the remittance, and recollect well that I felt not a little annoyed at this; the more so, when, on picking up a newspaper, I learned that Thackeray had sailed for home. The day after he had gone, when there could be no refusal, I received a certificate of deposit on his New York bankers for an amount quite sufficient to meet any loss incurred, as he thought, on his behalf. I give the accompanying note, merely suppressing the name of the gentleman in question. There are some little things in this note — its blanks and dates — to which a fac-simile alone would do justice: —

"*April* 24.

"MY DEAR REED, — When you get this, ... remum-mum-ember me to kick-kick-kind ffu-fffu-ffriends . . . . a sudden resolution — to—mummum-morrow . . . . in the Bu-bu-baltic.

"Good-by, my dear kind friend, and all kind friends in Philadelphia. I did n't think of going away when I left home this morning; but it 's the best way.

"I think it is best to send back 25 per cent. to poor ——. Will you kindly give him the inclosed; and depend on it I shall go and see Mrs. Booth when I go to London, and tell her all about you. My heart is uncommonly heavy; and I am yours gratefully and affectionately. "W. M. T."

And thus, with an act and words of kindness, he left America, never to return!

It was during this visit to the United States that, as he told me, the idea of his American novel "The Virginians," was conceived; and I have reason to think that some of the details in the story were due as well to Mr. Prescott's "Crossed Swords" as to conversations with me at a time when my mind was full of historical associations and suggestions, and when to think of my country's story was matter of pride and pleasure. In the letter of November 1854, on my brother's death, Mr. Thackeray speaks of "The Memoirs of Hester Reed," which he had found on his study-table. This was a little volume, privately printed a few years before, containing the biography of my paternal grandmother, Esther de Berdt, a young English girl, who had made the acquaintance of her American lover when, in colony times, he was a student in the Temple. They married — came to this country: he became a soldier of the Revolution, and she, sharing her husband's feelings and opinions and trials, died, still a young woman, in the middle of the war. As I have said, Esther Reed was my father's mother. Mr. Thackeray seemed pleased with the genuineness of the little book, and talked often of it. The names "Hetty" and "Theodosia" (the latter, I believe, in his family also), which appear in "The Virginians," are to be found in my homely narrative of Revolutionary times. One other suggestion I trace in "The Virginians." I recollect in one of our rambles telling him of a book which he did not seem to know; and I can hardly say that it is to my credit that I did — "The Memoirs of the Duke de Lauzun." We spoke of the dispute as to its genuineness (its authenticity as a record of the intrigues of a courtier of Louis XV. there was no reason to doubt), and I called his attention to the fact, very creditable to my countrywomen of ancient days, that while Lauzun's life, not only in France, where it was natural enough, but in England, was a continuity of atrocious licentiousness, with his victims' names revealed as only a Frenchman of that day was capable of doing, the moment he lands in America, accompanying Rochambeau's army to Rhode Island, the wicked spirit seems rebuked by the purity and simplicity of American women; and though he mentions the names of several ladies whom he met, there is not a word of indecorum or whispered thought of impurity. This idea the reader will find stated in "The Virginians" thus: —

"There lived during the last century a certain French duke

and marquis who distinguished himself in Europe, and America likewise, and has obliged posterity by leaving behind him a choice volume of memoirs, which the gentle reader is specially warned not to consult. Having performed the part of Don Juan in his own country, in ours, and in other parts of Europe, he has kindly noted down the names of many court beauties who fell victims to his powers of fascination; and very pleasing, no doubt, it must be for the grandsons and descendants of the fashionable persons among whom our brilliant nobleman moved, to find the names of their ancestresses adorning M. le Duc's sprightly pages, and their frailties recorded by the candid writer who caused them. In the course of the peregrinations of this nobleman he visited North America, and, as had been his custom in Europe, proceeded straightway to fall in love. And curious it is to contrast the elegant refinements of European society — where, according to Monseigneur, he had but to lay siege to a woman in order to vanquish her — with the simple lives and habits of the colonial folks, amongst whom the European enslaver of hearts did not, it appears, make a single conquest. Had he done so, he would as certainly have narrated his victories in Pennsylvania and New England as he described his successes in this and his own country. Travellers in America have cried quite loudly enough against the rudeness and barbarism of Transatlantic manners; let the present writer give the humble testimony of his experience, that the conversation of American gentlemen is generally modest, and, to the best of his belief, the lives of the women pure."

"The Virginians" appeared in monthly numbers while I was absent on my mission to China in 1858, and there I read it. In the tone of, I hope pardonable, egotism in which I have thus far written, I transcribe an entry in the little diary I kept in the East for the amusement of my wife and family at home: —

"*Friday, July* 23, *Shanghae.* — Read to-day No. VII. of 'The Virginians.' I still like it, though I fear my friend Lord Chesterfield will fare badly. I don't care what is said about old Q., or any of the Selwyn party. In one of his letters (this I have lost or mislaid, or some felonious autograph-hunter has purloined it) to me long ago, Thackeray, when he was projecting 'The Virginians,' told me he should use 'Esther de Berdt;' and now I see his heroines are 'Hetty' and 'Theodosia,' and from the same rank of life — almost the only pure one then — to which my 'Hetty' belonged. But what beautiful heart-stirring things one meets in his books! I can't help copying one: 'Canst thou, O friendly reader, count upon the fidelity of an artless or tender heart or two, and reckon among the blessings which Heaven hath bestowed on thee the love of faithful women? Purify thy own heart, and try to make it worthy theirs. On thy knees — on thy knees, give thanks for the blessings awarded thee! All the blessings of life are nothing compared with that one — all the rewards of ambition, pleasure, wealth, only vanity and disappointment grasped at greedily, and fought for fiercely, and over and over again found worthless by the weary winners. But love seems to survive life, and to reach beyond it. I think we take it with us past the grave. Do we not still give it to those who have left us? May we not hope that they feel it for us, and that we shall leave it here in one or two fond bosoms when we also are gone?' You will think I have very little to do or record to have time to make so long extracts; but I could not help it, for the magic words touched me."

On my appointment to China, Thackeray was among the first to congratulate me, at the same time begging me — as he seemed to take for granted that my route to the East would be what, by an odd misnomer, is called the "overland" — to stop with him in London. I went, however, by the Cape of Good Hope, and it was not till my return in the spring of 1859 that we met again. From Malta, or some point on the Continent, I wrote to ask him, having due regard to economy, my party being numerous, and to the odor of official station which still hung round me, to get me suitable lodgings in London, and the following perfectly characteristic note was the answer: —

MAURIGY'S HOTEL, 1 REGENT STREET, WATERLOO PLACE,
April 2, 1859.

"MY DEAR REED, — This is the best place for you, I think. Two bishops already in the house. Country-gentlefolks and American envoys especially affect it. Mr. Maurigy says you may come for a day at the rate of some ten guineas a-week, with rooms very clean and nice, which I have just gone over, and go away at the day's end if you disapprove.

"This letter [*referring to one inclosed*] is about the Athenæum, where you may like to look in. I wrote to Lord Stanhope, who is on the committee, to put you up.

"I won't bore you by asking you to dinner till we see how matters are, as of course you will consort with bigger wigs than yours always,

"W. M. THACKERAY."

No "bigger wigs" came between us. During my fortnight in London — for I was hastening home after two years' absence — we saw him nearly every day. He came regularly to our quarters, went with me to the Athenæum — that spot of brilliant association — where he pointed out the eminent men of whom I had heard and read; and then he would go to his working-table in the Club Library, and write for the 'Cornhill.' He would carry my son, a young man just of age, off with him to see the London world in odd "haunts." I dined with him twice: once at his modest house in Onslow Square, where we had the great pleasure of seeing his daughters; and once at Greenwich, at a bachelor's dinner, where I made the acquaintance, since ripened into intimacy, of another friend, who I am sure will excuse this distant allusion to him. We looked out on the Park, and the river where the Great Eastern was lying before her first voyage, and talked of America and American associations, and of the chance of his coming again.[1] And our last dinner was over. I left London on the 30th April, 1859. Mr. and Miss Thackeray were at the Euston Square station to say farewell. He took my son aside, and to his infinite confusion handed him a little *cadeau*, which I hope

[1] "When the magazine slavery was at an end."

he will always cherish with pride for the sake of the giver. We parted with a great deal of kindness, please God, and friendly talk of a future meeting. May it happen one day; for I feel sure he is a just man.

My pious duty is nearly done. On my return to America our correspondence naturally enough languished: each was much occupied; he with drudgery which was exhausting and engrossing. I often received kind messages and sometimes apologies. After the Civil War began, no letter passed between us. I had not the heart to write, and I don't believe he had; for I reject with emphasis the idea that his gentle nature could feel aught but horror at this war of brethren — "brothers speaking the same dear mother tongue."[1] His American novel and his pictures of life in ancient days at Castlewood on the Potomac, show this abundantly.[2] He had been in the South and met Southern ladies and gentlemen, the highest types of American civilization. This I may say now in their hour of suffering and possible disaster. He had visited Southern homes, and shared Southern hospitality.

As recently as February, 1862, in one of his fugitive essays, he referred to an incident of our days of sorrow, and thus embalmed his affectionate regard for a distant friend on whom the hand of arbitrary power was, or was supposed to be, laid. I have reason to believe the reference was to a gentleman long a resident of Savannah.

"I went to the play one night, and protest I hardly knew what was the entertainment which passed before my eyes. In the next stall was an American gentleman who knew me. . . . . And the Christmas piece which the actors were playing proceeded like a piece in a dream. To make the grand comic performance doubly comic, my neighbor presently informed me how one of the best friends I had in America — the most hospitable, kindly, amiable of men, from whom I had twice received the warmest welcome, and the most delightful

[1] More than any Englishman of letters I have ever known, he was free from that sentimental disease "abolitionism!"

[2] His estimate of Mrs. Stowe's evil-omened future in one of the letters that I have given, shows it.

hospitality — was a prisoner in Fort Warren on charges by which his life might be risked. I think it was the most dismal Christmas piece these eyes ever looked on."

One other memorandum I did receive from my friend. In the summer of 1863 an Anglo-Indian officer brought me the following note written on one of the little book-slips used in the Reading-Room of the British Museum.

"At sight pay any kindness you can to the bearer, Major F. Goldsmith, and debit the same to your old friend,

"W. M. THACKERAY."

My little memorial is finished. I have written it in a frame of mind distracted by all that in these last few days has been going on around me, with two objects: one, to embalm, I trust not unpleasantly to any one, the memories I happen to have of a friend who was dear to me; the other, to try by a desperate intellectual effort to throw aside, if but for a moment (and the date will show why I feel so), the burden of consciousness that bloody deeds are now doing which will bring new sorrow into many a home.

THACKERAY'S LITERARY CAREER.

That Mr. Thackeray was born in India in 1811; that he was educated at Charter House and Cambridge; that he left the University after a few terms' residence without a degree; that he devoted himself at first to art; that in pursuit thereof he lived much abroad "for study, for sport, for society;" that about the age of twenty-five, married, without fortune, without a profession, he began the career which has made him an English classic; that he pursued that career steadily till his death, — all this has, within the last few weeks, been told again and again.

It is a common saying that the lives of men of letters are uneventful. In an obvious sense this is true. They are seldom called on to take part in events which move the world, in politics, in the conflicts of nations; while the exciting incidents of sensation-novels are as rare in their lives as in the lives of other men. But men of letters are in no way exempt from the changes and chances of fortune; and the story of these, and of the effects which came from them, must possess an interest for all. Prosperity succeeded by cruel reverses; happiness, and the long prospect of it, suddenly clouded; a hard fight, with aims as yet uncertain, and powers unknown; success bravely won; the austerer victory of failure manfully borne, — these things make a life truly eventful, and make the story of that life full of interest and instruction. They will all fall to be narrated when Mr. Thackeray's life shall be written; we have only now to do with them so far as they illustrate his literary career, of which we propose to lay before our readers an account as complete as is in our power, and as impartial as our warm admiration for the great writer we have lost will allow.

Many readers know Mr. Thackeray only as the Thackeray of "Vanity Fair," "Pendennis," "The Newcomes," and "The Virginians," the quadrilateral of his fame, as they were called by the writer of an able and kindly notice in the "Illustrated News." The four volumes of "Miscellanies" published in 1857, though his reputation had been then established, are less known than they should be. But Mr. Thackeray wrote much which does not appear even in the "Miscellanies"; and some account of his early labors may not be unacceptable to our readers.

His first attempt was ambitious. He became connected as editor, and also, we suspect, in some measure, as proprietor, with a weekly literary journal, the fortunes of which were not prosperous. We believe the journal to have been one which bore the imposing title of "The National Standard and Journal of Literature, Science, Music, Theatricals, and the Fine Arts." Thackeray's editorial reign began about the 19th Number, after which he seems to have done a good deal of work, — reviews, letters, criticisms, and verses. As the "National Standard" is now hardly to be met with out of the British Museum, we give a few specimens of these first efforts. There is a mock sonnet by W. Wordsworth, illustrative of a drawing of Braham in stage nautical costume, standing by a theatrical sea-shore ; in the background an Israelite, with the clothes-bag and triple hat of his ancient race ; and in the sky, constellation-wise, appears a Jew's harp, with a chaplet of bays round it. The sonnet runs : —

"Say not that Judah's harp hath lost its tone,
Or that no bard hath found it where it hung
Broken and lonely, voiceless and unstrung,
Beside the sluggish streams of Babylon :
Slowman [1] repeats the strain his fathers sung,
And Judah's burning lyre is Braham's own !
Behold him here ! Here view the wondrous man,
Majestical and lonely, as when first,
In music on a wondering world he burst,
And charmed the ravished ears of Sov'reign Anne.[2]
Mark well the form, O reader ! nor deride
The sacred symbol — Jew's harp glorified —
Which, circled with a blooming wreath, is seen
Of verdant bays ; and thus are typified
The pleasant music, and the baize of green,
Whence issues out at eve Braham with front serene."

We have here the germ of a style in which Thackeray became famous, though the humor of attributing this nonsense to Wordsworth, and of making Braham coeval with Queen Anne, is not now very plain. There is a yet more characteristic touch in a review of Montgomery's "Woman the Angel of Life," winding up with a quotation of some dozen lines, the order of which he says has been reversed by the printer, but as they read quite as well the one way as the other, he does not think it worth while to correct the mistake ! A comical tale, called the "Devil's Wager," afterwards reprinted in the "Paris Sketch-Book," also appeared in the "National Standard," with a capital wood-cut, representing the Devil as sailing through the air, dragging after him the fat Sir Roger de Rollo

[1] "It is needless to speak of the eminent vocalist and improvisatore. He nightly delights a numerous and respectable audience at the Cider Cellar ; and while on this subject, I cannot refrain from mentioning the kindness of Mr. Evans, the worthy proprietor of that establishment. N. B. — A *table d'hôte* every Friday. — W. WORDSWORTH."

[2] "Mr. Braham made his first appearance in England in the reign of Queen Anne. — W. W."

by means of his tail, which is wound round Sir Roger's neck. The idea of this tale is characteristic. The venerable knight, already in the other world, has made a foolish bet with the Devil involving very seriously his future prospects there, which he can only win by persuading some of his relatives on earth to say an Ave for him. He fails to obtain this slight boon from a kinsman successor for obvious reasons; and from a beloved niece, owing to a musical lover whose serenading quite puts a stop to her devotional exercises; and succeeds at last, only when, giving up all hope from compassion or generosity, he appeals by a pious fraud to the selfishness of a brother and a monk. The story ends with a very Thackerean touch: "The moral of this story will be given in several successive numbers;" the last three words are in the Sketch-Book changed into "the second edition."

Perhaps best of all is a portrait of Louis Philippe, presenting the Citizen King under the Robert Macaire aspect, the adoption and popularity of which Thackeray so carefully explains and illustrates in his Essay on "Caricatures and Lithography in Paris." Below the portrait are these lines, not themselves very remarkable, but in which, especially in the allusion to Snobs by the destined enemy of the race, we catch glimpses of the future: —

"Like 'the king in the parlor' he 's fumbling his money,
Like 'the queen in the kitchen' his speech is all honey,
Except when he talks it, like Emperor Nap,
Of his wonderful feats at Fleurus and Jemappe;
But alas! all his zeal for the multitude 's gone,
And of no numbers thinking except Number One!
No huzzas greet his coming, no patriot club licks
The hand of 'the best of created republics:'
He stands in Paris, as you see him before ye,
Little more than a snob. That 's an end of the story."

The journal seems to have been an attempt to substitute vigorous and honest criticism of books and of art for the partiality and slipslop general then, and now not perhaps quite unknown. It failed, however, partly, it may be, from the inexperience of its managers, but doubtless still more from the want of the capital necessary to establish anything of the sort in the face of similar journals of old standing. People get into a habit of taking certain periodicals unconsciously, as they take snuff. The "National Standard," etc., etc., came into existence on the 5th January, 1833, and ceased to be on the 1st February, 1834.

His subsequent writings contain several allusions to this misadventure; from some of which we would infer that the breakdown of the journal was attended with circumstances more unpleasant than mere literary failure. Mr. Adolphus Simcoe [1] ("Punch," Vol. III.), when in a bad way from a love of literature and drink, completed his ruin by purchasing and conducting for six months that celebrated miscellany called the "Lady's Lute," after which time "its chords were rudely snapped asunder, and he who had swept them aside with such joy went forth a wretched and heart-broken man." And in "Lovel the Widower," Mr. Batchelor narrates similar experiences: —

"I dare say I gave myself airs as editor of that confounded "Museum," and proposed to educate the public taste, to diffuse morality and sound literature throughout the nation, and to pocket a liberal salary in return for my services. I dare say I printed my own sonnets, my own tragedy, my own verses (to a being who shall be nameless, but whose conduct has caused a faithful heart to bleed not a little). I dare say I wrote satirical articles, in which I piqued myself on the fineness of my wit and criticisms, got up for the nonce, out of encyclopædias and biographical dictionaries; so that I would be actually astonished at my own knowledge. I dare say I made a gaby of myself to the world; pray, my good friend, hast

[1] The portrait of Mr. Adolphus, stretched out, "careless diffused," — seedy, hungry, and diabolical, in his fashionable cheap hat, his dirty white duck trousers strapped tightly down, as being the mode and possibly to conceal his bare legs; a half-smoked, probably unsmokably bad cigar, in his hand, which is lying over the arm of a tavern bench, from whence he is casting a greedy and ruffian eye upon some unseen fellows, supping plenteously and with cheer, — is, for power and drawing, not unworthy of Hogarth.

thou never done likewise? If thou hast never been a fool, be sure thou wilt never be a wise man."

Silence for a while seems to have followed upon this failure; but in 1836 his first attempt at independent authorship appeared simultaneously at London and Paris. This publication, at a time when he still hoped to make his bread by art, is, like indeed everything he either said or did, so characteristic, and has been so utterly forgotten, that an account of it may not be out of place, perhaps more minute than its absolute merits deserve.

It is a small folio, with six lithographs, slightly tinted, entitled "Flore et Zephyr, Ballet Mythologique dédié à — par Théophile Wagstaffe." Between "à" and "par" on the cover is the exquisite Flore herself, all alone in some rosy and bedizened bower. She has the old Jaded smirk, and, with eyebrows up and eyelids dropt, she is looking down oppressed with modesty and glory. Her nose, which is long, and has a ripe droop, gives to the semicircular smirk of the large mouth, down upon the centre of which it comes in the funniest way, an indescribably sentimental absurdity. Her thin, sinewy arms and large hands are crossed on her breast, and her petticoat stands out like an inverted white tulip — of muslin — out of which come her professional legs, in the only position which human nature never puts its legs into; it is her special *pose*. Of course, also, you are aware, by that smirk, that look of being looked at, that though alone in maiden meditation in this her bower, and sighing for her Zephyr, she is in front of some thousand pairs of eyes, and under the fire of many double-barrelled lorgnettes, of which she is the focus.

In the first plate, "La Danse fait ses offrandes sur l' autel de l'harmonie," in the shapes of Flore and Zephyr coming trippingly to the footlights, and paying no manner of regard to the altar of harmony, represented by a fiddle with an old and dreary face, and a laurel-wreath on its head, and very great regard to the unseen but perfectly understood "house." Next is "Triste et abattu, les séductions des Nymphes le

(Zephyr) tentent en vain," Zephyr looking theatrically sad. Then "Flore" (with one lower extremity at more than a right angle to the other) "déplore l'absence de Zephyr." The man in the orchestra endeavoring to combine business with pleasure, so as to play the flageolet and read his score, and at the same time miss nothing of the deploring, is intensely comic. Next Zephyr has his turn, and "dans un pas seul exprime sa suprême désespoir," — the extremity of despair being expressed by doubling one leg so as to touch the knee of the other, and then whirling round so as to suggest the regulator of a steam-engine run off. Next is the rapturous reconciliation, when the faithful creature bounds into his arms, and is held up to the house by the waist in the wonted fashion. Then there is "La Retraite de Flore," where we find her with her mother and two admirers, — Zephyr, of course, not one. This is in Thackeray's strong, unflinching line. One lover is a young dandy without forehead or chin, sitting idiotically astride his chair. To him the old lady, who has her slight rouge, too, and is in a homely shawl and muff, having walked, is making faded love. In the centre is the fair darling herself still on tiptoe, and wrapped up, but not too much, for her *fiacre*. With his back to the comfortable fire, and staring wickedly at her, is the other lover, a big, burly, elderly man, probably well to do on the Bourse, and with a wife and family at home in their beds. The last exhibits "Les délassements de Zephyr." That hard-working and homely personage is resting his arm on the chimney-piece, taking a huge pinch of snuff from the box of a friend, with a refreshing expression of satisfaction, the only bit of nature as yet. A dear little innocent pot-boy, such as only Thackeray knew how to draw, is gazing and waiting upon the two, holding up a tray from the nearest tavern, on which is a great pewter-pot of foaming porter for Zephyr, and a rummer of steaming brandy and water for his friend, who has come in from the cold air. These drawings are lithographed by Edward Morton, son of "Speed the Plough," and are done with that delicate strength and truth for which this excellent but little known artist is always to be praised. In each corner is the monogram, which appears so often afterwards with the M added, and is itself superseded by the well-known pair of spectacles. Thackeray must have been barely five-and-twenty when this was published by Mitchell in Bond Street. It can hardly be said to have sold.

Now it is worth noticing how in this, as always, he ridiculed the ugly and the absurd in truth and pureness. There is, as we may well know, much that is wicked (though not so much as the judging community are apt to think) and miserable in such a life. There is much that a young man and artist might have felt and drawn in depicting it, of which in after years he would be ashamed; but "Théophile Wagstaffe" has done nothing of this. The effect of looking over these *juvenilia* — these first shafts from that mighty bow, now, alas! unbent — is good, is moral; you are sorry for the hard-wrought slaves; perhaps a little contemptuous towards the idle people who go to see them; and you feel, moreover, that the "Ballet," as thus done, is ugly as well as bad, is stupid as well as destructive of decency.

His dream of editorship being ended, Mr. Thackeray thenceforward contented himself with the more lowly, but less responsible, position of a contributor, especially to "Fraser's Magazine." The youth of "Fraser" was full of vigor and genius. We know no better reading than its early volumes, unsparing indeed, but brilliant with scholarship and originality and fire. In these days, the staff of that periodical included such men as Maginn, "Barry Cornwall," Coleridge, Carlyle, Hogg, Galt, Theodore Hook, Delta, Gleig, Edward Irving, and, now among the greatest of them all, Thackeray. The first of the "Yellowplush Correspondence" appeared in November, 1837. The world should be grateful to Mr. John Henry Skelton, who in that year wrote a book called "My Book, or the Anatomy of Conduct," for to him is owing the existence of Mr. Charles Yellowplush as a critic, and as a narrator of "fashnable fax and polite annygoats." Mr. Yellowplush on reading Mr. Skelton's book, saw at once that only a gentleman of his distinguished profession could competently criticise the same ; and this was soon succeeded by the wider conviction that the great subject of fashionable life should not be left to any "common writin creatures," but that an authentic picture thereof must he supplied by "ONE OF US." In the words of a note to the first paper, with the initials O. Y., but which it is easy to recognize as the work of Mr. Charles himself without the plush : "He who looketh from a tower sees more of the battle than the knights and captains engaged in it ; and, in like manner, he who stands behind a fashionable table knows more of society than the guests who sit at the board. It is from this source that our great novel-writers have drawn their experience, retailing the truths which they learned. It is not impossible that Mr. Yellowplush may continue his communications, when we shall be able to present the reader with the only authentic picture of fashionable life which has been given to the world in our time." The idea was not carried out very fully. The only pictures sketched by Mr. Yellowplush were the farce of "Miss Shum's Husband" and the terrible tragedy of "Deuceace," neither of them exactly "pictures of fashionable life." We rather fancy that, in the story of Mr. Deuceace, Mr. Yellowplush was carried away from his original plan, a return to which he found impossible after that wonderful medley of rascality, grim humor, and unrelieved bedevilry of all kinds. But in 1838 he reverted to his original critical tendencies, and demolished all that "The Quarterly" had left of a book which made some noise in its day, called "A Diary Illustrative of the Times of George the Fourth ;" and wrote from his pantry one of the "Epistles to the Literati," expressing his views of Sir Edward Lytton's "Sea Captain," than which we know of no more good-natured, trenchant, and conclusive piece of criticism. All the Yellowplush papers except the first are republished in the Miscellanies.

In 1839 appeared the story of "Catherine," by Ikey Solomon. This story is little known, and it throws us back upon one still less known. In 1832, when Mr. Thackeray was not more than twenty-one, "Elisabeth Brownrigge: a Tale," was narrated in the August and September numbers of "Fraser." This tale is dedicated to the author of "Eugene Aram," and the author describes himself as a young man who has for a length of time applied himself to literature, but entirely failed in deriving any emoluments from his exertions. Depressed by failure he sends for the popular novel of "Eugene Aram" to gain instruction therefrom. He soon discovers his mistake: —

"From the frequent perusal of older works of imagination I had learnt so to weave the incidents of my story as to interest the feelings of the reader in favor of virtue, and to increase his detestation of vice. I have been taught by 'Eugene Aram' to mix vice and virtue up together in such an inextricable confusion as to render it impossible that any preference should be given to either, or that the one, indeed, should be at all distinguishable from the other. . . . . In taking my subject from that walk of life to which you had directed my attention, many motives conspired to fix my choice on the heroine of the ensuing tale; she is a classic personage, — her name has been already 'linked to immortal verse' by the muse of Canning. Besides, it is extraordinary that, as you had commenced a tragedy under the title of 'Eugene Aram,' I had already sketched a burletta with the title of 'Elisabeth Brownrigge.' I had, indeed, in my dramatic piece, been guilty of an egregious and unpardonable error: I had attempted to excite the sympathies of the audience in favor of the murdered apprentices, but your novel has disabused me of so vulgar a prejudice, and, in my present version of her case, all the interest of the reader and all the pathetic powers of the author will be engaged on the side of the murderess."

According to this conception the tale proceeds, with incidents and even names taken directly from the "Newgate Calendar," but rivaling "Eugene Aram" itself in magnificence of diction, absurdity of sentiment, and pomp of Greek quotation. The trial scene and the speech for the defense are especially well hit off. If "Elisabeth Brownrigge" was written by Thackeray, and the internal evidence seems to us strong, the following is surprising criticism from a youth of twenty-one, — the very Byron and Bulwer age: —

"I am inclined to regard you (the author of "Eugene Aram") as an original discoverer in the world of literary enterprise, and to reverence you as the father of a new '*lusus naturæ* school.' There is no other title by which your manner could be so aptly designated. I am told, for instance, that in a former work, having to paint an adulterer, you described him as belonging to the class of country curates, among whom, perhaps, such a criminal is not met with once in a hundred years; while, on the contrary, being in search of a tender-hearted, generous, sentimental, high-minded hero of romance, you turned to the pages of the "Newgate Calendar," and looked for him in the list of men who have cut throats for money, among whom a person in possession of such qualities could never have been met with at all. Wanting a shrewd, selfish, worldly, calculating valet, you describe him as an old soldier, though he bears not a single trait of the character which might have been moulded by a long course of military service, but, on the contrary, is marked by all the distinguishing features of a bankrupt attorney, or a lame duck from the Stock Exchange. Having to paint a cat, you endow her with the idiosyncrasies of a dog."

At the end, the author intimates that he is ready to treat with any liberal publisher for a series of works in the same style, to be called "Tales of the Old Bailey, or Romances of Tyburn Tree." The proposed series is represented only by "Catherine," a longer and more elaborate effort in the same direction. It is the narrative of the misdeeds of Mrs. Catherine Hayes, — an allusion to whose criminality in after days brought down upon the author of "Pendennis" an amusing outpouring of fury from Irish patriotism, forgetting in its excitement that the name was borne by a heroine of the Newgate Calendar, as well as by the accomplished singer whom we all regret. The purpose of "Catherine" is the same as that of "Elisabeth Brownrigge,"—to explode the *lusus naturæ* school; but the plan adopted is slightly different. Things had got worse than they were in 1832. The public had called for coarse stimulants and had got them. "Jack Sheppard" had been acquiring great popularity in Bentley's "Miscellany;" and the true feeling and pathos of many parts of "Oliver Twist" had been marred by the unnatural sentimentalism of Nancy. Mr. Ikey Solomon objected utterly to these monstrosities of literature, and thought the only cure was a touch of realism; an attempt to represent blackguards in some measure as they actually are:—

"In this," he says, "we have consulted nature and history rather than the prevailing taste and the general manner of authors. The amusing novel of Ernest Maltravers, for instance, opens with a seduction; but then it is performed by people of the strictest virtue on both sides; and there is so much religion and philosophy in the heart of the seducer, so much tender innocence in the soul of the seduced, that—bless the little dears!—their very peccadilloes make one interested in them; and their naughtiness becomes quite sacred, so deliciously is it described. Now, if we are to be interested by rascally actions, let us have them with plain faces, and let them be performed, not by virtuous philosophers, but by rascals. Another clever class of novelists adopt the contrary system, and create interest by making their rascals perform virtuous actions. Against these popular plans we here solemnly appeal. We say, let your rogues in novels act like rogues, and your honest men like honest men; don't let us have any juggling and thimblerigging with virtue and vice, so that, at the end of three volumes, the bewildered reader shall not know which is which; don't let us find ourselves kindling at the generous qualities of thieves and sympathizing with the rascalities of noble hearts. For our own part, we know what the public likes, and have chosen rogues for our characters, and have taken a story from the "Newgate Calendar," which we hope to follow out to edification. Among the rogues at least, we will have nothing that shall be mistaken for virtue. And if the British public (after calling for three or four editions) shall give up, not only our rascals, but the rascals of all other authors, — we shall be content. We shall apply to government for a pension, and think that our duty is done."

Again, further on in the same story: —

"The public will hear of nothing but rogues; and the only way in which poor authors, who must live, can act honestly by the public and themselves, is to paint such thieves as they are; not dandy, poetical, rose-water thieves, but real downright scoundrels, leading scoundrelly lives, drunken, profligate, dissolute, low, as scoundrels will be. They don't quote Plato like Eugene Aram, or live like gentlemen, and sing the pleasantest ballads in the world, like jolly Dick Turpin; or prate eternally about τὸ καλόν, like that precious canting Maltravers, whom we all of us have read about and pitied; or die whitewashed saints, like poor Biss Dadsy, in "Oliver Twist." No, my dear madam, you and your daughters have no right to admire and sympathize with any such persons, fictitious or real; you ought to be made cordially to detest, scorn, loathe, abhor, and abominate all people of this kidney. Men of genius, like those whose works we have above alluded to, have no business to make these characters interesting or agreeable, to be feeding your morbid fancies, or indulging their own with such monstrous food. For our parts, young ladies, we beg you to bottle up your tears, and not waste a single drop of them on any one of the heroes or heroines in this history; they are all rascals, every soul of them, and behave 'as sich.' Keep your sympathy for those who deserve it; don't carry it, for preference, to the Old Bailey, and grow maudlin over the company assembled there."

Neither of these tales, though it is very curious to look back at them now, can be considered quite successful. And the reason of this is not hard to find. It was impossible that they could be attractive as stories; while, on the other hand, the humor was not broad enough to command attention for itself. They were neither sufficiently interesting nor sufficiently amusing. They are caricatures without the element of caricature. In "Elisabeth," we have little but the story of a crime committed by a criminal actuated by motives and overflowing with sentiments of the Eugene Aram type. "Catherine" is more ambitious. In it an attempt is made to construct a story, — to delineate character. The rival loves of Mr. Bullock and Mr. Hayes, and the adventures of the latter on his marriage-day, show, to some extent, the future novelist; while in the pictures of the manners of the times, slight though they are, in the characters of Corporal Brock and Cornet Galgenstein, and M. l'Abbé O'Flaherty, we can trace, or at least we now fancy we can trace, the author of "Barry Lyndon" and "Henry Esmond." Catherine herself, in her gradual progress from the village jilt to a murderess, is the most striking thing in the story, and is a sketch of remarkable power. But nothing could make a story interesting which consists of little more than the seduction of a girl, the intrigues of a mistress, the discontent of a wife growing into hatred and ending in murder. At the close, indeed, the writer resorts to the true way of making such a *jeu d'esprit* attractive, — burlesque. He concludes, though too late altogether to save the piece, in a blaze of theatrical blue-fire; and it was this idea of burlesque or extravagant caricature which led to the perfected successes of George de Barnwell and Codlingsby. In a literary point of view, it is well worth while to go back upon those early efforts; and we have dwelt upon them the more willingly that their purpose and the literary doctrine they contend for would be well remembered at this very time. We have given up writing about discovered criminals, only to write more about criminals not yet found out; the *lusus naturæ* school has given place to the sensational; the literature of the "Newgate Calendar" has been supplanted by the literature of the detective officer, — a style rather the worse and decidedly the more stupid of the two. The republication of "Catherine" might be a useful, and would be a not unpleasing specific in the present diseased state of literary taste. We have said that the hand of the master is traceable in the characters of this tale. We have also a good example of what was always a marked peculiarity, both in his narrative writing and in his representations of composite natures, what some one has called his "sudden pathos," an effect of natural and unexpected contrast always deeply poetical in feeling, such as the love of Barry Lyndon for his son, the association of a murderess eying her victim, with images of beauty and happiness and peace. We quote the passage, although, as is always the case with the best things of the best writers, it suffers greatly by separation from the context, the force of the contrast being almost entirely lost: —

"Mrs. Hayes sat up in the bed sternly regarding her husband. There is, to be sure, a strong magnetic influence in wakeful eyes so examining a sleeping person; do not you, as a boy, remember waking of bright summer mornings and finding your mother looking over you? had not the gaze of her tender eyes stolen into your senses long before you woke, and cast over your slumbering spirit a sweet spell of peace, and love, and fresh-springing joy?"

In 1840 the "Shabby Genteel Story" appeared in "Fraser," which broke off sorrowfully enough, as we are told, "at a sad period of the writer's own life," to be afterwards taken up in "The Adventures of Philip." The story is not a pleasant one, nor can we read it without pain, although we know that the after fortunes of the Little Sister are not altogether unhappy. But it shows clear indications of growing power and range; Brandon, Tufthunt, the Gann family, and Lord Cinqbars, can fairly claim the dignity of ancestors. The "Great Hoggarty Diamond" came in 1841. This tale was always, we are informed in the preface to a separate edition in 1849, a great favorite with the author, — a judgment, however, in which at first he stood almost alone. It was refused by one magazine before it found a place in "Fraser;" and when it did appear it was little esteemed, or, indeed, noticed in any way. The late Mr. John Sterling took a different view, and wrote Mr. Thackeray a letter which "at that time gave me great comfort and pleasure." Few will now venture to express doubts of Mr. Sterling's discernment. But in reality we suspect that this story is not very popular. It is said to want humor and power; but, on the other hand, in its beauty of pathos and tenderness of feeling, quite indescribable, it reaches a higher point of art than any of the minor tales; and these qualities have gained for it admirers very enthusiastic if not numerous. "Fraser" for June of the same year has a most enjoyable paper called "Memorials of Gormandizing," in which occurs the well-known adaptation of the "Persicos Odi,"—"Dear Lucy, you know what my wish is;" a paper better than anything in the "Original," better because simpler than Hayward's "Art of Dining," and which should certainly be restored to a dinner-eating world. To say nothing of its quiet humor and comical earnestness, it has a real practical value. It would be invaluable to all the hungry Britons in Paris who lower our national character, and, what is a far greater calamity, demoralize even French cooks, by their well-meant but ignorant endeavors to dine. There is a description of a dinner at the Café Foy altogether inimitable; so graphic that the reader almost fancies himself in the actual enjoyment of the felicity depicted. Several of the Fitz-Boodle papers, which appeared in 1842–43, are omitted in the Miscellanies. But in spite of the judgment of the author himself we venture to think that Mr. Fitz-Boodle's love experiences as recorded in "Miss Löwe" (October, 1842), "Dorothea" (January, 1843), and "Ottilia" (February, 1843), are not unworthy of a place beside the "Ravenswing," and should be preserved as a warning to all fervent young men. And during these hard-working years we have also a paper on "Dickens in France," containing an amazing description of Nicholas Nickleby, as translated and adapted (bless thee, Bottom, thou art translated indeed!)

to the Parisian stage, followed by a hearty defense of Boz against the criticism of Jules Janin; and "Bluebeard's Ghost," in its idea — that of carrying on a well-known story beyond its proper end — the forerunner of Rebecca and Rowena. "Little Travels" is the title of two papers, in May and October, 1844, — sketches from Belgium, closely resembling, certainly not inferior, to the roundabout paper called a "Week's Holiday;" and our enumeration of his contributions to "Fraser" closes with the incomparable "Barry Lyndon." "The Hoggarty Diamond" is better and purer, and must therefore rank higher; but "Barry Lyndon" in its own line stands, we think, unrivaled; immeasurably superior, if we must have comparative criticism, to "Count Fathom"; superior even to the history of "Jonathan Wild." It seems to us to equal the sarcasm and remorseless irony of Fielding's masterpiece, with a wider range and a more lively interest.

Mr. Thackeray's connection with "Punch" began very early in the history of that periodical, and he continued a constant contributor at least up to 1850. The acquisition was an invaluable one to "Mr. Punch." Without undue disparagement of that august dignitary, it may now be said that at first he was too exclusively metropolitan in his tone, too much devoted to "natural histories" of medical students and London idlers, — in fact, somewhat Cockney. Mr. Thackeray at once stamped it with a different tone; made its satire universal, adapted its fun to the appreciation of cultivated men. On the other hand, the connection with "Punch" must have been of the utmost value to Mr. Thackeray. He had the widest range, could write without restraint, and without the finish and completeness necessary in more formal publications. The unrestrained practice in "Punch," besides the improvement in style and in modes of thought which practice always gives, probably had no small share in teaching him wherein his real strength lay. For it is worthy of notice in Mr. Thackeray's literary career that this knowledge did not come easily or soon, but only after hard work and much experience. His early writings both in "Fraser" and "Punch" were as if groping. In these periodicals his happier efforts come last, and after many preludes, — some of them broken off abruptly. "Catherine" is lost in "George de Barnwell"; "Yellowplush" and "Fitz-Boodle" are the preambles to "Barry Lyndon" and "The Hoggarty Diamond"; Punch's "Continental Tour" and the "Wanderings of the Fat Contributor" close untimely, and are succeeded by the "Snob Papers" and the kindly wisdom of the elder Brown. Fame, indeed, was not now far off; but ere it could be reached there remained yet repeated effort and frequent disappointment. With peculiar pleasure we now recall the fact that these weary days of struggle and obscurity were cheered in no inconsiderable degree by the citizens of Edinburgh.

There happened to be placed in the window of an Edinburgh jeweler a silver statuette of "Mr. Punch," with his dress *en rigueur*, — his comfortable and tidy paunch, with all its buttons; his hunch; his knee-breeches, with their ties; his compact little legs, one foot a little forward; and the intrepid and honest, kindly little fellow firmly set on his pins, with his customary look of up to and good for anything. In his hand was his weapon, a pen; his skull was an inkhorn, and his cap its lid. A passer-by — who had long been grateful to our author, as to a dear unknown and enriching friend, for his writings in "Fraser" and in "Punch," and had longed for some way of reaching him, and telling him how his work was relished and valued — bethought himself of sending this inkstand to Mr. Thackeray. He went in, and asked its price. "Ten guineas, sir." He said to himself, "There are many who feel as I do; why should n't we send him up to him? I 'll get eighty several half-crowns, and that will do it" (he had ascertained that there would be discount for ready money). With the help of a friend, who says he awoke to Thackeray, and divined his great future, when he came, one evening, in "Fraser" for May, 1844, on the word *kinopium*,[1] the half-

[1] Here is the passage. It is from *Little Travels and Roadside Sketches*. Why are they not republished? We must have his *Opera Omnia*. He is on the top of the Richmond omnibus. "If I were a great prince, and rode outside of coaches (as

crowns were soon forthcoming, and it is pleasant to remember, that in the "octogint" are the names of Lord Jeffrey and Sir William Hamilton, who gave their half-crowns with the heartiest good will. A short note was written telling the story. The little man in silver was duly packed, and sent with the following inscription round the base:—

GULIELMO MAKEPEACE THACKERAY.

ARMA VIRUMQUE

GRATI NECNON GRATÆ EDINENSES

LXXX.

D. D. D.

To this the following reply was made:—

"13 YOUNG STREET, KENSINGTON SQUARE, *May* 11, 1848.

"MY DEAR SIR,—The arms and the man arrived in safety yesterday, and I am glad to know the names of two of the eighty Edinburgh friends who have taken such a kind method of showing their good-will towards me. If you are grati I am gratior. Such tokens of regard & sympathy are very precious to a writer like myself, who have some difficulty still in making people understand what you have been good enough to find out in Edinburgh, that under the mask satirical there walks

I should if I were a great prince), I would, whether I smoked or not, have a case of the best Havannas in my pocket, not for my own smoking, but to give them to the snobs on the coach, who smoke the vilest cheroots. They poison the air with the odor of their filthy weeds. A man at all easy in circumstances would spare himself much annoyance by taking the above simple precaution.

"A gentleman sitting behind me tapped me on the back, and asked for a light. He was a footman or rather valet. He had no livery, but the three friends who accompanied him were tall men in pepper-and-salt undress jackets, with a duke's coronet on their buttons.

"After tapping me on the back, and when he had finished his cheroot, the gentleman produced another wind instrument, which he called a 'kinopium,' a sort of trumpet, on which he showed a great inclination to play. He began puffing out of the kinopium an abominable air, which he said was the 'Duke's March.' It was played by the particular request of the pepper-and-salt gentry.

"The noise was so abominable, that even the coachman objected and said it was not allowed to play on *his* bus. 'Very well,' said the valet, '*we're only of the Duke of B——'s* establishment, THAT'S ALL.'"

about a sentimental gentleman who means not unkindly to any mortal person. I can see exactly the same expression under the vizard of my little friend in silver, and hope some day to shake the whole octogint by the hand gratos & gratas, and thank them for their friendliness and regard. I think I had best say no more on the subject, lest I should be tempted into some enthusiastic writing of wh I am afraid. I assure you these tokens of what I can't help acknowledging as popularity — make me humble as well as grateful — and make me feel an almost awful sense of the responsibility wh falls upon a man in such a station. Is it deserved or undeserved? Who is this that sets up to preach to mankind, and to laugh at many things wh men reverence? I hope I may be able to tell the truth always, & to see it aright, according to the eyes wh God Almighty gives me. And if, in the exercise of my calling I get friends, and find encouragement and sympathy, I need not tell you how much I feel and am thankful for this support. Indeed I can't reply lightly upon this subject or feel otherwise than very grave when people begin to praise me as you do. Wishing you and my Edinburgh friends all health and happiness believe me my dear Sir most faithfully yours

"W. M. THACKERAY."

How like the man is this gentle and serious letter, written these long years ago! He tells us frankly his "calling:" he is a preacher to mankind. He "laughs," he does not sneer. He asks home questions at himself as well as the world: "Who is this?" Then his feeling "not otherwise than very grave" when people begin to praise, is true conscientiousness. This servant of his Master hoped to be able "to tell the truth always, and to see it aright, according to the eyes which God Almighty gives me." His picture by himself will be received as correct *now*, "a sentimental gentleman, meaning not unkindly to any mortal person," — sentimental in its good old sense, and a gentleman in heart and speech. And that little touch about enthusiastic writing, proving all the more that the enthusiasm itself was there.

Of his work in "Punch," the "Ballads of Pleaceman X," the "Snob Papers," "Jeames' Diary," the "Travels and Sketches in London," a "Little Dinner at Timmins'," are now familiar to most readers. But besides these he wrote much which has found no place in the Miscellanies. M. de la Pluche discoursed touching many matters other than his own rise and fall. "Our Fat Contributor" wandered over the face of the earth gaining and imparting much wisdom and experience, if little information; Dr. Solomon Pacifico "prosed" on various things besides the "pleasures of being a Fogy;" and even two of the "Novels by Eminent Hands," "Crinoline" and "Stars and Stripes," have been left to forgetfulness. "Mrs. Tickletoby's Lectures on the History of England," in Vol. III., are especially good reading. Had they been completed, they would have formed a valuable contribution to the philosophy of history. His contributions to "Punch" became less frequent about 1850, but the connection was not entirely broken off till much later; we remember, in 1854, the "Letters from the Seat of War, by our own Bashi-Bazouk," who was, in fact, Major Gahagan again, always foremost in his country's cause. To the last, as Mr. Punch has himself informed us, he continued to be an adviser and warm friend, and was a constant guest at the weekly *symposia*.

In addition to all this work for periodicals, Mr. Thackeray had ventured on various independent publications. We have already alluded to "Flore et Zephyr," his first attempt. In 1840, he again tried fortune with "The Paris Sketch-Book," which is at least remarkable for a dedication possessing the quite peculiar merit of expressing real feeling. It is addressed to M. Aretz, Tailor, 27 Rue Richelieu, Paris; and we quote it the more readily that, owing to the failure of these volumes to attract public attention, the rare virtues of that gentleman have been less widely celebrated than they deserve: —

"SIR, — It becomes every man in his station to acknowledge and praise virtue wheresoever he may find it, and to point it out for the admiration and example of his fellow-men.

"Some months since, when you presented to the writer of these pages a small account for coats and pantaloons manufactured by you, and when you were met by a statement from your debtor that an immediate settlement of your bill would be extremely inconvenient to him, your reply was, 'Mon dieu, sir, let not that annoy you; if you want money, as a gentleman often does in a strange country, I have a thousand-franc note at my house, which is quite at your service.' History or experience, sir, makes us acquainted with so few actions that can be compared to yours, — an offer like this from a stranger and a tailor seems to me so astonishing, — that you must pardon me for making your virtue public, and acquainting the English nation with your merit and your name. Let me add, sir, that you live on the first floor, that your cloths and fit are excellent, and your charges moderate and just; and, as a humble tribute of my admiration, permit me to lay these volumes at your feet. Your obliged faithful servant,

"M. A. TITMARSH."

Some of the papers in these two volumes were reprints, as "Little Poinsinet" and "Cartouche," from "Fraser" for 1839; "Mary Ancel," from "The New Monthly" for 1839; others appeared then for the first time. They are, it must be confessed, of unequal merit. "A Caution to Travellers" is a swindling business, afterwards narrated in "Pendennis," by Amory or Altamont as among his own respectable adventures; "Mary Ancel" and "The Painter's Bargain" are amusing stories; while a "Gambler's Death" is a tale quite awful in the every-day reality of its horror. There is much forcible criticism on the French school of painting and of novel writing, and two papers especially good, called "Caricatures and Lithography in Paris," and "Meditations at Versailles," the former of which gives a picture of Parisian manners and feeling in the Orleans times in no way calculated to make us desire those days back again; the latter an expression of the thoughts called up by the splendor of Versailles and the beauty of the Petit Trianon, in its truth, sarcasm, and half-melancholy, worthy of his best days. All these the public, we think, would gladly welcome in a more accessible form. Of the rest of the "Sketch-Book" the same can hardly be said, and yet we should ourselves much regret never to have seen, for example, the four graceful imitations of Béranger.

The appreciative and acquisitive tendencies of our Yankee friends forced, we are told, independent authorship on Lord Macaulay and Sir James Stephen. We owe to the same cause the publication of the "Comic Tales and Sketches" in 1841; Mr. Yellowplush's memoirs having been more than once reprinted in America before that date. The memoirs were accompanied with "The Fatal Boots" (from the "Comic Almanack"); the "Bedford Row Conspiracy," and the Reminiscences of that astonishing Major Gahagan (both from the "New Monthly Magazine," 1838–1840, a periodical then in great glory, with Hood, Marryatt, Jerrold, and Laman Blanchard among its contributors); all now so known and so appreciated that the failure of this third effort seems altogether unaccountable. In 1843, however, the "Irish Sketch-Book" was, we believe, tolerably successful; and in 1846 the "Journey from Cornhill to Grand Cairo" was still more so; in which year also "Vanity Fair" began the career which has given him his place and name in English literature.

We have gone into these details concerning Mr. Thackeray's early literary life, not only because they seem to us interesting and instructive in themselves; not only because we think his severe judgment rejecting so many of his former efforts should in several instances be reversed; but because they give us much aid in arriving at a true estimate of his genius. He began literature as a profession early in life, — about the age of twenty-five, — but even then he was, as he says of Addison, "full and ripe." Yet it was long before he attained the measure of his strength, or discovered the true bent of his powers. His was no sudden leap into fame. On the contrary, it was by slow degrees, and after many and vain endeavors that he attained to anything like success. Were it only to show how hard these endeavors were, the above retrospect would be well worth while; not that the retrospect is anything like exhaustive. In addition to all we have mentioned, he wrote for the "Westminster," for the "Examiner," and the "Times"; was connected with the "Constitutional," and also, it is said, with the "Torch" and the "Parthenon,"— these last three being papers which enjoyed a brief existence, No man ever more decidedly refuted the silly notion which dissociates genius from labor. His industry must have been unremitting, for he worked slowly, rarely retouching, writing always with great thought and habitual correctness of expression. His writing would of itself show this; always neat and plain; capable of great beauty and minuteness. He used to say that if all trades failed, he would earn sixpences by writing the Lord's Prayer and the Creed (not the Athanasian) in the size of one. He considered and practiced caligraphy as one of the fine arts, as did Porson and Dr. Thomas Young. He was continually catching new ideas from passing things, and seems frequently to have carried his work in his pocket, and when a thought, or a turn, or a word struck him, it was at once recorded. In the fullness of his experience, he was well pleased when he wrote six pages of "Esmond" in a day; and he always worked in the day, not at night. He never threw away his ideas; if at any time they passed unheeded, or were carelessly expressed, he repeats them, or works them up more tellingly. In these earlier writings we often stumble upon the germ of an idea, or a story, or a character with which his greater works have made us already familiar; thus the swindling scenes during the sad days of Becky's decline and fall, and the Baden sketches in the "Newcomes," the Deuceaces, and Punters, and Loders, are all in the "Yellowplush Papers" and the "Paris Sketch-Book;" the University pictures of "Pendennis" are sketched, though slightly, in the "Shabby-Genteel Story"; the anecdote of the child whose admirer of seven will learn that she has left town "from the newspapers," is transferred from the "Book of Snobs" to Ethel Newcome; another child, in a different rank of life, whose acquisition of a penny gains for her half a dozen sudden followers and friends, appears, we think, three times; "Canute," neglected in "Punch," is incorporated in "Rebecca and Rowena." And his names, on which he bestowed no ordinary care, and which have a felicity almost deserving an article to themselves, are repeated again and again. He had been ten years engaged in literary work before the conception of "Vanity Fair" grew up. Fortunately for him it was declined by at least one magazine, and, as we can well believe, not without much anxiety and many misgivings he sent it out to the world alone. Its progress was at first slow; but we cannot think its success was ever doubtful. A friendly notice in the "Edinburgh," when eleven numbers had appeared, did something, the book itself did the rest; and before "Vanity Fair" was completed, the reputation of its author was established.

Mr. Thackeray's later literary life is familiar to all. It certanliy was not a life of idleness. "Vanity Fair," "Pendennis," "Esmond," "The Newcomes," "The Virginians," "Philip"; the Lectures on the "Humorists" and the "Georges"; and that wonderful series of Christmas stories, "Mrs. Perkins's Ball," "Our Street," "Dr. Birch," "Rebecca and Rowena," and "The Rose and the Ring," represent no small labor on the part of the writer, no small pleasure and improvement on the part of multitudes of readers. For the sake of the "Cornhill Magazine" he reverted to the editorial avocations of his former days, happily with a very different result both on the fortunes of the periodical and his own, but, we should think, with nearly as much discomfort to himself. The public, however, were the gainers, if only they owe to this editorship the possession of "Lovel the Widower." We believe that "Lovel" was written for the stage, and was refused by the management of the Olympic about the year 1854. Doubtless the decision was wise, and "Lovel" might have failed as a comedy. But as a tale it is quite unique, — full of humor, and curious experience of life, and insight; with a condensed vigor, and grotesque effects and situations which betray its dramatic origin. The tone of many parts of the book, particularly the description of the emotions of a disappointed lover, shows the full maturity of the author's powers; but there is a daring and freshness about other parts of it which would lead us to refer the dramatic sketch even to an earlier date than 1854. This imperfect sketch of his literary labors may be closed, not inappropriately, with the description which his "faithful old Gold Pen" gives us of the various tasks he set it to: —

"Since he my faithful service did engage
To follow him through his queer pilgrimage,
I've drawn and written many a line and page.

"Caricatures I scribbled have, and rhymes,
And dinner-cards, and picture pantomimes,
And merry little children's books at times.

"I've writ the foolish fancy of his brain;
The aimless jest that, striking, hath caused pain;
The idle word that he'd wish back again.

. . . .

"I've helped him to pen many a line for bread;
To joke, with sorrow aching in his head;
And make your laughter when his own heart bled.

"Feasts that were ate a thousand days ago,
Biddings to wine that long hath ceased to flow,
Gay meetings with good fellows long laid low;

"Summons to bridal, banquet, burial, ball,
Tradesman's polite reminders of his small
Account due Christmas last, — I've answered all.

"Poor Diddler's tenth petition for a half-
Guinea; Miss Bunyan's for an authograph;
So I refuse, accept, lament, or laugh,

"Condole, congratulate, invite, praise, scoff,
Day after day still dipping in my trough,
And scribbling pages after pages off.

. . . .

"Nor pass the words as idle phrases by;
Stranger! I never writ a flattery,
Nor signed the page that registered a lie."

"En réalité," says the writer of an interesting notice in "Le Temps," "l'auteur de 'Vanity Fair' (la *Foire aux vanités*) est un satiriste, un moraliste, un humoriste, auquel il a manqué, pour être tout-à-fait grand, d'être un artiste. Je dis tout-à-fait grand ; car s'il est douteux que, comme humoriste, on le puisse comparer soit à Lamb, soit à Sterne, il est bien certain, du moins, que comme satiriste, il ne connaît pas de supérieurs, pas même Dryden, pas même Swift, pas même Pope. Et ce qui le distingue d'eux, ce qui l'élève au dessus d'eux, ce qui fait de lui un génie essentiellement original, c'est que sa colère, pour qui est capable d'en pénétrer le secret, n'est au fond que la réaction d'une nature tendre, furieuse d'avoir été désappointée." Beyond doubt the French critic is right in holding Thackeray's special powers to have been those of a satirist or humorist. We shall form but a very inadequate conception of his genius if we look at him exclusively, or even chiefly, as a novelist. His gifts were not those of a teller of stories. He made up a story in which his characters played their various parts, because the requirement of interest is at the present day imperative, and because stories are well paid for, and also because to do this was to a certain extent an amusement to himself ; but it was often, we suspect, a great worry and puzzle to him, and never resulted in any marked success. It is not so much that he is a bad constructor of a plot, as that his stories have no plot at all. We say nothing of such masterpieces of constructive art as Tom Jones ; he is far from reaching even the careless power of the stories of Scott. None of his novels end with the orthodox marriage of hero and heroine, except "Pendennis," which might just as well have ended without it. The stereotyped matrimonial wind-up in novels can of course very easily be made game of ; but it has a rational meaning. When a man gets a wife and a certain number of hundreds a year, he grows stout, and his adventures are over. Hence novelists naturally take this as the crisis in a man's life to which all that has gone before leads up. But for Mr. Thackeray's purposes a man or woman is as good after marriage as before it,

— indeed, rather better. To some extent this is intentional; a character, as he says somewhere, is too valuable a property to be easily parted with. Besides, he is not quite persuaded that marriage concludes all that is interesting in the life of a man: "As the hero and heroine pass the matrimonial barrier, the novelist generally drops the curtain, as if the drama were over then, the doubts and struggles of life ended; as if, once landed in the marriage country, all were green and pleasant there, and wife and husband had nothing but to link each other's arms together, and wander gently downwards towards old age in happy and perfect fruition." But he demurs to this view; and as he did not look on a man's early life as merely an introduction to matrimony, so neither did he regard that event as a final conclusion. Rejecting, then, this natural and ordinary catastrophe, he makes no effort to provide another. His stories stop, but they don't come to an end. There seems no reason why they should not go on further, or why they should not have ceased before. Nor does this want of finish result from weariness on the part of the writer, or from that fear of weariness on the part of readers which Mr. Jedediah Cleishbotham expresses to Miss Martha Buskbody: "Really, Madam, you must be aware that every volume of a narrative turns less and less interesting as the author draws to a conclusion; just like your tea, which, though excellent hyson, is necessarily weaker and more insipid in the last cup. Now, as I think the one is by no means improved by the luscious lump of half-dissolved sugar usually found at the bottom of it, so I am of opinion that a history, growing already vapid, is but dully crutched up by a detail of circumstances which every reader must have anticipated, even though the author exhaust on them every flowery epithet in the language." It arises from the want of a plot, from the want often of any hero or heroine round whom a plot can centre. Most novelists know how to let the life out towards the end, so that the story dies quite naturally, having been wound up for so long. But his airy nothings, if once life is breathed into them, and they are made to speak and act, and love and hate, will not die; on the contrary, they grow in force and vitality under our very eye; the curtain comes sheer down upon them when they are at their best. Hence his trick of re-introducing his characters in subsequent works, as fresh and life-like as ever. He does not indeed carry this so far as Dumas, whose characters are traced with edifying minuteness of detail from boyhood to the grave; Balzac or our own Trollope afford, perhaps, a closer comparison, although neither of these writers — certainly not Mr. Trollope — rivals Thackeray in the skill with which such reappearances are managed. In the way of delineation of character we know of few things more striking in its consistency and truth than Beatrix Esmond grown into the Baroness Bernstein: the attempt was hazardous, the success complete.

Yet this deficiency in constructive art was not inconsistent with dramatic power of the highest order. Curiously enough, if his stories for the most part end abruptly, they also for the most part open well. Of some of them, as "Pendennis" and the "Newcomes," the beginnings are peculiarly felicitous. But his dramatic power is mainly displayed in his invention and representation of character. In invention his range is perhaps limited, though less so than is commonly said. He has not, of course, the sweep of Scott, and, even where a comparison is fairly open, he does not show Scott's creative faculty; thus, good as his high life below stairs may be, he has given us no Jenny Dennison. He does not attempt artisan life like George Eliot, nor, like other writers of the day, affect rural simplicity, or delineate provincial peculiarities (the Mulligan and Costigan are national), or represent special views or opinions. But he does none of these things, — not so much because his range is limited as because his art is universal. There are many phases of human life on which he has not touched; few developments of human nature. He has caught those traits which are common to all mankind, peer and artisan alike, and he may safely omit minor points of distinction. It is a higher art to draw men, than to draw noblemen or workingmen. If the specimen of our nature be brought before us, it matters little whether it be dressed in a lace coat or a fustian jacket.

Among novelists he stands, in this particular, hardly second to Scott. His pages are filled with those touches of nature which make the whole world kin. Almost every passion and emotion of the heart of man finds a place in his pictures. These pictures are taken mainly from the upper and middle classes of society, with an occasional excursion into Bohemia, sometimes even into depths beyond that pleasant land of lawlessness. In variety, truth, and consistency, they are unrivaled. They are not caricatures, they are not men of humors; they are the men and women whom we daily meet; they are, in the fullest sense of the word, representative; and yet they are drawn so sharply and finely that we never could mistake or confound them. Pendennis, Clive Newcome, Philip, are all placed in circumstances very much alike, and yet they are discriminated throughout by delicate and certain touches, which we hardly perceive even while we feel their effect. Only one English writer of fiction can be compared to Mr. Thackeray in this power of distinguishing ordinary characters, — the authoress of "Pride and Prejudice." But with this power he combines, in a very singular manner, the power of seizing humors, or peculiarities, when it so pleases him. Jos. Sedley, Charles Honeyman, Fred Bayham, Major Pendennis, are so marked as to be fairly classed as men of humors; and in what a masterly way the nature in each is caught and held firm throughout! In national peculiarities he is especially happy. The Irish he knows well: the French, perhaps, still better. How wonderfully clever is the sketch of "Mary, Queen of Scots" and the blustering Gascon, and the rest of her disreputable court at Baden! And what can those who object to Thackeray's women say of that gentle lady Madame de Florac, — a sketch of ideal beauty, with her early, never-forgotten sorrow, her pure, holy resignation? To her inimitable son no words can do justice. The French-English of his speech would make the fortune of any ordinary novel. It is as unique, and of a more delicate humor, than the orthography of Jeames. Perhaps more remarkable than even his invention is the fidelity with which the conception of his characters is preserved. This never fails. They seem to act, as it were, of themselves. The author having once projected them, appears to have nothing more to do with them. They act somehow according to their own natures, unprompted by him, and beyond his control. He tells us this himself in one of those delightful and most characteristic Roundabout Papers, which are far too much and too generally undervalued: "I have been surprised at the observations made by some of my characters. It seems as if an occult power was moving the pen. The personage does or says something, and I ask, How the dickens did he come to think of that? . . . . We spake anon of the inflated style of some writers. What also if there is an *afflated* style; when a writer is like a Pythoness, or her oracle tripod, and mighty words, words which he cannot help, come blowing, and bellowing, and whistling, and moaning through the speaking pipes of his bodily organ?" Take one of his most subtle sketches, — though it is but a sketch, — Elizabeth, in "Lovel the Widower." The woman has a character, and a strong one; she shows it, and acts up to it; but it is as great a puzzle to us as the character of Hamlet; the author himself does not understand it. This is, of course, art; and it is the highest perfection of art; it is the art of Shakespeare; and hence it is that Thackeray's novels are interesting irrespective of the plot, or story, or whatever we choose to call it. His characters come often without much purpose: they go often without much reason; but they are always welcome, and for the most part we wish them well. Dumas makes up for the want of a plot by wild incident and spasmodic writing; Thackeray makes us forget a like deficiency by the far higher means of true conceptions, and consistent delineations of human nature. "Esmond," alone of all his more important fictions is artistically constructed. The marriage indeed of Esmond and Lady Castlewood marks no crisis in their lives; on the contrary, it might have happened at any time, and makes little change in their relations; but the work derives completeness from the skill with which the events of the time are connected with the fortunes of the chief actors in the story, — the historical plot leading up to the catastrophe of Beatrix, the failure of the conspiracy, and the exile of the conspirators. In "Esmond," too, Thackeray's truth to nature is especially conspicuous. In all his books the dialogue is surprising in its naturalness, in its direct bearing on the subject in hand. Never before, we think, in fiction did characters so uniformly speak exactly like the men and women of real life. In "Esmond" — owing to the distance of the scene — this rare excellence was not easy of attainment, yet it has been attained. Every one not only acts, but speaks in accordance certainly with the ways of the time, but always like a rational human being; there is no trace of that unnaturalness which offends us even in Scott's historical novels, and which substitutes for intelligible converse long harangues in pompous diction, garnished with strange oaths, — a style of communicating their ideas never adopted, we may be very sure, by any mortals upon this earth. Add to these artistic excellences a tenderness of feeling and a beauty of style which even Thackeray has not elsewhere equaled, and we come to understand why the best critics look on "Esmond" as his master-piece.

Nor, in speaking of Thackeray as a novelist, should we forget to mention — though but in a word — his command of the element of tragedy. The parting of George Osborne with Amelia, the stern grief of old Osborne for the loss of his son, the later life of Beatrix Esmond, the death of Colonel Newcome, are in their various styles perfect, and remarkable for nothing more than for the good taste which controls and subdues them all.

But, as we said before, to criticise Mr. Thackeray as a novelist is to criticise what was in him only an accident. He wrote stories, because to do so was the mode; his stories are natural and naturally sustained, because he could do nothing otherwise than naturally; but to be a teller of stories was not his vocation. His great object in writing was to express himself, — his notions of life, all the complications and variations which can be played by a master on this one everlasting theme.

Composite human nature as it is, that sins and suffers, enjoys and does virtuously, that was "the main haunt and region of his song." To estimate him fairly, we must look at him as taking this wider range; must consider him as a humorist, using the word as he used it himself. "The humorous writer professes to awaken and direct your love, your pity, your kindness; your scorn for untruth, pretension, imposture; your tenderness for the weak, the poor, the oppressed, the unhappy. To the best of his means and ability, he comments on all the ordinary actions and passions of life almost. He takes upon himself to be the week-day preacher, so to speak. Accordingly, as he finds and speaks and feels the truth best, we regard him, esteem him, — sometimes love him." Adopting this point of view, and applying this standard, it seems to us that no one of the great humorists of whom he has spoken is deserving equally with himself of our respect, esteem, and love; respect for intellectual power, placing him on a level even with Swift and Pope; esteem for manliness as thorough as the manliness of Fielding, and rectitude as unsullied as the rectitude of Addison; love for a nature as kindly as that of Steele. Few will deny the keen insight, the passion for truth of the week-day preacher we have lost; few will now deny the kindliness of his disposition, but many will contend that the kindliness was too much restrained; that the passion for truth was allowed to degenerate into a love of detecting hidden faults. The sermons on women have been objected to with especial vehemence and especial want of reason. No one who has read Mr. Brown's letters to his nephew, — next to the Snob Papers and Sydney Smith's Lectures, the best modern work on moral philosophy, — will deny that Mr. Thackeray can at least appreciate good women, and describe them: —

"Sir, I do not mean to tell you that there are no women in the world, vulgar and ill-humored, rancorous and narrow-minded, mean schemers, son-in-law hunters, slaves of fashion, hypocrites; but I do respect, admire, and almost worship good women; and I think there is a very fair number of such to be found in this world, and I have no doubt, in every educated Englishman's circle of society, whether he finds that circle in palaces in Belgravia and May Fair, in snug little suburban villas, in ancient comfortable old Bloomsbury, or in back parlors behind the shop. It has been my fortune to meet with excellent English ladies in every one of these places, — wives graceful and affectionate, matrons tender and good, daughters happy and pure-minded, and I urge the society of such to you, because I defy you to think evil in their company. Walk into the drawing-room of Lady Z., that great lady; look at her charming face, and hear her voice. You know that she can't but be good, with such a face and such a voice. She is one of those fortunate beings on whom it has pleased Heaven to bestow all sorts of its most precious gifts and richest worldly favors. With what grace she receives you; with what a frank kindness and natural sweetness and dignity! Her looks, her motions, her words, her thoughts, all seem to be beautiful and harmonious quite. See her with her children, what woman can be more simple and loving? After you have talked to her for a while, you very likely find that she is ten times as well read as you are: she has a hundred accomplishments which she is not in the least anxious to show off, and makes no more account of them than of her diamonds, or of the splendor round about her, — to all of which she is born, and has a happy, admirable claim of nature and possession, — admirable and happy for her and for us too; for is it not a happiness for us to admire her? Does anybody grudge her excellence to that paragon? Sir, we may be thankful to be admitted to contemplate such consummate goodness and beauty: and as, in looking at a fine landscape or a fine work of art every generous heart must be delighted and improved, and ought to feel grateful afterwards, so one may feel charmed and thankful for having the opportunity of knowing an almost perfect woman. Madam, if the gout and the custom of the world permitted, I would kneel down and kiss the hem of your ladyship's robe. To see your gracious face is a comfort — to see you walk to your carriage is a holiday. Drive her faithfully, O thou silverwigged coachman! drive to all sorts of splendors and honors and royal festivals. And for us, let us be glad that we should have the privilege to admire her.

"Now, transport yourself in spirit, my good Bob, into another drawing-room. There sits an old lady of more than fourscore years, serene and kind, and as beautiful in her age now, as in her youth, when History toasted her. What has she not seen, and is she not ready to tell? All the fame and wit, all the rank and beauty, of more than half a century, have passed through those rooms where you have the honor of making your best bow. She is as simple now as if she had never had any flattery to dazzle her: she is never tired of being pleased and being kind. Can that have been anything but a good life which after more than eighty years of it are spent, is so calm? Could she look to the end of it so cheerfully, if its long course had not been pure? Respect her, I say, for being so happy, now that she is old. We do not know what goodness and charity, what affections, what trials, may have gone to make that charming sweetness of temper and complete that perfect manner. But if we do not admire and reverence such an old age as that, and get good from contemplating it, what are we to respect and admire.

"Or shall we walk through the shop (while N. is recommending a tall copy to an amateur, or folding up a twopenny-worth of letter-paper, and bowing to a poor customer in a jacket and apron with just as much respectful gravity as he would show while waiting upon a duke), and see Mrs. N. playing with the child in the back parlor until N. shall come in to tea? They drink tea at five o'clock; and are actually as well-bred as those gentlefolks who dine three hours later. Or will you please to step into Mrs J.'s lodgings, who is waiting, and at work, until her husband comes home from Chambers? She blushes and puts the work away on hearing the knock, but when she sees who the visitor is, she takes it with a smile from behind the sofa cushion, and behold, it is one of J.'s waist-coats on which she is sewing buttons. She might have been a countess blazing in diamonds, had Fate so willed it, and the higher her station the more she would have adorned it. But she looks as charming while plying her needle as the great lady in the palace whose equal she is — in beauty, in goodness, in high-bred grace and simplicity; at least, I can't fancy her better, or any peeress being more than her peer."

But then he is accused of not having represented this. "It is said," to quote a friendly critic in the "Edinburgh Review" for 1848, "that having with great skill put together a creature of which the principal elements are indiscriminating affection, ill-requited devotion, ignorant partiality, a weak will and a narrow intellect, he calls on us to worship his poor idol as the type of female excellence. This is true." Feminine critics enforce similar charges yet more vehemently. Thus, Miss Brontë says: "As usual, he is unjust to women, quite unjust. There is hardly any punishment he does not deserve for making Lady Castlewood peep through a keyhole, listen at a door, and be jealous of a boy and a milkmaid." Mrs. Jameson criticises him more elaborately: "No woman resents his Rebecca, — inimitable Becky! No woman but feels and acknowledges with a shiver the completeness of that wonderful and finished artistic creation; but every woman resents the selfish, inane Amelia. . . . . Laura in 'Pendennis' is a yet more fatal mistake. She is drawn with every generous feeling, every good gift. We do not complain that she loves that poor creature Pendennis, for she loved him in her childhood. She grew up with that love in her heart; it came between her and the perception of his faults; it is a necessity indivisible from her nature. Hallowed, through its constancy, therein alone would lie its best excuse, its beauty and its truth. But Laura, faithless to that first affection; Laura waked up to the appreciation of a far more manly and noble nature, in love with Warrington, and then going back to Pendennis, and marrying *him!* Such infirmity might be true of some women, but not of such a woman as Laura; we resent the inconsistency, the indelicacy of the portrait. And then Lady Castlewood, — so evidently a favorite of the author, what shall we say of her? The virtuous woman *par excellence*, who 'never sins and never forgives'; who never resents, nor relents, nor repents; the mother who is the rival of her daughter; the mother, who for years is the confidante of a man's delirious passion for her own child, and then consoles him by marrying him herself! O Mr. Thackeray! this will never do! Such women may exist, but to hold them up as examples of excellence, and fit objects of our best sympathies, is a fault, and proves a low standard in ethics and in art."

But all these criticisms, even if sound, go to this only, that Mr. Thackeray's *representations* of women are unjust: they are confined solely to his novels. Now, if the view we have taken of Mr. Thackeray's genius be the true one, such a limitation is unfair. He is not to be judged only by his novels as a representer of character, he must be judged also by all his writings together as a describer and analyzer of character. In the next place, the said criticisms are based upon wonderfully hasty generalizations. Miss Brontë knew that *she* would not have listened at a keyhole, and she jumps at once to the conclusion that neither would Lady Castlewood. But surely the character of that lady is throughout represented as marred by many feminine weaknesses falling little short of unamiability. Is the existence of a woman greedy of affection, jealous, and unforgiving, an impossibility? Her early love for Esmond we cannot quite approve; her later marriage with him we heartily disapprove; but neither of these things is the fault of the writer. With such a woman as Lady Castlewood, deprived of her husband's affection, the growth of an attachment towards her dependent into a warmer feeling, was a matter of extreme probability; and her subsequent marriage to Esmond, affectionate, somewhat weak, and above all, disappointed elsewhere, was, in their respective relations, a mere certainty. Not to have married them would have been a mistake in art. Thus, when a friend remonstrated with him for having made Esmond "marry his mother-in-law," he replied, "*I* did n't make him do it; they did it themselves." But as to Lady Castlewood's being a favorite with the author, which is the gravamen of the charge, that is a pure assumption on the part of Mrs. Jameson. We confess to having always received, in reading the book, a clear impression to the contrary. Laura, again, we do not admire vehemently; but we cannot regard her returning to her first love, after a transient attachment to another, as utterly unnatural. Indeed, we think it the very thing a girl of her somewhat commonplace stamp of character would certainly have done. She never is much in love with Pendennis either first or last, but she marries him nevertheless. She might have loved Warrington had the Fates permitted it, very differently; and as his wife, would never have displayed those airs of self-satisfaction and moral superiority which make her so tediously disagreeable. But all this fault-finding runs up into the grand objection, that Thackeray's good women are denied brains; that he preserves an essential alliance between moral worth and stupidity; and it is curious to see how women themselves dislike this, — how, in their admiration of intellect, they admit the truth of Becky willingly enough, but indignantly deny that of Amelia. On this question Mr. Brown thus expresses himself: —

"A set has been made against clever women from all times. Take all Shakespeare's heroines: they all seem to me pretty much the same, affectionate, motherly, tender, that sort of thing. Take Scott's ladies, and other writers, each man seems to draw from one model: an exquisite slave is what we want for the most part, a humble, flattering, smiling, child-loving, tea-making, pianoforte-playing being, who laughs at our jokes however old they may be, coaxes and wheedles us in our humors, and fondly lies to us through life."

In the face of Rosalind, Beatrice, and Portia, it is impossible to concur with Mr. Brown in his notions about Shakespeare's women; but otherwise he is right. Yet it is but a poor defense for the deficiences of a man of genius, that others have shown the like short-comings. And on Mr. Thackeray's behalf a much better defense may be pleaded;

though it may be one less agreeable to the sex which he is said to have maligned. That defense is a simple plea of not guilty; a denial that his women as a class, want intellectual power to a greater extent than is consistent with truth. They vary between the extremes of pure goodness and pure intellect — Becky and Amelia — just as women do in real life. The moral element is certainly too prominent in Amelia; but not more so than in Colonel Newcome, and we can't see anything much amiss in Helen Pendennis. Laura, as Miss Bell, is clever enough for any man; and, though she afterwards becomes exceedingly tiresome and a prig, she does not become a fool. And what man would be bold enough to disparage the intellectual powers of Ethel Newcome? Her moral nature is at first incomplete owing to a faulty education; but when this has been perfected through sorrow, wherein is the character deficient? Besides, we must bear in mind that virtue in action is undoubtedly "slow." Goodness is not in itself entertaining, while ability is; and the novelist, therefore, whose aim is to entertain, naturally labors most with the characters possessing the latter, in which characters the reader too is most interested. Hence they acquire greater prominence both as a matter of fact in the story and also in our minds. Becky, Blanche Amory, 'Trix are undeniably more interesting, and in their points of contrast and resemblance afford far richer materials for study than Amelia, Helen Pendennis, and Laura. But this is in the nature of things; and the writer must not be blamed for it any more than the readers. Taking, however, the Thackerean gallery as a whole, we cannot admit that either in qualities of heart or head his women are inferior to the women we generally meet. Perhaps he has never — not even in Ethel — combined these qualities in their fullest perfection; but then how often do we find them so combined? It seems to us that Thackeray has drawn women more carefully and more truly than any novelist in the language, except Miss Austen; and it is small reproach to any writer, that he has drawn no female character so evenly good as Anne Elliot or Elizabeth Bennet.

If this is true of his women, we need not labor in defense of his men. For surely it cannot be questioned that his representations of the ruder sex are true, nay, are on the whole an improvement on reality? The ordinary actors who crowd his scene are not worse than the people we meet with every day; his heroes, to use a stereotyped expression, are rather better than the average; while one such character as George Warrington is worth a wilderness of commonplace excellence called into unnatural life. But then it is said his general tone is bitter; he settles at once on the weak points of humanity, and to lay them bare is his congenial occupation. To a certain extent this was his business. "Dearly beloved," he says, "neither in nor out of this pulpit do I profess to be bigger, or cleverer, or wiser, or better than any of you." Nevertheless he was a preacher, though an unassuming one; and therefore it lay upon him to point out faults, to correct rather than to flatter. Yet it must be confessed that his earlier writings are sometimes too bitter in their tone, and too painful in their theme. This may be ascribed partly to the infectious vehemence of "Fraser" in those days, partly to the influence of such experiences as are drawn upon in some parts of the "Paris Sketch-Book;" but, however accounted for, it must be condemned as an error in art. As a disposition to doubt and despond in youth betrays a narrow intellect, or a perverted education; so in the beginning of a literary career, a tendency towards gloom and curious research after hidden evil reveals artistic error, or an unfortunate experience. Both in morals and art these weaknesses are generally the result of years and sorrow; and thus the common transition is from the joyousness of youth to sadness, it may be to moroseness, in old age. But theirs is the higher and truer development, who reverse this process, — who, beginning with false tastes or distorted views, shake these off as they advance into a clearer air, in whom knowledge but strengthens the nobler powers of the soul, and whose kindliness and generosity, based on a firmer foundation than the buoyancy of mere animal life, are purer and more enduring. Such, as it appears to us, was the history of Thackeray's genius. Whatever may have been the severity of his earlier writings, it was latterly laid aside. In the "Newcomes" he follows the critical dogma which he lays down, that "fiction has no business to exist unless it be more beautiful than reality;" and truthful kindliness marks all his other writings of a later date, from the letters of Mr. Brown and Mr. Spec in "Punch," down to the pleasant egotism of the "Roundabout Papers." He became disinclined for severe writing even where deserved: "I have militated in former times, and not without glory, but I grow peaceable as I grow old." The only things towards which he never grew peaceable were pretentiousness and falsehood. But he preferred to busy himself with what was innocent and brave, to attacking even these; he forgot the satirist, and loved rather honestly to praise or defend. The "Roundabout Papers" show this on every page, especially, perhaps, those on Tunbridge Toys, on Ribbons, on a Joke I heard from the late Thomas Hood, and that entitled "Nil nisi bonum." The very last paper of all was an angry defense of Lord Clyde against miserable club gossip, unnecessary perhaps, but a thing one likes now to think that Thackeray felt stirred to do. "To be tremblingly alive to gentle impressions," says Foster, "and yet be able to preserve, when occasion requires it, an immovable heart, even amidst the most imperious causes of subduing emotion, is perhaps not an impossible constitution of mind, but it is the utmost and rarest condition of humanity." These words do not describe the nature of a man who would pay out of his own pocket for contributions he could not insert in the "Cornhill;" but if for heart we substitute intellect, they will perfectly describe his literary genius. He was always tremblingly alive to gentle impressions, but his intellect amidst any emotions remained clear and immovable; so that good taste was never absent, and false sentiment never came near him. He makes the sorrows of Werther the favorite reading of the executioner at Strasbourg.[1]

[1] Among his ballads we have the following somewhat literal analysis of this work: —

"Werther had a love for Charlotte
Such as words could never utter;

Few men have written so much that appeals directly to our emotions, and yet kept so entirely aloof from anything tawdry, from all falsetto. "If my tap," says he, "is not genuine, it is naught, and no man should give himself the trouble to drink it." It was at all times thoroughly genuine, and is therefore everything to us. Truthfulness, in fact, eager and uncompromising, was his main characteristic; truthfulness not only in speech, but, what is a far more uncommon and precious virtue, truth in thought. His entire mental machinery acted under this law of truth. He strove always to find and show things as they really are, — true nobleness apart from trappings, unaffected simplicity, generosity without ostentation; confident that so he would best convince every one that what is truly good pleases most, and lasts longest, and that what is otherwise soon becomes tiresome, and, worst of all, ridiculous. A man to whom it has been given consistently to devote to such a purpose the highest powers of sarcasm, ridicule, sincere pathos, and, though sparingly used, of exhortation, must be held to have fulfilled a career singularly honorable and useful. To these noble ends he was never unfaithful. True, he made no boast of this. Disliking cant of all kinds, he made no exception in favor of the cant of his own profession. "What the deuce," he writes to a friend, "our twopenny

Would you know how first he met her?
She was cutting bread and butter.

"Charlotte was a married lady,
And a moral man was Werther,
And, for all the wealth of Indies,
Would do nothing for to hurt her.

"So he sighed and pined and ogled,
And his passion boiled and bubbled,
Till he blew his silly brains out,
And no more was by it troubled.

"Charlotte, having seen his body
Borne before her on a shutter,
Like a well-conducted person,
Went on cutting bread and butter."

reputations get us at least twopence-halfpenny; and then comes *nox fabulæque manes*, and the immortals perish." The straightforward Mr. Yellowplush stoutly maintains, in a similar strain, that people who write books are no whit better, or actuated by more exalted motives, than their neighbors: "Away with this canting about great motifs! Let us not be too prowd, and fansy ourselves marters of the truth, marters or apostels. We are but tradesmen, working for bread, and not for righteousness' sake. Let's try and work honestly; but don't let us be prayting pompisly about our 'sacred calling.'" And George Warrington, in "Pendennis," is never weary of preaching the same wholesome doctrine. Thackeray had no sympathy with swagger of any kind. His soul revolted from it; he always talked under what he felt. At the same time, indifference had no part in this want of pretense. So far from being indifferent, he was peculiarly sensitive to the opinions of others; too much so for his own happiness. He hated to be called a cynical satirist; the letter we have quoted to his Edinburgh friends shows how he valued any truer appreciation. Mere slander he could despise like a man; he winced under the false estimates and injurious imputations too frequent from people who should have known better. But he saw his profession as it really was, and spoke of it with his innate simplicity and dislike of humbug. And in this matter, as in the ordinary affairs of life, those who profess little, retaining a decent reserve as to their feelings and motives, are far more to be relied on than those who protest loudly. Whether authors are moved by love of fame, or a necessity for daily bread, does not greatly signify. The world is not concerned with this in the least; it can only require that, as Mr. Yellowplush puts it, they should "try to work honestly;" and herein he never failed. He never wrote but in accordance with his convictions; he spared no pains that his convictions should be in accordance with truth. For one quality we cannot give him too great praise; that is the sense of the distinction of right and of wrong. He never puts bitter for sweet, or sweet for bitter; never calls evil things good, or good things evil; there is no haziness or muddle; no "topsyturvifications," like Madame Sand's, in his moralities: — with an immense and acute compassion for all suffering, with a power of going out of himself, and into almost every human feeling, he vindicates at all times the supremacy of conscience, the sacredness and clearness of the law written in our hearts.

His keenness of observation and his entire truthfulness found expression in a style worthy of them in its sharpness and distinctness. The specimens we have quoted of his earlier writings show that these qualities marked his style from the first. He labored to improve those natural gifts. He steadily observed Mr. Yellowplush's recommendation touching poetical composition: "Take my advise, honrabble sir — listen to a humble footmin: it 's genrally best in poatry to understand puffickly what you mean yourself, and to ingspress your meaning clearly afterwoods — in the simpler words the better, praps." He always expressed his meaning clearly and in simple words. But as, with increasing experience, his meanings deepened and widened, his expression became richer. The language continued to the last simple and direct, but it became more copious, more appropriate, more susceptible of rythmical combinations: in other words, it rose to be the worthy vehicle of more varied and more poetical ideas. This strange peculiarity of soberness in youth, of fancy coming into being at the command and for the service of the mature judgment, has marked some of the greatest writers. The words in which Lord Macaulay has described it with regard to Bacon may be applied, with little reservation, to Thackeray: "He observed as vigilantly, meditated as deeply, and judged as temperately, when he gave his first work to the world, as at the close of his long career. But in eloquence, in sweetness and variety of expression, and in richness of illustration, his later writings are far superior to those of his youth." Confessedly at the last he was the greatest master of pure English in our day. His style is never ornate, on the contrary is always marked by a certain reserve which surely betokens thought and real feeling; is never forced or loaded, only entirely appropriate and entirely beautiful; like crystal, at once clear and splendid. We quote two passages, both from books written in his prime, not merely as justifying these remarks, but because they illustrate qualities of his mind second only to his truthfulness, — his sense of beauty and his sense of pathos. And yet neither passage has any trace of what he calls the "sin of grandiloquence, or tall-talking." The first is the end of the "Kickleburys on the Rhine": —

"The next morning we had passed by the rocks and towers, the old familiar landscapes, the gleaming towers by the river-side, and the green vineyards combed along the hills; and when I woke up, it was at a great hotel at Cologne, and it was not sunrise yet. Deutz lay opposite, and over Deutz the dusky sky was reddened. The hills were veiled in the mist and the gray. The gray river flowed underneath us, the steamers were roosting along the quays, a light keeping watch in the cabins here and there, and its reflection quivering in the water. As I look, the sky-line towards the east grows redder and redder. A long troop of gray horsemen winds down the river road, and passes over the bridge of boats. You might take them for ghosts, those gray horsemen, so shadowy do they look; but you hear the trample of their hoofs as they pass over the planks. Every minute the dawn twinkles up into the twilight; and over Deutz the heaven blushes brighter. The quays begin to fill with men; the carts begin to creak and rattle; and wake the sleeping echoes. Ding, ding, ding, the steamers' bells begin to ring; the people on board to stir and wake; the lights may be extinguished, and take their turn of sleep; the active boats shake themselves, and push out into the river; the great bridge opens, and gives them passage; the church-bells of the city begin to clink; the cavalry trumpets blow from the opposite bank; the sailor is at the wheel, the porter at his burden, the soldier at his musket, and the priest at his prayers. . . . . And lo! in a flash of crimson splendor, with blazing scarlet clouds running before his chariot, and heralding his majestic approach, God's sun rises upon the world, and all nature wakens and brightens. O glorious spectacle of light and life! O beatific symbol of Power, Love, Joy, Beauty! Let us look at thee with humble wonder, and thankfully acknowledge and adore. What gracious forethought is it, — what generous and loving provision, that deigns to prepare for our eyes and to soothe our hearts with such a splendid morning festival! For these magnificent bounties of Heaven to us, let us be thankful, even that we can feel thankful (for thanks surely is the noblest effort, as it is the greatest delight, of the gentle soul); and so, a grace for this feast, let all say who partake of it. . . . . See! the mist clears off Drachenfels, and it looks out from the distance, and bids us a friendly farewell."

Our second quotation describes Esmond at his mother's grave, — one of the most deeply affecting pieces of writing in the language: —

"Esmond came to this spot in one sunny evening of spring, and saw, amidst a thousand black crosses, casting their shadows across the grassy mounds, that particular one which marked his mother's resting-place. Many more of those poor creatures that lay there had adopted that same name with which sorrow had rebaptized her, and which fondly seemed to hint their individual story of love and grief. He fancied her, in tears and darkness, kneeling at the foot of her cross, under which her cares were buried. Surely he knelt down, and said his own prayer there, not in sorrow so much as in awe (for even his memory had no recollection of her), and in pity for the pangs which the gentle soul in life had been made to suffer. To this cross she brought them; for this heavenly bridegroom she exchanged the husband who had wooed her, the traitor who had left her. A thousand such hillocks lay round about, the gentle daisies springing out of the grass over them, and each bearing its cross and *requiescat.* A nun, veiled in black, was kneeling hard by, at a sleeping sister's bedside (so fresh made, that the spring had scarce had time to spin a coverlid for it); beyond the cemetery walls you had glimpses of life and the world, and the spires and gables of the city. A bird came down from a roof opposite, and lit first on a cross, and then on the grass below it, whence it flew away presently with a leaf in its mouth: then came a sound of chanting, from the chapel of the sisters hard by: others had long since filled the place which poor Mary Magdalene once had there, were kneeling at the same stall and hearing the same hymns and prayers in which her stricken heart had found consolation. Might she sleep in peace, — might she sleep in peace; and we, too, when our struggles and pains are over! But the earth is the Lord's as the heaven is; we are alike his creatures here and yonder. I took a little flower off the hillock and kissed it, and went my way like the bird that had just lighted on the cross by me, back into the world again. Silent receptacle of death! tranquil depth of calm, out of reach of tempest and trouble. I felt as one who had been walking below the sea, and treading amidst the bones of shipwrecks."

Looking at Mr. Thackeray's writings as a whole, he would be more truthfully described as a sentimentalist than as a cynic. Even when the necessities of his story compel him to draw bad characters, he gives them as much good as he can. We don't remember in his novels any utterly unredeemed scoundrel except Sir Francis Clavering. Even Lord Steyne has something like genuine sympathy with Major Pendennis's grief at the illness of his nephew. And if reproof is the main burden of his discourse, we must remember that to reprove, not to praise, is the business of the preacher. Still further, if his reproof appears sometimes unduly severe, we must remember that such severity may spring from a belief that better things are possible. Here lies the secret of Thackeray's seeming bitterness. His nature was, in the words of the critic in "Le Temps," "furieuse d'avoir été désappointée." He condemns sternly men as they often are, because he had a high ideal of what they might be. The feeling of this contrast runs through all his writings. "He could not have painted 'Vanity Fair' as he has, unless Eden had been shining brightly before his eyes."[1] And this contrast could never have been left, the glories of Eden could never have been seen, by the mere satirist or by the misanthrope. It has been often urged against him that he does not make us think better of our fellow-men. No, truly. But he does what is far greater than this,—he makes us think worse of ourselves. There is no great necessity that we should think well of other people; there is the utmost necessity that we should know ourselves in our every fault and weakness; and such knowledge his writings will supply.

In Mr. Hannay's Memoir,[2] which we have read with admiration and pleasure, a letter from Thackeray is quoted, very illustrative of this view of his character: "I hate Juvenal; I mean, I think him a truculent brute, and I love Horace better than you do, and rate Churchill much lower; and as for Swift, you have n't made me alter my opinion. I admire, or rather admit, his power as much as you do; but I don't admire that kind of power so much as I did fifteen years ago, or twenty shall we say. *Love is a higher intellectual exercise than hatred.*" We think the terrible Dean had love as well as hate strong within him, and none the worse in that it was more special than general; "I like Tom, Dick, and Harry," he used to say; "I hate the race;" but nothing can be more characteristic of Thackeray than this judgment. Love was the central necessity of his understanding as well as of his affections; it was his fulfilling of the law; and unlike the Dean, he could love Tom, and also like and pity as well as rebuke the race.

Mr. Thackeray has not written any history formally so called. But it is known that he purposed doing so, and in "Esmond"

[1] Essays by George Brimley. Second edition. Cambridge, 1860. A collection of singularly good critical papers.

[2] *A Brief Memoir of the late Mr. Thackeray.* By James Hannay, Edinburgh, 1864.

and the "Lectures" he has given us much of the real essence of history. The "Saturday Review," however, in a recent article, has announced that this was a mistake; that history was not his line. Such a decision is rather startling. In one or two instances of historical representation, Mr. Thackeray may have failed. Johnson and Richardson do not appear in the "Virginians" with much effect. But surely in the great majority of instances, he has been eminently successful. Horace Walpole's letter in the "Virginians," the fictitious "Spectator" in "Esmond," are very felicitous literary imitations. Good-natured trooper Steele comforting the boy in the lonely country-house; Addison, serene and dignified, "with ever so slight a touch of *merum* in his voice" occasionally; Bolingbroke, with a good deal of *merum* in his voice talking reckless Jacobitism at the dinner at General Webbe's, are wonderful portraits. And, though the estimate of Marlborough's character may be disputed, the power with which that character is represented cannot be questioned. But the historical genius displayed in "Esmond" goes beyond this. We know of no history in which the intrigues and confusion of parties at the death of Queen Anne are sketched so firmly as in the third volume of that work; in fact, a more thorough historical novel was never written. It is not loaded with historical learning; and yet it is most truly, though or rather *because* unpretendingly, a complete representation of the time. It reads like a veritable memoir. And it will hardly be disputed, that a good historical novel cannot be written save by one possessed of great historical powers. What are the qualities necessary to a historian? Knowledge, love of truth, insight into human nature, imagination to make alive before him the times of which he writes. All these Mr. Thackeray had. His knowledge was accurate and minute, — indeed, he could not have written save of what he knew well; a love of truth was his main characteristic; for insight into human nature he ranks second to Shakespeare alone; and, while he wanted that highest creative imagination which makes the poet, he had precisely that secondary imagination which serves the historian, which can realize the past and make the distant near. Had he been allowed to carry out his cherished design of recording the reign of Queen Anne, a great gap in the history of our country would have been filled up by one of the most remarkable books in the language. We might have had less than is usual of the "dignity of history," of battles and statutes and treaties; but we should have had more of human nature, — the actors in the drama would have been brought before us living and moving, their passions and hidden motives made clear; the life of England would have been sketched by a subtle artist; the literature of England, during a period which this generation often talks about, but of which it knows, we suspect, very little, would have been presented to us lighted up by appreciative and competent criticism. The Saturday Reviewer gives a reason for Mr. Thackeray's failure as a historian, which will seem strange to those who have been accustomed to regard him as a cynic. He was so carried away by worth, says this ingenious critic bent on fault-finding, and so impatient of all moral obliquity, that he could not value fairly the services which had been rendered by bad men. And the instance given is that a sense of what we owe to the Hanoverian succession was not allowed to temper the severity of the estimate given of the first two Georges; — an unfortunate instance, as the critic would have discovered had he read the following passage in the lecture on George the Second: —

"But for Sir Robert Walpole, we should have had the Pretender back again. But for his obstinate love of peace, we should have had wars which the nation was not strong enough nor united enough to endure. But for his resolute counsels and good-humored resistance, we might have had German despots attempting a Hanoverian regimen over us; we should have had revolt, commotion, want, and tyrannous misrule, in place of a quarter of a century of peace, freedom, and material prosperity, such as the country never enjoyed, until that corrupter of parliaments, that dissolute, tipsy cynic, that courageous lover of peace and liberty, that great citizen, patriot, and statesman governed it."

The truth is, that Mr. Thackeray, while fully appreciating the blessings of the Hanoverian succession, knew well that the country did not in the least degree owe the stability of that succession to the Hanoverian kings, but, on the contrary, to that great minister, whose character is sketched, in a powerful passage, of which the above quotation is a part. In fact, Mr. Thackeray judged no man harshly. No attentive student of his works can fail to see that he understood the duty of "making allowance," not less with regard to historical characters, than with regard to characters of his own creation. He does full justice, for example, to the courage and conduct of Marlborough, as to whose moral character the opinion of Colonel Esmond is in curious accordance with the historical judgment given later to the public by Lord Macaulay.

These "Lectures on the Georges" were made the ground of a charge against Mr. Thackeray of disloyalty. This charge was urged with peculiar offensiveness by certain journals, which insinuated that the failings of English kings had been selected as a theme grateful to the American audiences who first heard the lectures delivered. Mr. Thackeray felt this charge deeply, and repelled it in language which we think worthy to be remembered. At a dinner given to him in Edinburgh, in 1857, he said:—

"I had thought that in these lectures I had spoken in terms, not of disrespect or unkindness, and in feelings and in language not un-English, of her Majesty the Queen; and wherever I have had to mention her name, whether it was upon the banks of the Clyde or upon those of the Mississippi, whether it was in New England or in Old England, whether it was in some great hall in London to the artisans of the suburbs of the metropolis, or to the politer audiences of the western end, —wherever I had to mention her name, it was received with shouts of applause, and with the most hearty cheers. And why was this? It was not on account of the speaker; it was on account of the truth; it was because the English and the Americans — the people of New Orleans a year ago, the people of Aberdeen a week ago — all received and acknowledged with due allegiance the great claims to honor which that lady has who worthily holds that great and awful situation which our Queen occupies. It is my loyalty that is called in question, and it is my loyalty that I am trying to plead to you. Suppose, for example, in America, — in Philadelphia or in New York, — that I had spoken about George IV. in terms of praise and affected reverence, do you believe they would have hailed his name with cheers, or have heard it with anything like respect? They would have laughed in my face if I had so spoken of him. They know what I know and you know, and what numbers of squeamish loyalists who affect to cry out against my lectures know, that that man's life was not a good life, — that that king was not such a king as we ought to love, or regard, or honor. And I believe, for my part, that, in speaking the truth, as we hold it, of a bad sovereign, we are paying no disrespect at all to a good one. Far from it. On the contrary, we degrade our own honor and the Sovereign's by unduly and unjustly praising him; and the mere slaverer and flatterer is one who comes forward, as it were, with flash notes, and pays with false coin his tribute to Cæsar. I don't disguise that I feel somehow on my trial here for loyalty, for honest English feeling."

The judgment pronounced by the accomplished Scotch judge who presided at this dinner-trial, a man far removed, both by tastes and position, from any sympathy with vulgar popularity-hunting, will be accepted by every candid person as just: —

"I don't," said Lord Neaves, "for my part, regret if there are some painful truths told in these lectures to those who had before reposed in the pleasing delusion that everything royal was immaculate. I am not sorry that some of the false trappings of royalty or of a court life should be stripped off. We live under a Sovereign whose conduct, both public and private, is so unexceptionable, that we can afford to look all the facts connected with it in the face; and woe be to the country or to the crown when the voice of truth shall be stifled as to any such matters, or when the only tongue that is allowed to be heard is that of flattery."

It was said of Fontenelle that he had as good a heart as could be made out of brains. Adapting the observation, we may say of Thackeray that he was as good a poet as could be made out of brains. The highest gifts of the poet of course he wanted. His imagination, to take Ruskin's distinction, was more penetrative than associative or contemplative. His mind was too much occupied with realities for persistent ideal work. But manliness and common sense, combined with a perfect mastery of language, go a long way at least to the making of very excellent verses. More than this, he had the sensibility, the feeling of time and of numbers essential to versifying; and his mind fulfilled the condition required by our greatest living poet: —

"Clear and bright it should be ever,
Flowing like a crystal river."

His verse-making was a sort of pleasaunce, — a flower-garden in the midst of spacious policies. It was the ornamentation of his intellect. His ballads do not perhaps show poetic feeling more profound than is possessed by many men; they derive, for the most part, their charm from the same high qualities as mark his prose, with the attraction of music and rhyme superadded. Writing them seems to have given him real pleasure. The law of self-imposed restraint, of making the thought often wait upon the sound, necessary in rhythmical composition, rather than, as in prose, the sound upon the sense, — this measuring of feeling and of expression had plainly a great charm for his rich and docile genius. His verses give one the idea of having been a great delight to himself, like humming a favorite air; there is no trace of effort, and yet the trick of the verse is perfect. His rhymes are often as good as Swift's and Hood's. This feeling of enjoyment, as also the abounding fertility in strange rhymes, is very marked in the White Squall; and hardly less in the ease and gayety of Peg of Limavaddy. Take, for instance, the description of the roadside inn where Peg dispenses liquor: —

> "Limavaddy inn's
>   But a humble baithouse,
> Where you may procure
>   Whiskey and potatoes;
> Landlord at the door
>   Gives a smiling welcome
> To the shivering wights
>   Who to his hotel come.
> Landlady within
>   Sits and knits a stocking,
> With a wary foot
>   Baby's cradle rocking.
> To the chimney nook,
>   Having found admittance,
> There I watch a pup
>   Playing with two kittens;
> (Playing round the fire,
>   Which of blazing turf is,
> Roaring to the pot
>   Which bubbles with the murphies)
> And the cradled babe
>   Fond the mother nursed it,
> Singing it a song
>   As she twists the worsted!"

Peg herself and her laugh, —

> "Such a silver peal!
>   In the meadows listening,
> You who 've heard the bells
>   Ringing to a christening;
> You who ever heard
>   Caradori pretty,
> Smiling like an angel,
>   Singing 'Giovinetti';
> Fancy Peggy's laugh,
>   Sweet, and clear, and cheerful,
> At my pantaloons
>   With half a pint of beer full!
> See her as she moves!
>   Scarce the ground she touches,

Airy as a fay,
  Graceful as a duchess;
Bare her rounded arm,
  Bare her little leg is,
Vestris never showed
  Ankles like to Peggy's;
Braided is her hair,
  Soft her look and modest,
Slim her little waist
  Comfortably boddiced."

In a similar light and graceful style are the "Cane-Bottomed Chair," "Piscator and Piscatrix," the "Carmen Lilliense," etc.; and all the Lyra Hibernica, especially the rollicking "Battle of Limerick," are rich in Irish absurdity. That compact little epic, the "Chronicle of the Drum," the well-known "Bouillabaisse," and "At the Church Gate,"—the first literary effort of Mr. Arthur Pendennis,— seem to us in their various styles to rise into the region of real poetry. The "Chronicle of the Drum" is a grand martial composition, and a picture of the feelings of the French soldiery which strikes on us at once as certainly true. The ballads of Pleaceman X. are unique in literature, —as startlingly original as "Tam O'Shanter." "Jacob Homnium's Hoss" is perhaps the most amusing, the "Foundling of Shoreditch" the most serious; but through them all there runs a current of good sense, good feeling, and quaint fun which makes them most pleasant reading. They remind one somehow of John Gilpin,—indeed there is often the same playful fancy and delicate pensiveness in Thackeray as in Cowper. We should like to quote many of these; but we give in preference Miss Tickletoby's ballad on King Canute, long though it be, because it is not included in the collected ballads, and has not, we fear, obtained great popularity by being incorporated into "Rebecca and Rowena,"—a rendering of poetical justice less generally read than it should be:—

KING CANUTE

King Canute was weary-hearted; he had reigned for years a score;
Battling, struggling, pushing, fighting, killing much and robbing more,
And he thought upon his actions, walking by the wild sea-shore.

'Twixt the chancellor and bishop walked the king with steps sedate,
Chamberlains and grooms came after, silver sticks and gold sticks great,
Chaplains, aides-de-camp, and pages, — all the officers of state.

Sliding after like his shadow, pausing when he chose to pause ;
If a frown his face contracted, straight the courtiers dropped their jaws ;
If to laugh the king was minded, out they burst in loud hee-haws.

But that day a something vexed him, that was clear to old and young,
Thrice his grace had yawned at table, when his favorite gleeman sung,
Once the queen would have consoled him, but he bade her hold her tongue.

" Something ails my gracious master," cried the keeper of the seal ;
"Sure, my lord, it is the lampreys served at dinner, or the veal ! "
"Psha ! " exclaimed the angry monarch, " keeper, 't is not that I feel.

" 'T is the *heart* and not the dinner, fool, that doth my rest impair ;
Can a king be great as I am, prithee, and yet know no care?
Oh, I 'm sick, and tired, and weary." — Some one cried, "The king's arm-chair ! "

Then towards the lackeys turning, quick my lord the keeper nodded,
Straight the king's great chair was brought him, by two footmen able-bodied,
Languidly he sank into it : it was comfortably wadded.

"Leading on my fierce companions," cried he, "over storm and brine,
I have fought and I have conquered ! Where was glory like to mine ! "
Loudly all the courtiers echoed, " Where is glory like to thine ? "

" What avail me all my kingdoms? Weary am I now, and old,
Those fair sons I have begotten long to see me dead and cold ;
Would I were, and quiet buried, underneath the silent mould !

"O remorse, the writhing serpent ! at my bosom tears and bites :
Horrid, horrid things I look on, though I put out all the lights ;
Ghosts of ghastly recollections troop about my bed of nights.

"Cities burning, convents blazing, red with sacrilegious fires ;
Mothers weeping, virgins screaming, vainly for their slaughtered sires" —
" Such a tender conscience," cries the bishop, " every one admires."

" But for such unpleasant bygones, cease, my gracious lord, to search,
They 're forgotten and forgiven by our holy Mother Church ;
Never, never does she leave her benefactors in the lurch.

" Look ! the land is crowned with ministers, which your Grace's bounty raised ;
Abbeys filled with holy men, where you and heaven are daily praised ;
You, my lord, to think of dying ? on my conscience, I 'm amazed ! "

"Nay, I feel," replied King Canute, "that my end is drawing near;"
"Don't say so," exclaimed the courtiers (striving each to squeeze a tear),
"Sure your Grace is strong and lusty, and may live this fifty year."

"Live these fifty years!" the bishop roared, with actions made to suit,
"Are you mad, my good lord keeper, thus to speak of King Canute!
Men have lived a thousand years, and sure his Majesty will do't.

"Adam, Enoch, Lamech, Canan, Mahaleel, Methusela,
Lived nine hundred years apiece, and may n't the king as well as they?"
"Fervently," exclaimed the keeper, "fervently, I trust he may."

"*He* to die," resumed the bishop. "He a mortal like to us?
Death was not for him intended, though *communis omnibus;*
Keeper, you are irreligious, for to talk and cavil thus.

"With his wondrous skill in healing ne'er a doctor can compete,
Loathsome lepers, if he touch them, start up clean upon their feet;
Surely he could raise the dead up, did his Highness think it meet.

"Did not once the Jewish captain stay the sun upon the hill,
And the while he slew the foemen, bid the silver moon stand still?
So, no doubt, could gracious Canute, if it were his sacred will."

"Might I stay the sun above us, good Sir Bishop?" Canute cried;
"Could I bid the silver moon to pause upon her heavenly ride?
If the moon obeys my orders, sure I can command the tide.

"Will the advancing waves obey me, bishop, if I make the sign?"
Said the bishop, bowing lowly, "Land and sea, my lord, are thine."
Canute turned towards the ocean,—"Back!" he said, "thou foaming brine

"From the sacred shore I stand on, I command thee to retreat;
Venture not, thou stormy rebel, to approach thy master's seat;
Ocean, be thou still! I bid thee come not nearer to my feet!"

But the sullen ocean answered with a louder, deeper roar,
And the rapid waves drew nearer, falling sounding on the shore;
Back the keeper and the bishop, back the king and courtiers bore.

And he sternly bade them never more to kneel to human clay,
But alone to praise and worship that which earth and seas obey;
And his golden crown of empire never wore he from that day.
King Canute is dead and gone: parasites exist alway.

We must say a few words on his merits as an artist and a critic of art. We can hardly agree with those who hold that he failed as an artist, and then took to his pen. There is no proof of failure; his art accomplishes all he sets it to. Had he, instead of being a gentleman's son, brought up at the Charter-house and Cambridge, been born in the parish of St. Bartholomew the Great, and apprenticed, let us say, when thirteen years old, to Raimbach the engraver, we might have had another, and in some ways a subtler Hogarth. He draws well; his mouths and noses, his feet, his children's heads, all his ugly and queer "mugs," are wonderful for expression and good drawing. With beauty of man or woman he is not so happy; but his fun is, we think, even more abounding and *funnier* in his cuts than in his words. The love of fun in him was something quite peculiar. Some writers have been more witty; a few have had a more delicate humor; but none, we think, have had more of that genial quality which is described by the homely word *fun*. It lay partly in imitation, as in the "Novels by Eminent Hands." There were few things more singular in his intellectual organization than the coincidence of absolute originality of thought and style with exquisite mimetic power. But it oftener showed itself in a pure love of nonsense, — only nonsense of the highest order. He was very fond of abandoning himself to this temper; witness the "Story *à la Mode*" in the "Cornhill," some of the reality-giving touches in which would have done credit to Gulliver. Major Gahagan is far funnier than Baron Munchausen; and where is there more exquisite nonsense than "The Rose and the Ring," with the "little beggar baby that laughed and sang as droll as may be?" There is much of this spirit in his ballads, [1] especially, as we have already said, the series by

[1] We subjoin an astonishing piece of nonsense, — a species of song, or ditty, which he chanted, we believe, *extempore*, [in singing, each line to be repeated twice]: —

LITTLE BILLEE.

There were 3 sailors in Bristol city,
Who took a boat and went to sea.

But first with beef and captain's biscuit,
And pickled pork they loaded she.

There was guzzling Jack and gorging Jimmy,
And the youngest he was little Billee.

Pleaceman X.; but we are inclined to think that it finds most scope in his drawings. We well remember our surprise on coming upon some of his earlier works for "Punch." Best of

Now very soon, they were so greedy,
They didn't leave not one split pea.

Says guzzling Jack to gorging Jimmy
"I am extremely hungaree."

Says gorging Jim to guzzling Jacky,
"We have no provisions, so we must eat we."

Says guzzling Jack to gorging Jimmy,
"O gorging Jim, what a fool you be!

"There's little Bill is young and tender,
We're old and tough, so let's eat he."

"O Bill, we're going to kill and eat you,
So undo the collar of your chemie."

When Bill received this infumation
He used his pocket-handkerchie.

"O let me say my catechism,
As my poor mammy taught to me."

"Make haste, make haste," says guzzling Jacky,
While Jim pulled out his snickersnee.

So Bill went up the maintop-gallant mast,
Where down he fell on his bended knee.

He scarce had come to the Twelfth Commandment,
When up he jumps, "There's land, I see.

"There's Jerusalem and Madagascar,
And North and South Amerikee.

"There's the British fleet a riding at anchor,
With Admiral Nelson, K. C. B."

"So when they came to the admiral's vessel,
He hanged fat Jack and flogged Jimmee.

But as for little Bill, he made him
The captain of a seventy-three.

all was an impressive series illustrative of the following passage in the "Times" of December 7, 1843: "The agents of the tract societies have lately had recourse to a new method of introducing their tracts into Cadiz. The tracts were put into glass bottles *securely corked;* and, taking advantage of the tide flowing into the harbor, they were committed to the waves, on whose surface they floated towards the town, where the inhabitants eagerly took them up on their arriving at the shore. The bottles were then uncorked, and the tracts they contain are *supposed to have been* read with much interest." The purpose of the series is to hold up to public odium the Dissenting tract-smuggler,—Tractistero dissentero contrabandistero. The first cut represents a sailor, "thirsty as the seaman naturally is," rushing through the surf to seize the bottle which has been bobbing towards him. "Sherry, perhaps," he exclaims to himself and his friend. Second cut: the thirsty expectant has the bottle in position, and is drawing the cork, another mariner, and a little wondering boy, capitally drawn, looking on. "Rum, I hope," is the thought of each. Lastly we have the awful result: our friend holds up on the corkscrew to his companion and the universe "a Spanish translation of the Cow-boy of Kensington Common," with an indignant "Tracts, by jingo!" Then there is John Balliol, in "Miss Tickletoby's Lectures," "cutting" into England on a ragged sheltie, which is trotting like a maniac over a series of boulders, sorely discomposing the rider, whose kilt is of the shortest. Even better is the cut illustrative of the ballad of "King Canute," the king and his courtiers on the shore, with bathing-machines and the Union-Jack in the distance; and a most preposterous representation of the *non Angli sed Angeli* story. We wish Mr. Thackeray's excellent friends, the proprietors of "Punch," would reprint all his odds and ends, with their wood-cuts. They will get the laughter and gratitude of mankind if they do.

He is, as far as we recollect, the only great author who illustrated his own works. This gives a singular completeness to the result. When his pen has said its say, then comes his pencil and adds its own felicity. Take the original edition of the Book of Snobs, all those delicious Christmas little quartos, especially "Mrs. Perkins's Ball" and the "Rose and the Ring" (one of the most perfectly realized ideas we know of), and see how complete is the duet between the eye and the mind, between word and figure. There is an etching in the "Paris Sketch-Book" which better deserves to be called "high art" than most of the class so called. It is Majesty in the person of "Le Grand Monarque" in and stripped of its externals, which are there also by themselves. The lean and slippered old pantaloon is tottering peevishly on his staff, his other hand in his waistcoat pocket; his head absolutely bald; his whole aspect pitiable and forlorn, querulous and absurd. To his left is his royal self, in all his glory of high-heeled boots, three-storied flowing wig, his orders, and sword, and all his "dread magnificence," as we know him in his pictures; on his right we behold, and somehow feel as if the old creature, too, is in awe of them, — his clothes, *per se*, — the "properties" of the great European actor, set ingeniously up, and looking as grand and much steadier than with him inside. The idea and the execution are full of genius. The frontispiece of the same book contains a study of Heads, than which Hogarth certainly never did anything better. These explanatory lines are below the picture: —

> "Number 1 's an ancient Carlist; number 3 a Paris artist;
> Gloomily there stands between them number 2, a Bonapartist;
> In the middle is King Louis Philip standing at his ease,
> Guarded by a loyal grocer, and a serjeant of police;
> 4 's the people in a passion; 6 a priest of pious mien;
> 5 a gentleman of fashion copied from a magazine."

No words can do justice to the truth and power of this group of characters: it gives a history of France during the Orleans dynasty.

It would not be easy to imagine better criticisms of art than those from Mr. Thackeray's hand in "Fraser," in "Punch," in a kindly and beautiful paper on our inimitable John Leech in the "Quarterly," in a Roundabout on Rubens, and throughout his stories, — especially the "Newcomes," — wherever art comes in. He touches the matter to the quick, — and touches nothing else; and, while sensitive to all true and great art, he detects and detests all that is false or mean. He is not so imaginative, not so impassioned and glorious, not so amazing in illustration, and in painting better than pictures, as Mr. Ruskin, who has done more for art and its true interests than all other writers. But he is more to be trusted because he is more objective, more cool, more critical in the true sense. He sees everything by the *lumen siccum*, though it by no means follows that he does not feel as well as see; but here, as in everything else, his art "has its seat in reason, and is judicious." Here is his description of Turner's Old Téméraire, from a paper on the Royal Academy in "Fraser." We can give it no higher praise than that it keeps its own with Ruskin's: —

"I must request you to turn your attention to a noble river piece, by J. W. M. Turner, Esq., R. A., 'The Fighting Téméraire,' as grand a painting as ever figured on the walls of any academy, or came from the easel of any painter. The old Téméraire is dragged to her last home by a little, spiteful, diabolical steamer. A mighty red sun, amidst a host of flaring clouds, sinks to rest on one side of the picture, and illumines a river that seems interminable, and a countless navy that fades away into such a wonderful distance as never was painted before. The little demon of a steamer is belching out a volume (why do I say a volume? not a hundred volumes could express it) of foul, lurid, red-hot, malignant smoke, paddling furiously, and lashing up the water round about it; while behind it (a cold, gray moon looking down on it), slow, sad, and majestic, follows the brave old ship, with death, as it were, written on her. . . . . It is absurd, you will say (and with a great deal of reason), for Titmarsh or any other Briton to grow so politically enthusiastic about a four-foot canvas, representing a ship, a steamer, a river, and a sunset. But herein surely lies the power of the great artist. He makes you see and think of a great deal more than the objects before you; he knows how to soothe or to intoxicate, to fire or to depress, by a few notes, or forms, or colors, of which we cannot trace the effect to the source, but only acknowledge the power. I recollect some years ago, at the theatre at Weimar, hearing Beethoven's 'Battle of Vittoria,' in which, amidst a storm of glorious music, the air of 'God save the King' was introduced. The very instant it begun, every Englishman in the house was bolt upright, and so stood reverently until the air was played out. Why so? From some such thrill of excitement as makes us glow and rejoice over Mr. Turner and his 'Fighting Téméraire,' which I am sure, when the art of translating colors into poetry or music shall be discovered, will be found to be a magnificent national ode or piece of music."

When speaking of "The Slave Ship" by the same amazing artist, he says, with delightful *naïveté:* "I don't know whether it is sublime or ridiculous," — a characteristic instance of his outspoken truthfulness; and he lays it down that the "first quality of an artist is to have a large heart," believing that all art, all imaginative work of the highest order, must originate in and be addressed to the best powers of the soul, must "submit the shows of things to the desires of the mind."

Mr. Trollope says, in the "Cornhill" for this February, "That which the world will most want to know of Thackeray is the effect which his writings have produced." In one sense of the word, the world is not likely ever to find this out; it is a matter which each man must determine for himself. But the world can perhaps ascertain what special services Mr. Thackeray has rendered; and it is this probably which Mr. Trollope means. His great service has been in his exposure of the prevailing faults of his time. Among the foremost are the faults of affectation and pretense, but there is one yet more grievous than these, — the skeptical spirit of the age. This he has depicted in the gentlest and saddest of all his books, "Pendennis": —

"And it will be seen that the lamentable stage to which his logic at present has brought him" (Arthur Pendennis) "is one of general skepticism and sneering acquiescence in the world as it is; or if you like so to call it, a belief qualified with scorn in all things extant. . . . . And to what does this easy and skeptical life lead a man? Friend Arthur was a Sadducee, and the Baptist might be in the wilderness shouting to the poor, who were listening with all their might and faith to the preacher's awful accents and denunciations of wrath or woe or salvation; and our friend the Sadducee would turn his sleek mule with a shrug and a smile from the crowd, and go home to the shade of his terrace, and muse over preacher and audience, and turn to his roll of Plato, or his pleasant Greek song-book babbling of honey and Hybla, and nymphs and fountains and love. To what, we say, does this skepticism lead? It leads a man to a shameful loneliness and selfishness, so to speak, — the more shameful, because it is so good-humored and conscienceless and serene. Conscience! What is conscience? Why accept remorse? What is public or private faith? Mythuses alike enveloped in enormous tradition."

The delineation is not a pleasant one, but it is true. The feeling hardly deserves to be called skepticism; it is rather a calm indifferentism, a putting aside of all things sacred. And as the Sadducees of Judea were, on the whole, better men than the Pharisees, so this modern Sadducean feeling prevails not only among the cultivated classes, but among those conspicuously honorable and upright. These men, in fact, want spiritual guides and teachers. The clergy do not supply this want; most of them refuse to acknowledge its existence; Mr. Thackeray, with his fearless truthfulness, sees it and tells it. To cure it is not within his province. As a lay-preacher, only the secondary principles of morality are at his command. "Be each, pray God, a gentleman," is his highest sanction. But though he cannot tell the afflicted whither to turn, it is no slight thing to have laid bare the disorder from which so many suffer, and which all, with culpable cowardice, study to conceal. And he does more than lay bare the disorder; he convinces us how serious it is. He does this by showing us its evil effect on a good and kindly nature. No teaching can be more impressive than the contrast between Pendennis under the influence of this skeptical spirit, and Warrington, over whom, crushed as he is by hopeless misfortune, it has no power.

The minor vices of affectation and pretension he assails directly. To do this was his especial mission from the first. What success may have attended his efforts we cannot certainly tell. It is to be feared, however, that, despite his teaching, snobs, like poverty, will never cease out of the land. But all who feel guilty, — and every one of us is guilty more or less, — and who desire to amend, should use the means: the "Book of Snobs" should be read carefully at least once a year. His was not the hortatory method. He had no notion that much could be done by telling people to be good. He found it more telling to show that by being otherwise they were in danger of becoming unhappy, ridiculous, and contemptible. Yet he did not altogether neglect positive teaching. Many passages might be taken from his works — even from the remorseless "Book of Snobs" itself — which inculcate the beauty of goodness; and the whole tendency of his writings, from the first to the last line he penned during a long and active literary life, has invariably been to inspire reverence for manliness and purity and truth. And to summon up all, in representing after his measure the characteristics of the age, Mr. Thackeray has discharged one of the highest functions of a writer. His keen insight into modern life has enabled him to show his readers that life fully; his honesty and high tone of mind has enabled him to do this truly. Hence he is the healthiest of writers. In his pages we find no false stimulus, no pernicious ideals, no vulgar aims. We are led to look at things as they really are, and to rest satisfied with our place among them. Each man learns that he can do much if he preserves moderation; that if he goes beyond his proper sphere he is good for nothing. He teaches us to find a fitting field for action in our peculiar studies or business, to reap lasting happiness in the affections which are common to all. Our vague longings are quieted; our foolish ambitions checked; we are soothed into contentment with obscurity, — encouraged in an honest determination to do our duty.

A "Roundabout Paper" on the theme *Nil nisi bonum* concludes thus: —

"Here are two literary men gone to their account; and, *laus Deo,* as far as we know, it is fair, and open, and clean. Here is no need of apologies for shortcomings, or explanations of vices which would have been virtues but for unavoidable, etc. Here are two examples of men most differently gifted: each pursuing his calling; each speaking his truth as God bade him; each honest in his life; just and irreproachable in his dealings; dear to his friends; honored by his country; beloved at his fireside. It has been the fortunate lot of both to give incalculable happiness and delight to the world, which thanks them in return with an immense kindliness, respect, affection. It may not be our chance, brother-scribe, to be endowed with such merit or rewarded with such fame. But the rewards of these men are rewards paid to our service. We may not win the baton or epaulettes; but God give us strength to guard the honor of the flag!"

The prayer was granted: he had strength given him always to guard the honor of the flag; and now his name is worthy to be placed beside the names of Washington Irving and Lord Macaulay, as of one no whit less deserving the praise of these noble words.

We have seen no satisfactory portrait of Mr. Thackeray. We like the photographs better than the prints; and we have an old daguerreotype of him without his spectacles which is good; but no photograph can give more of a man than is in any one ordinary — often very ordinary — look of him; it is only Sir Joshua and his brethren who can paint a man liker than himself. Laurence's first drawing has much of his thoroughbred look, but the head is too much tossed up and *vif.* The photograph from the later drawing by the same hand we like better: he is alone, and reading with his book close up to his eyes. This gives the prodigious size and solidity of his head, and the sweet mouth. We have not seen that by Mr. Watts, but, if it is as full of power and delicacy as his Tennyson, it will be a comfort.

Though in no sense a selfish man, he had a wonderful interest in himself as an object of study, and nothing could be more delightful and unlike anything else than to listen to him on himself. He often draws his own likeness in his books. In the "Fraserians," by Maclise, in "Fraser," is a slight sketch of him in his unknown youth; and there is an excessively funny and not unlike extravaganza of him by Doyle or Leech, in the "Month," a little short-lived periodical, edited by Albert Smith. He is represented lecturing, when certainly he looked his best.

The foregoing estimate of his genius must stand instead of any special portraiture of the man. Yet we would mention two leading traits of character traceable, to a large extent, in his works, though finding no appropriate place in a literary criticism of them. One was the deep steady melancholy of his nature. He was fond of telling how on one occasion, at Paris, he found himself in a great crowded *salon;* and looking from the one end across the sea of heads, being in Swift's place of calm in a crowd,[1] he saw at the other end a strange visage, staring at him with an expression of comical woebegoneness. After a little he found that this rueful being was himself in the mirror. He was not, indeed, morose. He was alive to and thankful for every-day blessings, great and small; for the happiness of home, for friendship, for wit and music, for beauty of all kinds, for the pleasures of the "faithful old gold pen"; now running into some felicitous expression, now playing itself into some droll initial letter; nay, even for the creature comforts. But his persistent state, especially for the

1 "An inch or two above it."

later half of his life, was profoundly *morne*, — there is no other word for it. This arose in part from temperament, from a quick sense of the littleness and wretchedness of mankind. His keen perception of the meanness and vulgarity of the realities around him contrasted with the ideal present to his mind could produce no other effect. This feeling, embittered by disappointment, acting on a harsh and savage nature, ended in the *sæva indignatio* of Swift; acting on the kindly and too sensitive nature of Mr. Thackeray, it led only to compassionate sadness. In part, too, this melancholy was the result of private calamities. He alludes to these often in his writings, and a knowledge that his sorrows were great is necessary to the perfect appreciation of much of his deepest pathos. We allude to them here, painful as the subject is, mainly because they have given rise to stories, — some quite untrue, some even cruelly injurious. The loss of his second child in infancy was always an abiding sorrow, — described in the "Hoggarty Diamond," in a passage of surpassing tenderness, too sacred to be severed from its context. A yet keener and more constantly present affliction was the illness of his wife. He married her in Paris when he was "mewing his mighty youth," preparing for the great career which awaited him. One likes to think on these early days of happiness, when he could draw and write with that loved companion by his side: he has himself sketched the picture: "The humblest painter, be he ever so poor, may have a friend watching at his easel, or a gentle wife sitting by with her work in her lap, and with fond smiles or talk or silence, cheering his labors." After some years of marriage, Mrs. Thackeray caught a fever, brought on by imprudent exposure at a time when the effects of such ailments are more than usually lasting both on the system and the nerves. She never afterwards recovered so as to be able to be with her husband and children. But she has been from the first intrusted to the good offices of a kind family, tenderly cared for, surrounded with every comfort by his unwearied affection. The beautiful lines in the ballad of the "Bouillabaisse" are well known: —

"Ah me! how quick the days are flitting!
I mind me of a time that 's gone,
When here I 'd sit as now I 'm sitting,
In this same place, — but not alone.
A fair young form was nestled near me,
A dear, dear face looked fondly up,
And sweetly spoke and smiled to cheer me, —
There 's no one now to share my cup."

In one of the latest "Roundabouts" we have this touching confession: "I own for my part that, in reading pages which this hand penned formerly, I often lose sight of the text under my eyes. It is not the words I see; but that past day; that by-gone page of life's history; that tragedy, comedy it may be, which our little home-company was enacting; that merry-making which we shared; that funeral which we followed; that bitter, bitter grief which we buried." But all who knew him know well, and love to recall, how these sorrows were soothed and his home made a place of happiness by his two daughters and his mother, who were his perpetual companions, delights, and blessings, and whose feeling of inestimable loss now will be best borne and comforted by remembering how they were everything to him, as he was to them.

His sense of a higher Power, his reverence and godly fear, is felt more than expressed — as indeed it mainly should always be — in everything he wrote. It comes out at times quite suddenly, and stops at once, in its full strength. We could readily give many instances of this. One we give, as it occurs very early, when he was probably little more than six-and-twenty; it is from the paper, "Madam Sand and the New Apocalypse." Referring to Henri Heine's frightful words, "Dieu qui se meurt," "Dieu est mort," and to the wild godlessness of "Spiridion," he thus bursts out: "O awful, awful name of God! Light unbearable! mystery unfathomable! vastness immeasurable! Who are these who come forward to explain the mystery, and gaze unblinking into the depths of the light, and measure the immeasurable vastness to a hair? O name that God's people of old did fear to utter! O light that God's prophet would have perished had he seen!

who are these now so familiar with it?" In ordinary intercourse the same sudden "Te Deum" would occur, always brief and intense, like lightning from a cloudless heaven; he seemed almost ashamed, — not of it, but of his giving it expression.

We cannot resist here recalling one Sunday evening in December, when he was walking with two friends along the Dean road to the west of Edinburgh, — one of the noblest outlets to any city. It was a lovely evening, — such a sunset as one never forgets: a rich dark bar of cloud hovered over the sun, going down behind the Highland hills, lying bathed in amethystine bloom; between this cloud and the hills there was a narrow slip of the pure ether, of a tender cowslip color, lucid, and as if it were the very body of heaven in its clearness; every object standing out as if etched upon the sky. The northwest end of Corstorphine Hill, with its trees and rocks, lay in the heart of this pure radiance, and there a wooden crane, used in the quarry below, was so placed as to assume the figure of a cross; there it was, unmistakable, lifted up against the crystalline sky. All three gazed at it silently. As they gazed, he gave utterance in a tremulous, gentle, and rapid voice, to what all were feeling, in the word "CALVARY!" The friends walked on in silence, and then turned to other things. All that evening he was very gentle and serious, speaking, as he seldom did, of divine things, — of death, of sin, of eternity, of salvation; expressing his simple faith in God and in his Saviour.

There is a passage at the close of the "Roundabout Paper," No. XXIII., "De Finibus," in which a sense of the ebb of life is very marked: the whole paper is like a soliloquy. It opens with a drawing of Mr. Punch, with unusually mild eye, retiring for the night; he is putting out his high-heeled shoes, and before disappearing gives a wistful look into the passage, as if bidding it and all else good-night. He will be in bed, his candle out, and in darkness, in five minutes, and his shoes found next morning at his door, the little potentate all the while in his final sleep. The whole paper is worth the most careful study; it reveals not a little of his real nature, and unfolds very curiously the secret of his work, the vitality, and abiding power of his own creations; how he "invented a certain *Costigan*, out of scraps, heel-taps, odds and ends of characters," and met the original the other day, without surprise, in a tavern parlor. The following is beautiful: "Years ago I had a quarrel with a certain well-known person (I believed a statement regarding him which his friends imparted to me, and which turned out to be quite incorrect). To his dying day that quarrel was never quite made up. I said to his brother, 'Why is your brother's soul still dark against me? *It is I who ought to be angry and unforgiving, for I was in the wrong.*'" *Odisse quem læseris* was never better contravened. But what we chiefly refer to now is the profound pensiveness of the following strain, as if written with a presentiment of what was not then very far off: "Another Finis written; another milestone on this journey from birth to the next world. Sure it is a subject for solemn cogitation. Shall we continue this story-telling business, and be voluble to the end of our age?" "Will it not be presently time, O prattler, to hold your tongue?" And thus he ends: —

"Oh, the sad old pages, the dull old pages; oh, the cares, the *ennui*, the squabbles, the repetitions, the old conversations over and over again! But now and again a kind thought is recalled, and now and again a dear memory. Yet a few chapters more, and then the last; after which, behold Finis itself comes to an end, and the Infinite begins."

He sent the proof of this paper to his "dear neighbors," in Onslow Square, to whom he owed so much almost daily pleasure, with his corrections, the whole of the last paragraph in manuscript, and above a first sketch of it also in MS., which is fuller and more impassioned. His fear of "enthusiastic writing" had led him, we think, to sacrifice something of the sacred power of his first words, which we give with its interlineations: —

"Another Finis, another slice of life which *Tempus edax* has devoured! And I may have to write the word once or twice perhaps, and then an end of Ends. ~~Finite is over, and Infinite beginning.~~ Oh the troubles, the cares, the *ennui*, the ~~complications,~~ disputes, the repetitions, the old conversations over and over again, and here and there and oh the delightful passages, the dear, the brief, the forever remembered! ~~And then~~ A few chapters more, and then the last, and then behold Finis itself coming to an end and the Infinite beginning!"

How like music this, — like one trying the same air in different ways; as it were, searching out and sounding all its depths. "The dear, the brief, the forever remembered;" these are like a bar out of Beethoven, deep and melancholy as the sea! He had been suffering on Sunday from an old and cruel enemy. He fixed with his friend and surgeon to come again on Tuesday; but with that dread of anticipated pain, which is a common condition of sensibility and genius, he put him off with a note from "yours unfaithfully, W. M. T." He went out on Wednesday for a little, and came home at ten. He went to his room suffering much, but declining his man's offer to sit with him. He hated to make others suffer. He was heard moving, as if in pain, about twelve, on the eve of

> "The happy morn,
> Wherein the Son of Heaven's eternal King,
> Of wedded maid, and virgin-mother born,
> Our great redemption from above did bring."

Then all was quiet, and then he must have died — in a moment. Next morning his man went in, and opening the windows found his master dead, his arms behind his head, as if he had tried to take one more breath. We think of him as of our Chalmers; found dead in like manner; the same childlike, unspoiled open face; the same gentle mouth; the same spaciousness and softness of nature; the same look of power. What a thing to think of, — his lying there alone in the dark, in the midst of his own mighty London; his mother and his daughters asleep, and, it may be, dreaming of his goodness. God help them, and us all! What would become of us, stumbling along this our path of life, if we could not, at our utmost need, stay ourselves on Him?

Long years of sorrow, labor, and pain had killed him before his time. It was found after death how little life he had to live. He looked always fresh with that abounding silvery hair, and his young, almost infantine face, but he was worn to a shadow, and his hands wasted as if by eighty years. With him it is the end of Ends; finite is over, and infinite begun. What we all felt and feel can never be so well expressed as in his own words of sorrow for the early death of Charles Buller: —

> "Who knows the inscrutable design?
>   Blessed be He who took and gave!
> Why should your mother, Charles, not mine,
>   Be weeping at her darling's grave?
> We bow to Heaven that willed it so,
>   That darkly rules the fate of all,
> That sends the respite or the blow,
>   That's free to give, or to recall."

Some Recollections of Thackeray.

"You have asked me to give you my recollections of Thackeray, but not, I trust, with the expectation that they would consist of a string of piquant anecdotes and witticisms, or contain any new and striking revelations in regard to his life or character. For the former object a better memory and more pointed pen — perhaps I might rather say, a more active imagination — than mine would be required, and for the latter a more extended and intimate knowledge of the man.

"I saw him for the first time a day or two after his arrival in America on his first visit, and I saw him for the last time a few weeks before his death.

"Like the rest of the world, I had exclaimed, on reading the opening chapters of 'Vanity Fair,' 'Fielding redivivus!' and it was therefore with a feeling of curiosity and elation, the capacity for which has been seriously impaired by time, that I accepted the invitation of a friend, himself a man of eminence in the world of letters, to meet the author who had given me so much delight, and whose fame had just reached its zenith.

"It is rarely that the appearance of a distinguished man corresponds with our expectations; but the fault is in ourselves, or rather in the nature of things. People are often disappointed in their first view of the Alps: they expect to be enraptured or stunned *before* their eyes or their minds have grasped the features which constitute the beauty and sublimity of the scene; whereas this effect can only *follow* a process in which the first step is to get rid of one's false impressions, and there is nothing more jarring to the mind than a rectification of its misconceptions. Let us afterward compare the reality, full of force and character, with the vague and colorless image we had formed for ourselves, and we shall know what we have gained.

"Good portraits of Thackeray are so common, and so many of your readers saw him in the lecture-room, that I need not describe his person. The misshaped nose, so broad at the bridge, and stubby at the end, was the effect of an early accident. His near-sightedness, unless hereditary, must have had, I think, a similar origin, for no man had less the appearance of a student who had weakened his sight by application to books. In his gestures — especially in the act of bowing to a lady — there was a certain awkwardness, made more conspicuous by his tall, well-proportioned, and really commanding figure. His hair, at forty, was already gray, but abundant and massy; the cheeks had a ruddy tinge and there was no sallowness in the complexion; the eyes, keen and kindly even when they wore a sarcastic expression, twinkled sometimes through and sometimes over the spectacles. What I should call the predominant expression of the countenance was courage — a readiness to face the world on its own terms, without either bawling or whining, asking no favors, yielding, if at all, from magnanimity. I have seen but two faces in which this expression, coupled with that of high intellectual power, was equally striking — those of Daniel Webster and Thomas Carlyle. But the former had a saturnine gloom even in its animation, and the latter a variety and intensity of expression, which were absent from Thackeray's.

"On the evening of which I speak I sat beside him some time in the library — an apartment of which he has made mention in the opening sentence of 'The Virginians.' A variety of topics, chiefly literary, were discussed. His own manner soon made it impossible, even for one who in every sense looked up to him, to be otherwise than familiar in tone. No one was more thoroughly high-bred, but no one more averse to formality, and there was consequently no fencing required before one could feel at ease with him. His expressions at times were tolerably blunt. Speaking of Carlyle, he said, 'Why don't he hang up his d——d old fiddle?' adding, however, in reference to the "Life of Sterling," then recently published, 'Yes, a wonderful writer! What could *you or I* (!) have made of such a subject?' He went on to praise Carlyle's dignity of character: '*He* would not go round making a show of himself, as I am doing.' 'But he *has* lectured.' 'He did it once, and was done with it.'

"When I was going away, and had reached the farther end of a vacant drawing-room, a voice, which had already grown familiar to my ear, called after me from the half-opened glass door of the library, 'I say! come and dine with me to-morrow at two-thirty.' While I was gladly accepting the invitation the host came out and took us both back to smoke, the ladies and other guests having in the mean time left. We sat till a late, or rather early, hour. Thackeray was at that time a furious smoker, choosing the strongest cigars and dispatching them in rapid succession. Part of the talk ran on Dickens, of whom he spoke in a somewhat different strain from what he used in public. Our host had introduced the subject by saying, after some censure of that popular novelist's extravagancies, 'But I like Dickens personally: he is so genial and frank.' 'Genial, yes,' was the reply; 'but frank' — and a twinkle came from over the spectacles — 'well, frank as an oyster.' — 'Dickens,' he said afterwards, apropos of some remarks on literary genius, 'is making ten thousand pounds a year. He is very angry at me for saying so, but I *will* say it, for it is true. He does n't like me: he knows that my books are a protest against his — that if the one set are true, the other must be false. But 'Pickwick' is an exception: it is a capital book. It is like a glass of good English ale. I wish I had it to read before going to bed to-night.' And he made a slight inaudible motion with his lips, as if tasting the beverage he had mentioned.

"During his stay in Boston at that time, as well as on a second visit, I saw a good deal of him, both in company and *tête-à-tête*. In his general manner he gave one the impression of having a very large amount of vitality, without that excess which makes some people restless and others boisterous. I never heard him laugh heartily or talk vehemently, nor do I believe that breeding or a deep experience of life had so much to do with this as natural temperament. But neither was there any appearance of *ennui*, though a lassitude — the effect of ill-health, from which, though you would never have suspected it, he was seldom free — came over him at times, especially in the small hours. In society he was almost always animated, and he had the power of diffusing animation over a somewhat frigid circle.

"One evening, when he was expected at a large dinner-party, where the other guests were already assembled, a general conversation sprung up — we were sitting in a semicircle before a bright coal fire — in reference to his lectures. Two or three extremely well-read men, of a rather formal turn of mind, did most of the talk, and indulged in a good deal of carping criticism. It was not his depreciation of Swift and Sterne, or his exaggerated laudation of Addison, of which they complained, but of his calling Sir William Temple a prig — whereas Temple was in truth the very model of a gentleman, who had written in a style which was charming, though a little incorrect — his talking of 'a place in the Pipe Office' in evident and deplorable ignorance of what the Pipe Office was or had been, and similar matters. At the height, or rather depth, of the discussion the subject of it entered, and going round the circle shook hands with those he knew, and finding they were by far the greater number, turned back to exchange the same greeting with those to whom he had merely bowed when introduced. In a moment it seemed as if a new spirit had taken possession of the company. It was not that the theme was changed: on the contrary, though dropped for a moment, most of the mooted points were again taken up. But there was a life in the conversation which it had wanted before. It was no longer a dry debate. On some of the questions Thackeray owned himself wrong. He admitted with a quizzical look his lack of information in regard to the Pipe Office. But he stuck to the assertion that Stella was a natural daughter of Temple, went over the facts from which the inference was drawn, and in answer, not to a counter-statement, but a demand for more sufficient proof, said, 'I cannot prove it: it is apparent, like the broken nose in my face.'

"The French draw a distinction between *l'homme de génie* and *l'homme d'esprit*, meaning by the latter term not so much the witty man, or the man of talent or even of intellect, but rather the man whose powers, without being great or profound, are always at his service, who is never embarrassed or at a loss in his particular line, which line, in a land where the *salon* is an institution, always includes sparkling conversation. Thackeray was a man of genius, but he possessed as much of *esprit* as is compatible with genius. If seldom brilliant, he was always self-possessed and ready. It is doubtful whether those who knew him best and longest could make out a list of his bon-mots which would bear repeating; but he could always say a thing sufficiently good for the occasion, and in a manner which set it off to advantage. Being challenged by a lady for a rhyme to *liniment*, he replied immediately, with a reference to the customary physician's fee in England,

'When the doctor writes for liniment,
There is nothing but a guinea meant.'

Another fair one going into raptures, on shipboard, over the appearance of the foam-crested waves, and demanding a simile in default of imagination on her own part, he said, 'They look like white ponies racing over green fields.' With a sly look he would take quick advantage of any slip of the tongue committed by another. He told a story on one occasion of the head-master of Eton having flogged over a hundred boys in continuous succession for some joint offense. 'One would have thought such a performance would have raised a rebellion,' said a listener. 'What were the boys' — meaning the rest of the school — 'about? Didn't they know what was going on?' 'No, not till the next morning, when they woke up and found they had been flogged.'

"Such things, I well know, are not at all worth citing for themselves, but, like his bright look and springing gait, they were, in their abundance, indications of a quality which is obvious enough in Thackeray's writings — at least in the earlier ones — but which was more conspicuous in his conversation — a quality which, for lack of a better term, I must call animal spirits, though this carries with it a notion of effusiveness and loud gayety that would not at all suit the description. When a subject was seriously discussed he could talk gravely, though with diminished fire, and was apt, when pressed, to have recourse to banter. I doubt whether any one ever induced him to say much about matters of religious belief or feeling. What is called his cynicism showed itself occasionally. He defined the difference between Shakespeare and an ordinary mind as a difference in the length of two maggots. But much of his light talk was intended, not so much to conceal as to keep down a sensibility amounting almost to womanliness which belonged to his nature, and which contrasted, one might almost say, struggled, with the manliness which was equally its characteristic. He could not read anything pathetic without actual discomfort, and was unable, for example, to go through with the "Bride of Lammermoor."[1] I have heard him allude to some early sorrows, especially the loss of a child, in a way which showed how sharp and painful

[1] Yet Hawthorne expresses his surprise that Thackeray should have been able to read some of his own pathos — the final number of "The Newcomes" — aloud, and compares this coolness with his own emotion when he had read the last scene of "The Scarlet Letter" to his wife.

was the recollection after the lapse of many years. That he could sympathize warmly with others I infer from much that I have heard. His well-known sensitiveness sprung perhaps from the same root as his sensibility. 'I like Thackeray,' an English critic once said in my hearing, 'but I cannot respect him — he is so sensitive.' But his sensitiveness made harsh things distasteful to him even when he was not himself the object of them. 'You fiend!' he said to a friend who was laughing over a sharp attack on an acquaintance of both, and refused to hear or read a word of it.

"Hawthorne says in his 'English Note-Books' that he had heard Thackeray could not endure to have servants about him, feeling uneasy in their presence, and he goes on, *à la Hawthorne*, to analyze the feeling. On his second visit to America he brought with him an attendant who looked like a good specimen of the best English domestics. 'I don't call him my servant,' he told me: 'I call him my companion. I found he didn't like the company down-stairs' (this was at a hotel), 'so I make him sit beside me at the *table d' hôte*.' Yet Thackeray was a man of aristocratic feelings, and the last person in the world to be *hail fellow well met* with every one who chose to accost him. A touch on the shoulder from a railway conductor — after the manner of those 'gentlemanly' officials — made the blood tingle in his finger-ends, and left a feeling of indignation which burned anew as he recounted the occurrence. He demanded civil treatment, but hauteur or condescension was not in his disposition. Standing in no awe of the highest, he had no wish to inspire awe in the lowest. One day, after we had lunched together at Parker's, he handed a gold-piece to the waiter, saying, 'My friend, will you do me the favor to accept a sovereign?' 'I am very much obliged to you, *Mr. Thackeray*,' was the man's reply: he had not read "Vanity Fair" or "Esmond" I imagine, but he had probably tasted their author's bounty on former occasions. Yet Thackeray would sometimes be whimsically economical for others. 'Don't leave this bit of paper,' he would say to a visitor who was laying down a card on the table; 'it has cost you two cents, and will be just as good for your next call.'

"It was on a bright day, though the month was November and the place London, in 1863, that I called upon Thackeray at his red-brick house — the only one of the kind (so he thought) in the metropolis — looking out on the old oaks of Kensington Gardens. There had been no correspondence between us since I had seen him last, but two or three kindly messages had reached me, and I had read a passage in a letter to a friend at whose house we had met, in which he wrote, 'How often I think I should like to be sitting with you and Z. at the table in —— street, with that old butler putting on another bottle of the '35!' It was a little past noon, and I was shown up to his bedroom, a large and cheerful apartment, with little furniture besides the bed — the bed in which so shortly after he was to be found lying calm in death. There was a dressing-room behind, to which he went at times while making his toilette, keeping up the conversation through the open door. His appearance showed a change for which I was not prepared. It is hard to understand how his medical men should have allowed him to continue writing with signs of impending apoplexy so apparent to the unprofessional eye. In answer to my inquires about his health, he said he felt 'infernally old.' What was missing in his manner was a sort of light glee with which in former days he had been wont to tell an anecdote or say a good thing. The twinkle, too, was less bright, the lassitude more decided, and the sadness which lay deep in his nature, and against which, I think, he always fought, seemed to be gaining the upper hand. However, the sarcastic power was not extinct, and he expended several flings on the editor of a well-known literary paper — a person of infinite conceit and of never-failing ignorance. The war in America formed, of course, one of the topics of talk. Thackeray expressed no decided opinion, but his leanings were evidently on the side of the South. Speaking of letter-writing, 'I had left off,' he said, 'corresponding with everybody but Sally Fairfax, and you have killed her — sweet creature!' He asked whether I thought the North would ultimately beat, and on my assurance that its superior resources, combined with its persistent spirit, admitted of little doubt on that point, answered, with a half sigh, 'I suppose so: you will tire them out at last.' He took a volume from a book-case to show me the autograph of Washington on the fly-leaf. 'You have forgotten all about *him*,' he said: 'you care nothing now for his warnings.' I laughed, reminding him that I had always protested against his idolatry for Washington. After chatting for an hour or more, he changed his dressing-gown for a coat, and asked me to go down to his library — or rather to the room he had built for this object, but which was not well suited to it, making him consequently discontented with the house. An old lady in black entered: 'My mother,' he said, and presented me to her. There was no strong resemblance that I noticed; but her face had a look of placid resoluteness inherent, I fancy, in the stock, and she gave a vigorous description of a combat she had carried on in the night with the agile insects that disturb slumber. She was the widow of a second husband, and bore the name of Smith. She looked likely to survive her son, and did in fact, though only by a few months. After a while she went out, and Thackeray produced a box of Manillas, but did not smoke himself. 'I envy you,' he said — and I cannot help thinking, if the doctors had taken away his pen instead of his cigar, they would have done at least equally well. It was on this occasion that he mentioned the child who had died so many years before. 'Even now,' he said, 'I cannot bear to think of it.' When he shook hands with me on the door-step, he pointed to the oaks and said, 'You have no such trees in America; but they are dying.' The appearance of the top branches indicated as much; and he too, from indications not less apparent — he in whose character and intellect the strength of the oak was united with the beauty and the sweetness of the lily — he too was dying.

"It was with a shock, but not of surprise, that going into Galignani's on Christmas morning I received the announcement that Thackeray was dead. Returning through the Rue Rivoli, I passed a tailor's shop, which I had sometimes entered without recollecting till then that the name of the proprietor, M. Arendt, stands at the head of a characteristic dedication in one of the great novelist's books."

A Friend of my Childhood.

I suppose I must have pulled the bell very hard that day, for otherwise I don't think she would have kept me waiting twenty minutes, as she did. *She* was only my mother's servant-woman, whose duty was to wait upon the dinner-table and the door, the latter function being the more onerous one. Looking back at my conduct over the lapse of eighteen years, I am disposed to acknowledge that she was right in the abstract in punishing the inconsiderate impatience which made me keep the door-bell upon a continuous ring till I was let in. But how wrong did the event prove her! Scarcely was I warmed up to my work, when, turning my head, I saw a tall gentleman with broad shoulders and a round face, whose look, at first one of inquiry, and perhaps bewilderment as he tried to distinguish the house he was in search of from among a dozen, all characterized by that unity of design which in Philadelphia strikes forcibly the intelligent foreigner, suddenly changed to one of amusement, not, I thought then, unmixed with approval, as he caught sight of me at my reprehensible employment. And as I rang with a persistency which nothing can now call from me, he stood on the bottom step (for it was my mother whom he had come to see) with that expression in which I found so little discouragement, still looking forth from those great eyes of his, which had pierced deeply and sternly so many of the false and hollow things of this world, and which now, not, I am sure, for the first time, were bent kindly down upon a rude boy and his ruder pranks. How little did the latter know about the tall gentleman, and how little too would he have cared even if he had known all there was to know about him: known that then the age was beginning to recognize its philosopher, whose lessons, sharp and bitter enough at first, were to make it better and truer and purer, if such a thing were possible of accomplishment.

But that he was tall I did know, and my standard of eminence was a purely physical one. Five feet eight I did not despise, but six feet alone commanded absolute and genuine respect; and he, I believe, stood six feet one. The presumption which could keep such a height of perfection waiting at the front door shocked me beyond expression. No, not beyond expression, for the triumphant yell with which the hapless servant-girl was greeted when at last she admitted me, and I burst in exclaiming, "You have kept the tall gentleman waiting half an hour!" must have given, I think, some adequate idea of my feelings. To that incident may I not justly look back with satisfaction? Am I not right in taking pride to myself for having amused for so long a time one whose momentary attention the witty and the wise have thought it no slight thing to have gained? And — who knows? — perhaps he himself did not altogether forget it, and with the two sturdy *Buben* on the Rhine-boat, and those little men he used to meet at Eton or on the play-ground of the Charterhouse, may not the American boy also have found a place in his kindly memory? But I wish it clearly understood that I did not force myself upon his acquaintance: no lion-hunting can be laid to my charge. On the contrary, after giving him a glance of approbation for proving such an effectual weapon to me in subduing my enemy in the gate — or rather the enemy whose offense was that she was anywhere but in the gate — I did not, I can truly say, bestow another thought upon him till I was sent for to afford him, at his own special request, the honor of knowing me. Were there no servants in the kitchen to be tormented? No cats in the back yard to be chased with wild halloo? No rowdy boys in the alley with whom to fraternize over pies of communistic mud? No little sister up-stairs much nicer than any tall gentleman, even though he might have come from across the ocean and be thought a great deal of by the grown-up people, that I should go out of my way to see him, and abandon my cherished pursuits to listen to him talking of what I did not understand, and did not believe was worth understanding? No: my position was a high one, and I kept to it, for, though I gave up my occupations a little while and went down to the parlor, it was simply because politeness and filial obedience were the ruling motives of my conduct. Of the first formal introduction to my friend I have but a shadowy recollection. He said, I think, that he wanted to know the impetuous little boy he had met outside; but nothing more which I can recall. My own share in the conversation has entirely faded from my memory: it is probable indeed that I had no share in it at all, being less at my ease in the conventional sphere of a drawing-room than in the more unconstrained atmosphere of a back alley. Yet in hours of depression, when, in spite of the most sincere desire to think favorably of mankind, I cannot fail to notice that I am not appreciated as I should be by the undiscerning world, and my soul seeks consolation and forgetfulness from higher sources, I half believe that when he went back to his own country, and spoke there, as I have heard he did very often, of the pleasant people he had met here, of the American friends he valued so much, it was perhaps not without an *arrière-pensée* of his noisy acquaintance of the doorstep in Locust Street.

The intercourse so tempestuously begun was threatened with an early extinction, for my newly acquired friend returned soon after this to his home, where were the two little girls whom he was fond of describing while saying that he would not dare to bring them to this country, lest they should come to despise the simple muslin gowns with which they were then quite content; home to the toil of the hard-worked brain, the steady labor of the untiring pen, which was to give us before it rested forever nothing indeed like his earlier works, but much which we shall not willingly let die; home to England, in truth, but only that, having written the story of certain of its kings, as he had before written the worthier history of some of its unsceptred monarchs, whose sovereign sway is over our spirits still, he might come again across the ocean to greet all who should wish to hear him tell of the Britain of a century past, when our own history had as yet scarcely seen the conclusion of its opening chapter; giving as he did, so minute, life-like details relating to the great men of that time, whose familiar names were to most of his hearers not much more than names, but which, thanks in great part to him, are now as household words. And so we met, and being two years older, I was accorded the honor of becoming one of his auditors, going with my mother to hear each of his lectures. We sat in a box on one side of the stage in Concert Hall, and at this moment I recall the tall, dignified figure standing before the desk on which were placed his notes, and the crowded room full of indistinguishable attentive faces. I sometimes fancy too that I cannot have forgotten what are now favorite passages from those lectures — passages read and re-read, and then read again, till they are known almost by heart. I cannot acknowledge to myself that I do not remember his voice and look, and the tribute of listening silence which waited upon him while he spoke.

One at least of these evenings is well remembered. Its distinguishing feature was my being tipped. My mother and I had gone on this occasion quite early to our places — half an hour or three quarters before the time when the lecture should begin — and we found the lecturer already at his post. He, with head thrown back, had been walking with long strides up and down the little waiting-room, and talking in bright spirits to my mother, when a sudden thought seemed to strike him, and diving into one of his pockets he brought out a sovereign — perhaps it was a five-dollar gold piece — and insisted upon giving it to me; but the proposal produced at once a most severe parental resistance, while I disinterestedly looked on — a resistance apparently quite unlooked for by " my illustrious friend," who had much trouble in explaining that this species of beneficence was a thing of course in England. But American pride was silenced at last, though not convinced, as will be seen, for it planned on the spot a compromise which should reconcile the differences of national feeling, though *I* was induced to suppose that the sovereign was as far out of my reach as ever; and being then, as I said before, above or below such things, I turned all my attention to the lecture, which began soon afterward, and whose subject, the royal bugbear of patriotic school-boys of that time, I imagined I knew all about. It was therefore with astonished awe that I heard the peroration, when the speaker said, appealing directly to us all: "O brothers! speaking the same dear mother tongue! O comrades! enemies no more, let us take a mournful hand together, as we stand by this royal corpse and call a truce to battle! Low he lies to whom the proudest used to kneel once, and who was cast lower than the poorest: dead, whom millions prayed for in vain. Driven off his throne; buffeted by rude hands; with his children in revolt; the darling of his old age killed before him untimely; our Lear hangs over her breathless lips and cries, 'Cordelia! Cordelia! stay a little!'

> 'Vex not his ghost: oh, let him pass! He hates him
> That would upon the rack of this rough world
> Stretch him out longer."

Hush! strife and quarrel, over the solemn grave! Sound, trumpets, a mournful march! Fall, dark curtain, upon his pageant, his pride, his grief, his awful tragedy." This view of the subject was altogether new.

The compromise just spoken of—and I must bring to an end my story, already too long—consisted in the expenditure of the five-dollar piece in two of the books written by the bestower of that inflammatory coin. I open the volumes of "Pendennis" and "Vanity Fair" which have been lying at my elbow, and across the title-page of each I see written, in curiously small and delicate hand, "—— ——, with W. M. Thackeray's kind regards. April, 1856." These were the books.

A Child's Glimpse of Thackeray.

So many years ago that I do not care to count them I was taken by my guardian to an evening party at the house of a distinguished physician in Philadelphia. Though too much of a boy at the time to appreciate or understand thoroughly what was going on, there were certain little occurrences which made an impression on me then, and which have dwelt in my memory ever since.

The agreeable occupation of munching sponge-cake in which I spent the first part of the evening did not prevent my noticing a personage, tall, large, spectacled, slightly gray, leaning against one of the folding doors, and engaged in conversation with a number of gentlemen, among whom I recognized Mr. Peter, then British consul. What it was that attracted me I cannot exactly tell, but there certainly must have been something to beguile me out from a "coign of vantage" well adapted both for seeing and eating — a snug ambuscado behind the piano.

"Who is that man?" said I to my guardian, with indicating forefinger.

"That *gentleman* is Mr. Thackeray," was the smiling reply as the forefinger yielded to gentle pressure and fell by my side; "and when your mouth is empty I wish to take you up and present you to him. I will come back for you in a few minutes."

Forthwith I retreated again to my fastness to finish the cake and prepare for the ordeal, curiously eyeing the Transatlantic author all the time.

It seems strange, but even now — and I have visited many scenes and mixed with many people since that night — I can perfectly remember the tenor of my boyish cogitations. They were about as follows: So, that was Mr. Thackeray? What had I heard about him?

I knew that he had written a book called "Vanity Fair," because a charming lady (that is, she seemed charming to me in those halcyon days) had talked about it in my hearing, and said it was very clever. That was all I knew. How the people pressed round him and looked at him, while those across the room pointed and whispered! Was it, then, so very hard to write a book? How those girls on the sofa were pointing, and my guardian had just told me it was very rude to point!

I wonder if the manner in which fame first breaks upon him who achieves it is the same in which the reputation of another first looms upon the mind of a thinking boy? I had not yet learned that those talents which win power and position for their possessor compel alike admiration from equals and obsequiousness from inferiors. Before many years had passed over me I had learned that lesson by heart; but it is pleasant to recall those independent hours when my little mind indulged in such unbiased speculations, as heedless of the future as the sponge-cake I had just devoured.

My guardian came back, and after due inspection of hands, mouth, and clothes, took me up to the chatting group between the folding doors. The group separated, and I stood face to waistcoat with the great novelist, he looking kindly down on me through his glasses; I, after gazing up in his face for a moment, dropping my eyes and beginning a minute inspection of the watch-chain with which his left hand was playing, his right meanwhile holding my little pair tight in its mighty grasp. What he said to me I forget. It was probably more his manner than his words that induced me to stay at his side and listen to what others were talking about.

It struck me, from his languid position, that, without wishing to appear so, he was fatigued, and sometimes a little annoyed by the trivial questions so often put to him. At last he took me with him across the room, where he sat down on a sofa, and soon made me feel quite at home beneath his genial sway. Some young ladies were sitting near, with whom he entered into some little talk about music, and flowers, and such things as women love. Anon, a dashing young secretary of legation made his appearance — keen, pert, semi-witty, just from abroad, perfectly satisfied with himself, ready to show the latest fashions to all true believers. He lounged on the other end of the sofa, picked up the thread of conversation immediately, and was soon in the middle of a fluent speech, oratorically instructing everybody. Mr. Thackeray waited patiently till he was through, rather glad, I think, to be relieved from talking himself, and then, in reply to some new and extraordinary doctrine the young diplomat had broached, laughed and said, "Bravo, jeune homme! à la bonne heure! Vraiment, on fait des progrès dans ce pays ci!"

Then, somehow there coming a little lull in the noisy talk, he turned to me and asked how old I was, where I lived, and what I wanted to do in the great world some day — whether I had ever been in England, and where I had learned to speak French ; all which I answered, much to his apparent amusement and to the best of my small ability.

Then came supper, when I lost him in the crowd. If I felt any sorrow at losing him, it must have been a boyish sorrow, easily assuaged by the sight of divers comfits and good things on a well-spread table. I suppose there must have been a sense of gratified pride at being noticed by a distinguished man so publicly. Perhaps the sorrow has come with maturer years. At all events, I only saw him again just as he was taking his departure, when he turned and said a few kind words to me, and then was gone.

Hodder's Recollections of Thackeray.

In approaching the name of William Makepeace Thackeray I feel a degree of delicacy, and even timidity, which his absence from the scene of his world-wide renown does not tend to diminish ; for Thackeray was a man of such large mental proportions, and such far-seeing power in his mode of anatomizing and criticising human character, that one seems to be treading on volcanic ground in venturing to deal with him at all. But of what is biography composed ? Assuredly not of the knowledge and experience of one privileged person, but of the aggregate contributions of many, who are willing, when occasion offers, to state what they know for the information and benefit of posterity. A hundred admirers of Thackeray might undertake to write a memoir of him, and yet the task of doing full justice to his character and career must necessarily be left to a chosen future historian, who shall zealously gather together all the bits and fragments to be found scattered among books and men, and blend them into a substantial and permanent shape. But it must be admitted that there is an exceptional difficulty in regard to Thackeray, inasmuch as there were few whom he allowed to *know* him, in the true sense of the phrase — that is to say, there was a constitutional reserve in his manner, accompanied, at times, by a cold austerity, which led to some misgivings as to the possibility of his being the pleasant social companion his intimates often described him to be. And yet it is well known to those who saw much of Thackeray in his familiar moments that he could be essentially "jolly" (a favorite term of his) when the humor suited him, and that he would, on such occasions, open his heart as freely as if the word "reticence" formed no part of his vocabulary; whereas, at other times, he would keep himself entirely within himself, and answer a question by a monosyllable, or peradventure by a significant movement of the head. At one moment he would look you full in the face and greet you jauntily; at another he would turn from you with a peculiar waving of the hand, which of course indicated that he had no desire to talk. Men who were members of the same club with him have been heard to say that sometimes he would pass them in the lobbies unnoticed, and at others he would cheerfully initiate a conversation, and leave behind him an impression that sullenness or *hauteur* was wholly foreign to his nature. It should be stated, however, that his health for many years had never been entirely unimpaired, and that his acute sensibility often rendered it irksome to him to come in contact with his fellow-men. In short, he was essentially of a nervous temperament, and altogether deficient in that vigorous self-possession which enables a man to shine in public assemblies; for it was absolute pain to him to be called upon to make a speech, and even in ordinary conversation he showed no particular desire to hold a prominent place. But, the above considerations apart, it would be easier to know many men in a few days than it would be thoroughly to understand Thackeray in the same number of years. Douglas Jerrold, dating his acquaintance with Thackeray from the time that the latter, by some curious hazard, illustrated his book of "Men of Character," was often heard to say, "I have known Thackeray eighteen years, and I don't know him yet." But that the great novelist and satirist had a generous and sympathetic heart can hardly, I think, be disputed; and even the few brief letters which I received from him are sufficient to prove that, however austere he sometimes appeared to be externally, he was very rarely wanting in readiness to perform a kind office.

At one period of my intercourse with Mr. Thackeray I had been reading his "Journey from Cornhill to Grand Cairo," and, having always been an enthusiastic admirer of his writings, long before I knew that the "Michael Angelo Titmarsh" of "Fraser's Magazine" was identical with W. M. Thackeray, I could not refrain from expressing to him by letter the delight I had drawn from his Egyptian pages. Among other things, I remember being deeply impressed by the graphic power displayed in the poem of "The White Squall," and by the charming burst of parental feeling with which it concludes.[1]

Mr. Thackeray's answer was as follows: —

"DEAR HODDER, — I thank you very much for your note, and am very glad that my little book has given you pleasure. I hope that the future works of the same author will please you, and, indeed, am quite anxious to have as many people as may be of your opinion. It is not my intention to return to Constantinople at present, and when there I hope I shall be more moral than in former days, and have no desire to fling the handkerchief to any members whatsoever of his Highness's seraglio. Yours truly,

"W. M. THACKERAY."

I cannot at this distant date precisely call to mind the circumstances under which I continued, at intervals, to meet Mr. Thackeray, but the various letters I received from him contain the most gratifying proof that he was always well affected toward writers who could not possibly aspire to his

[1] "And when, its force expended,
The harmless storm was ended,
And as the sunrise splendid
Came blushing o'er the sea;
I thought as day was breaking,
My little girls were waking,
And smiling, and making
A prayer at home for me."

own rank in the literary army; and the following extract is one of the best evidences of this fact I can adduce, because, at the time he wrote it, my knowledge of him did not extend beyond that which was derived from a few brief conversations with him at the chambers of a friend, upon matters in no way relating to business, such as afterward brought me more closely in contact with him.

The letter refers to a loss which had just befallen me, in consequence of some changes which had taken place in a newspaper establishment with which I was then connected. It is dated May 19, 1855, and says: —

"I am sincerely sorry to hear of your position, and send the little contribution which came so opportunely from another friend whom I was enabled once to help. When you are well-to-do again I know you will pay it back, and I dare say somebody else will want the money, which is meanwhile most heartily at your service."

It was afterward explained to me that Mr. Thackeray made a practice of acting upon the principle embodied in the above note. Like many other generous men, he had always a few pounds floating about among friends and acquaintances whom he had been able to oblige in their necessity, and whenever he received back money which he had lent, he did not put it into his pocket with a glow of satisfaction at having added so much to his exchequer; but congratulated himself that he could transfer the same sum to another person who he knew was in need of it.

To my great satisfaction I received one evening a note from Mr. Thackeray, which I had been expecting for several days, as he had promised to write to me on the subject; but, as the delay seemed ominous, I began to think he had changed his determination, and would not require my services as now suggested. In this note, which is dated Onslow Square, September 6, 1855, he says, after referring to other matters: —

"I want a little work done in the way of arranging papers, copying at the B. M., etc. — if you are free, and will come here on Tuesday morning next, I can employ your services, and put some money in your way."

To Onslow Square I accordingly went on the morning fixed upon, and found Mr. Thackeray in his study to receive me; but, instead of entering upon business in that part of the house, he took me up-stairs to his bedroom, where every arrangement had been made for the convenience of writing. I then learned that he was busily occupied in preparing his lectures on the "Four Georges," and that he had need of an amanuensis to fill the place of one who was now otherwise occupied. In that capacity, it was my task to write to his dictation, and to make extracts from books, according to his instructions, either at his own house or at the British Museum. This duty called me to his bedchamber every morning, and, as a general rule, I found him up and ready to begin work, though he was sometimes in doubt and difficulty as to whether he should commence operations sitting, or standing, or walking about, or lying down. Often he would light a cigar, and, after pacing the room for a few minutes, would put the unsmoked remnant on the mantle-piece, and resume his work with increased cheerfulness, as if he had gathered fresh inspiration from the "gentle odors" of the "sublime tobacco."

It was not a little amusing to observe the frequency with which Mr. Thackeray, in the moments of dictation, would change his position, and I could not but think that he seemed most at his ease when one would suppose he was most uncomfortable. He was easy to "follow," as his enunciation was always clear and distinct, and he generally "weighed his words before he gave them breath," so that his amanuensis seldom received a check during the progress of his pen. He never became energetic, but spoke with that calm deliberation which distinguished his public readings; and there was one peculiarity which, among others, I especially remarked, viz., that when he made a humorous point, which inevitably caused me to laugh, his own countenance was unmoved, like that of the comedian Liston, who, as is well known, looked as if he wondered what had occurred to excite the risibility of his audience.

Many authors have often declared that they could not write to dictation. Thackeray was one who *could*, and liked to do so; and no better proof need be afforded of his power in that respect than is to be found in his "Four Georges," which contain some of the most thoughtful and vigorous passages that ever emanated from his brain.

While I was thus daily engaged with Mr. Thackeray he sometimes required my assistance on a Sunday afternoon; and I call to mind one Sunday in particular — I think it was the last before he started for America — when I found him in exceptionally high spirits, and much more inclined to talk than to write. He spoke of the journey he was about to commence, and of the money he should probably make by his readings in America. He wanted a few thousands more, he said, for he had not yet made enough. True, he added, that he possessed a small share of the world's goods, and he was happy to think that he had paid off one moiety of the cost of his house (which he then occupied), and that he should be able before he left the country to discharge the remainder of the liability. He then went on to relate some of his literary experiences, and the circumstances under which his fortunes had improved during the last few years, observing that lecturing was certainly more profitable than magazine writing. He next alluded to his friends, the contributors to "Punch," and passed in review many of their virtues and idiosyncrasies; and was at some pains to show that he held the humorous brotherhood in high esteem.

In speaking of periodical literature, he said he contemplated producing a magazine or journal in his own name after his return from America; and upon my venturing to observe that I hoped he did not intend to encourage the anonymous system in regard to his contributors, as the conductors of other publications of the day seemed resolved to do, he replied, "No. I think that's hard lines."[1] Our conversation

[1] On his return to England, the *Cornhill Magazine* was started under the editorship of Mr. Thackeray.

next turned upon his mission to the United States; and when he hinted at the probability of his taking a secretary with him, as he had done on his former visit to that country, I suggested that I should be delighted to fill that office, if he had not already selected some one. He promised to consider my suggestion, and let me know what determination he had arrived at; but, in the mean time, he feared he should require a valet more than a secretary. On the following morning he said he had turned the matter over in his mind, and had come to the conclusion that, in consequence of the state of his health, he should be obliged to take a servant with him instead of a secretary; adding, dryly, "I can ask a servant to hold a basin to me; but I doubt if I could so treat a secretary — at least, he *might* object." He smiled as he made this droll observation, but I too well knew that it was a true word spoken in jest; for he was subject to periodical illnesses which rendered the services of a valet most essential to him; and the young man who filled that situation at the time was fortunately one in whom he placed implicit confidence; and he was thankful for the gentle way in which his servant tended him.

It was but natural to suppose that, considering Mr. Thackeray's popularity among his friends, and the interest which attached to the object of his visit to America, a desire would be shown to invite him to a farewell dinner. The project being initiated, Mr. Peter Cunningham undertook the duties of secretary; and all the preliminary arrangements were of the most satisfactory kind, care being taken that the party should be entirely private, and that it should consist exclusively of Mr. Thackeray's intimates.

On the morning of the banquet he was in a state of great nervous anxiety, saying that it was very kind of his friends to give him a dinner, but that he wished it was over, for such things always set him trembling. "Besides," he exclaimed, "I have to make a speech, and what am I to say? Here, take a pen in your hand and sit down; and I'll see if I can hammer out something. It's hammering now; I'm afraid it will be *stammering* by and by." I did as he requested, and he dictated with much ease and fluency a speech — or rather the heads of a speech — which he proposed delivering in response to the inevitable toast of his own health.

This was on a morning in the first week of October, 1855, and the dinner took place at the London Tavern in the evening of the same day, the duties of chairman being delegated to Mr. Charles Dickens, who from the very beginning of his public career had always manifested a remarkable aptitude for that responsible office.

The following account of the affair was afterward published by a gentleman who was present on the occasion : —

"The Thackeray dinner was a triumph. Covers, we are assured, were laid for sixty; and sixty and no more sat down precisely at the minute named to do honor to the great novelist. Sixty very hearty shakes of the hand did Thackeray receive from sixty friends on that occasion ; and hearty cheers from sixty vociferous and friendly tongues followed the chairman's — Mr. Charles Dickens — proposal of his health, and of wishes for his speedy and successful return among us. Dickens — the best after-dinner speaker now alive — was never happier. He spoke as if he was fully conscious that it was a great occasion, and that the absence of even one reporter was a matter of congratulation, affording ample room to unbend. The table was in the shape of a horseshoe, having two vice-chairmen, and this circumstance was wrought up and played with by Dickens in the true Sam Weller and Charles Dickens manner. Thackeray, who is far from what is called a good speaker, outdid himself. There was his usual hesitation ; but this hesitation becomes his manner of speaking and his matter, and is never unpleasant to his hearers, though it is, we are assured, most irksome to himself. This speech was full of pathos and humor and oddity, with bits of prepared parts imperfectly recollected, but most happily made good by the felicities of the passing moment. Like the 'Last Minstrel,'

> 'Each blank in faithless memory's void
> The poet's glowing thought supplied.'

It was a speech to remember for its earnestness of purpose and its undoubted originality. Then the chairman quitted, and many near and at a distance quitted with him. Thackeray was on the move with the chairman, when, inspired by the moment, Jerrold took the chair, and Thackeray remained. Who is to chronicle what now passed? — what passages of wit — what neat and pleasant sarcastic speeches in proposing healths — what varied and pleasant, aye, and at times, sarcastic acknowledgments? Up to the time when Dickens left, a good reporter might have given all, and with ease, to future ages; but there could be no reporting what followed. There were words too nimble and too full of flame for a dozen Gurneys, all ears, to catch and preserve. Few will forget that night. There was an 'air of wit' about the room for three days after. Enough to make the two companies, though downright fools, right witty."

I am now fortunately enabled to give the original draft of the speech thus pictured, and which as I have just stated, was written by me to Mr. Thackeray's dictation on the morning of the dinner. It will be seen, from the occasional vacant spaces, that the writer of the above was correct in assuming that the speaker had intentionally left blanks with the view of supplying them at the moment. Some few sentences will be found to be quite incomplete; but it is not very difficult to conjecture how Mr. Thackeray would fill them up; though I believe I am right in saying that the speech as delivered fell far short of the speech as written. The latter has never been out of my possession since it came from Mr. Thackeray's lips; for, having once tested his power, and brought to light the thoughts which animated him, he did not care for the MS., and did not even read it. I subjoin it, *ipsissima verba:* —

"I know great numbers of us here present have been invited to a neighboring palace where turtle, champagne, and all good things are as plentiful almost as here, and where there reigns a civic monarch with a splendid court of officers, etc. — The sort of greeting that I had myself to-day — this splendor, etc. — the bevy in the ante-room — have filled my bosom with an elation with which no doubt Sir Francis Graham Moon's throbs.[1] I am surrounded by respectful friends, etc. — and I feel myself like a Lord Mayor. To his lordship's delight and magnificence there is a drawback. In the fountain of *his* pleasure there surges a bitter. He is thinking about the 9th of November, and I about the 13th of October.[2]

"Some years since, when I was younger and used to frequent jolly assemblies, I wrote a Bacchanalian song, to be chanted after dinner, etc. — I wish some one would sing that song now to the tune of the 'Dead March in Saul,' etc. — not for me — I am miserable enough; but for you, who seem in a great deal too good spirits. I tell you I am not — all the drink in Mr. Bathe's [3] cellar won't make me. There may be sherry there 500 years old — Columbus may have taken it out from Cadiz with him when he went to discover America, and it won't make me jolly, etc. — and yet, entirely unsatisfactory as this feast is to me, I should like some more. Why can't you give me some more? I don't care about them costing two guineas a head. It is not the turtle I value. Let us go to Simpson's fish ordinary — or to Bertolini's or John o'Groat's, etc. — I don't want to go away — I cling round the mahogany-tree.

"In the course of my profound and extensive reading I have found it is the habit of the English nation to give dinners to the unfortunate. I have been living lately with some worthy singular fellows 150 or 160 years old. I find that upon certain occasions the greatest attention was always paid them. They might call for anything they liked for dinner. My friend Simon Frazer, Lord Lovat, about 109 years since, I think, partook very cheerfully of minced veal and sack before he was going on his journey [4] — Lord Ferrers (Rice) [5] — I could

[1] Sir F. G. Moon, Bart., was at that time Lord Mayor of London.

[2] The day on which he was to start for America.

[3] The then proprietor of the London Tavern.

[4] He was beheaded in the year 1745 for fighting in the cause of the Pretender, in the Scottish rebellion of 1745.

[5] Executed at Tyburn in the year 1760 for the murder of one Johnson, the re-

tell you a dozen jolly stories about feasts of this sort. I remember a particular jolly one at which I was present, and which took place at least 900 years ago. My friend Mr. Macready gave it at Fores Castle, North Britain, Covent Garden. That was a magnificent affair indeed. The tables were piled with most splendid fruits — gorgeous dish-covers glittered in endless perspective — Macbeth — Macready, I mean — taking up a huge gold beaker, shining with enormous gems that must have been worth many hundred millions of money, filled it out of a gold six-gallon jug, and drank courteously to the general health of the whole table. Why did he put it down? What made him, in the midst of that jolly party, appear so haggard and melancholy? It was because he saw before him the ghost of John Cooper, with chalked face and an immense streak of vermilion painted across his throat! No wonder he was disturbed. In like manner I have before me at this minute the horrid figure of a steward, with a basin perhaps, or a glass of brandy and water, which he will press me to drink, and which I shall try and swallow, and which won't make me any better — I know it won't.

"Then there 's the dinner, which we all of us must remember in our school-boy days, and which took place twice or thrice a year at home, on the day before Dr. Birch expected his young friends to reassemble at his academy, Rodwell Regis. Don't you remember how the morning was spent? How you went about taking leave of the garden, and the old mare and foal, and the paddock, and the pointers in the kennel; and how your little sister wistfully kept at your side all day; and how you went and looked at that confounded trunk which old Martha was packing with the new shirts, and at that heavy cake packed up in the play-box; and how kind 'the governor' was all day; and how at dinner he said, 'Jack — or Tom — pass the bottle' in a very cheery voice; and

ceiver of his estates. His lordship was allowed to ride from the Tower to the scaffold in his own landau, and appeared gayly dressed in a light-colored suit of clothes, embroidered with silver. It was doubtless to this circumstance that Mr. Thackeray intended to allude in filling up the vacuum.

how your mother had got the dishes she knew you liked best; and how you had the wing instead of the leg, which used to be your ordinary share; and how that dear, delightful, hot raspberry rolly-polly pudding, good as it was, and fondly beloved by you, yet somehow had the effect of the notorious school stick-jaw, and choked you and stuck in your throat; and how the gig came; and then, how you heard the whirl of the mail-coach wheels, and the tooting of the guard's horn, as with an odious punctuality the mail and the four horses came galloping over the hill. — Shake hands, good-by! God bless everybody! Don't cry, sister. — Away we go! and to-morrow we begin with Dr. Birch, and six months at Rodwell Regis!

"But after six months came the holidays again![1] etc., etc., etc."

There is small chance of it being denied that the above is as fully characteristic of Mr. Thackeray's peculiar style as any passage to be found in his works. Not a doubt or question could possibly be raised in regard to its authorship; for there spoke Thackeray in his own original way — heart, lips, tone, and language.

That Mr. Thackeray was sometimes given to the "melting mood" may be shown by a little incident, in the relation of which I trust I shall violate no confidence, or throw myself open to the charge of ascribing to the great author a larger share of the milk of human kindness than often falls to the lot of ordinary mortals.

One morning I was making my way to 36 Onslow Square, at an earlier hour than usual, when, to my great surprise, I met Mr. Thackeray pacing up and down the footway in a state of great mental uneasiness. It was so entirely contrary to his custom — at least as far as my experience told me — to leave his house at so early an hour, and I was so much concerned at seeing him in such depression, that I was naturally induced to say that I hoped nothing very serious had happened to his

[1] Mr. Thackeray was to be absent from England for that space of time.

household. He answered, "Poor Marochetti's child is dying." Having said this, tears came to his relief, and he speedily returned home. He was on terms of close friendship with the Baron Marochetti (his next-door neighbor), and he sympathized with that well-known sculptor in the deep love he bore for his dying child. He was in a cheerless mood for the remainder of the day, and in the course of his work reverted many times to the calamity which he so much deplored.[1]

Again, on the morning of his departure for America. He was to start by an early train, and when I arrived (for it had been previously arranged that I should see him before he left) I found him in his study, and his two daughters in the dining-room — all in a very tearful condition; and I do not think I am far wrong in saying that if ever man's strength was overpowered by woman's weakness it was so upon this occasion; for Mr. Thackeray could not look at his daughters without betraying a moisture in his eyes, which he in vain strove to conceal. Nevertheless he was enabled to attend to several money transactions which it was necessary he should arrange before leaving; and to give me certain instructions about the four volumes of his "Miscellanies" then in course of publication, and which he begged me to watch in their passage through the press, with a view to a few foot-notes that might be thought desirable. Then came the hour for parting! A cab was at the door, the luggage had all been properly disposed of, and the servants stood in the hall, to notify, by their looks, how much they regretted their master's departure. "This is the moment I have dreaded!" said Thackeray, as he entered the dining-room to embrace his daughters; and when he hastily descended the steps of the door he *knew* that they would be at the window to

"Cast one longing, lingering look behind."

"Good-by," he murmured, in a suppressed voice, as I followed him to the cab; "keep close behind me, and let me try to jump in unseen."

[1] It will be recollected that the tablet to Thackeray's memory in Westminster Abbey was the design and workmanship of the late Baron Marochetti.

The instant the door of the vehicle was closed behind him he threw himself back into a corner and buried his face in his hands. That was the last I saw of Mr. Thackeray before he left London on his second visit to the United States; and I think I have given sufficient proof that, great as was his power of poising the shafts of ridicule at the follies and vices of the day, and coldly reserved as he sometimes was in his demeanor, he was full of that gentleness of heart to which his writings constantly bear testimony; and it was his instinct to be actuated by the kindliest impulses which do honor to our common nature.

On Mr. Thackeray's return from a successful tour in the United States, he sought to make arrangements for the reading of his lectures on "The Four Georges" in London and the provinces. He had fulfilled his purpose of delivering them in America in the first instance, and he had now no reason to think that they would not be listened to with satisfaction in his own country. To undertake the responsibility of organizing any plan of proceeding, of appointing agents, of superintending the publication of advertisements, and settling the various other preliminary matters incidental to what is technically called a "lecturing tour," was, of course, more than could possibly be expected from a man of Mr. Thackeray's intellectual calibre. It soon, therefore, became known that he was "in the market," as it were, ready to accept engagements for the reading of his lectures; and Mr. Frederick Beale, belonging to a musical firm of some note, expressed his desire to Mr. Thackeray, through me, to make the speculation his own, and to "farm" the lecturer at a given sum for each reading. Mr. Thackeray appeared pleased at the proposition, and a morning was appointed for Mr. Beale to accompany me to his house, with a view of my introducing him to the celebrated writer, and witnessing the arrangement of the terms.

Mr. Thackeray was in his dressing-gown and slippers, and received us in his bedroom, where, as I have already stated, he generally passed his mornings and wrote his books. His study being a small back-room behind the dining-room, on the ground floor, and being exposed to the noises from the street, he had caused his writing-table and appliances to be carried up-stairs to the second floor, where two rooms had been thrown into one — the back to be used as a sleeping-chamber, and the front, which was considerably larger than the other, as a sitting-room. The dimensions of this apartment being capacious, Mr. Thackeray was enabled to move about in the intervals of writing, and to extend his limbs on a couch; and, in fine, to change his attitude as often as his convenience demanded, for the operation of dictating necessarily spared him the pain of confining himself to a sitting posture. On the morning in question some domestic annoyance had ruffled the serenity of his mind; and it was evident, from the abruptness of his manner, that he had no idea of being other than thoroughly "business-like" in the negotiations we were about to commence. After a little preparatory interchange of civilities (which it was pretty evident Mr. Thackeray would have described as a "bore" had it been possible to ascertain his candid opinion at the moment), Mr. Beale, in his usual courteous manner, suggested the terms himself; and Mr. Thackeray, like a true diplomatist as he was, never allowed it to be supposed that he thought them more than reasonably remunerative.

The payment proposed was fifty guineas for each reading, and Mr. Thackeray was to appear a certain number of times in London — at the Surrey Music Hall, for instance — and to undertake a tour of three weeks in the provinces. That he was well satisfied with his arrangement with Mr. Beale is best proved by the fact that, when he saw me on the following day, he exclaimed, "What terms! fifty guineas a night! Why, I should n't have received one half that sum for an article in 'Fraser' a few years ago."

As I was travelling entirely in an official character, and was not responsible to Mr. Thackeray, I studiously avoided forcing myself on his company, but always took especial care to select a carriage he did *not* occupy, and to plant myself in an hotel he did *not* patronize. Hence — if I may speak paradoxically — we pulled remarkably well together; and although the arrangements for a public reading every evening at eight o'clock left little opportunity for social enjoyment — that is to say, at a time when it would be most in accordance with his usual habit — Mr. Thackeray occasionally invited me to dine with him. "This is a nice room," he would say, if the apartment allotted to him chanced to have a rural aspect, with trees and flowers bobbing in at the window; "I could *write* here!" And where was it, it may be asked, that he could *not* write? for the twenty-two handsome volumes of his works lately issued bear sufficient presumptive evidence that his labor was done in various places and climes. May it not be fairly supposed that Titmarsh's "Carmen Lilliense," date Lille, September 2, 1843, and published in "Fraser's Magazine," was written on the identical spot where he was visited by the sad pecuniary misfortune which he so humorously deplores in the *refrain* of the ballad?

"My heart is weary, my peace is gone;
How shall I e'er my woes reveal?
I have no money; I lie in pawn,
A stranger in the town of Lille."

At the time of the publication of "Vanity Fair," Thackeray's great contemporary, Charles Dickens (for in spite of all remonstrance it has always been the fashion to place the two writers in the same category, and often to sacrifice one at the shrine of the other, according to the particular taste of the person addressing himself to the subject), was producing, in the accustomed monthly form — the green cover in the one instance, against the yellow cover in the other — his story of "Dombey and Son;" and it was Thackeray's delight to read each number with eagerness as it issued from the press. He had often been heard to speak of the work in terms of the highest praise. When it had reached its fifth number, wherein Mr. Charles Dickens described the end of little Paul with a depth of pathos which produced a vibratory emotion in the hearts of all who read it, Mr. Thackeray seemed electrified at the thought that there was one man living who could exercise so complete a control over him. Putting No. 5 of "Dombey and Son" in his pocket, he hastened down to Mr. Punch's printing-office, and entering the editor's room, where I chanced to be the only person present except Mr. Mark Lemon himself, he dashed it on the table with startling vehemence, and exclaimed, "There's no writing against such power as this — one has no chance! Read that chapter describing young Paul's death: it is unsurpassed — it is stupendous!"

Long after this, and during the period that I acted as his amanuensis, I went into his chamber one morning, as usual, and found him in bed (for, lest it should be supposed that Mr. Thackeray was what is commonly called a late riser, I should state at once that my visits to him were somewhat early, that is to say, before nine o'clock), a little pot of tea and some dry toast on a table by his side. I therefore remained at a distance from him, but Mr. Thackeray called me forward, and I discovered that he had passed a very restless night. "I am sorry," said I, "that you do not seem very well this morning." "*Well!*" he murmured — "no, I am not well. I have got to make that confounded speech to-night." I immediately recollected that he was to preside at the annual dinner of the General Theatrical Fund — an undertaking which I well knew was entirely repugnant to his taste and wishes. "Don't let that trouble you, Mr. Thackeray," said I; "you will be sure to be all right when the time comes." "Nonsense!" he replied, "it won't come all right — I can't make a speech. Confound it! That fellow Jackson let me in for this! Why don't they get Dickens to take the chair? He *can* make a speech, and a good one. *I'm* of no use." I told him that I thoroughly appreciated his remark in regard to Mr. Dickens, but that at the same time he was giving little credit to those whose discernment had selected him as the chairman of the evening; and they could not very well ask Mr. Dickens, as he had only a year or two since occupied that position at an anniversary dinner of the same institution. "They little think how nervous I am," said Thackeray; "and Dickens does n't know the meaning of the word."

In confirmation of this remark I observed that I once asked Mr. Dickens if he ever felt nervous on public occasions when called upon to speak; and his instant reply was, "Not in the least. The first time I took the chair at a public dinner I felt just as much confidence as if I had done the same thing a hundred times before." [1]

The result of Mr. Thackeray's chairmanship on the evening in question may here be recorded, with all respect to his memory, and with that desire to be strictly correct which he himself would have been the first to encourage. True to his engagement he took the post assigned to him, and commenced his duties as if he had resolved to set difficulties at defiance, and to show that the task was *not* quite impossible with him; but, unhappily for his nervous and sensitive temperament, Mr. Charles Dickens, as the president of the institution, sat at his right hand, and when he came to the all-absorbing toast of the evening, the terrifying fact rushed across his mind that his great contemporary would witness all his short-comings and his sad inferiority. He had prepared his speech, and he commenced with some learned allusions to the car of Thespis and the early history of the drama, when he suddenly collapsed, and brought his address to a close in a few commonplace observations which could scarcely be called coherent. He too painfully felt the weakness of his position; and notwithstanding a particularly kind and complimentary speech in which Mr. Dickens proposed his health as chairman, he could not recover the *prestige* he believed he had lost, and he left the room in company with an old friend at as early a moment as he could consistently with the respect he owed to the company.

One other instance I may mention of the many which came

[1] Charles Dickens is as happy at intimate social gatherings as on great public occasions. A dinner was given to his eldest son on the occasion of his departure for China on a commercial mission. Blanchard Jerrold was in the chair, with Mr. Dickens on his left, and the guest of the evening on his right. The young gentleman became warmed with the wine; whereupon Dickens, in returning thanks for his own health, took the opportunity of observing that after such a generous dinner "a little transaction in tea" would do his son a world of good.

within my own knowledge of Mr. Thackeray's distrust of his own powers and his desire to exalt others at the expense of himself. I found him one morning in an unusually loquacious mood, and I had not been with him many minutes before he said he was not disposed to trouble himself with any work that day. He was more inclined to talk. Adverting by a natural transition from the subject he had first touched upon to the respective merits of various writers who were then daily before the world, he spoke of the great success of "Household Words," and of the ability displayed in its pages by some of its contributors. "There 's one man," for instance, he emphatically exclaimed, "who is a very clever fellow, and that is Sala. That paper of his, 'The Key of the Street,' is one of the best things I ever read. I could n't have written it. I wish I could."

It was a common practice in the towns we visited for quidnuncs, ambitious dowagers, and aspiring damsels pertaining to the order of blue-stockings, to pester Mr. Thackeray at the close of his lecture to insert his autograph in an album — a request with which he was not often willing to comply. On one occasion an album was placed before him by a young fellow, who thought to tempt him by calling attention to the fact that the signatures of several distinguished musicians, including that of one of our most celebrated tenors, were in the same book, and that therefore he would be in very good company. "What! among all these fiddlers!" exclaimed Thackeray, with pretended raillery. Having uttered the somewhat brusque phrase, he could not well do otherwise than satisfy the desire expressed; but he would not be prevailed upon to write more than the simple signature — "W. M. Thackeray." On another occasion the possessor of an album was much more fortunate. It belonged to a young lady of my acquaintance, and I had pleaded her cause so warmly that Mr. Thackeray opened the book, and I pointed out to him the names of certain contributors with whom I thought he might not object to be thus associated. He assented, and took the book home to his hotel, in order that he might have time to scan its contents. Among these he soon discovered the subjoined lines:

"Mont Blanc is the Monarch of Mountains —
They crown'd him long ago;
But who they got to put it on
Nobody seems to know.
"ALBERT SMITH.'

Under these lines Mr. Thackeray speedily wrote the following: —

"A HUMBLE SUGGESTION.
"I know that Albert wrote in hurry:
To criticise I scarce presume;
But yet methinks that Lindley Murray,
Instead of 'who,' had written *whom*.
"W. M. THACKERAY."

I need scarcely say that the young lady felt she had brought her album to a "very good market," and she could never afterward believe that Mr. Thackeray was other than the most amiable of authors and the most considerate of men.

If I remember rightly, Mr. Thackeray's engagement at Norwich required him to give four readings — that is to say, he was to introduce all "The Four Georges" — one each night — to the people of that city. He was received with much cordiality in that bustling capital, and his lectures were attended with a success justly proportioned to their merit; but it was evident that his health was much impaired, and that he was about to endure one of those sad periodical attacks to which he had long been liable. On the concluding night of the series he had some difficulty in getting to the Hall by the usual time, and when arrived there he was in great nervous trepidation, and expressed his fear that he should be quite unable to get through his work. I said what I could to make him more hopeful and cheerful, and when he made his appearance on the platform he was greeted with such a storm of applause, that he proceeded in his task with scarcely less vigor than he generally displayed; but as he approached the end of his discourse his voice faltered, and it was a severe struggle to him to reach the final sentence.

On the following morning, at an early hour, I received a message from him requesting that I would go and see him at his hotel, as he was laid up with one of his violent attacks. I lost no time in obeying his wish, and on entering his chamber I was much shocked to see him lying closely covered up in bed. He was suffering great pain, and begged that I would not look at him, as he knew he was a hideous object. I entreated that he would place my services entirely at his command, and he replied, with a waving of his hand, that all he wanted was some money out of the exchequer in my possession, as he should unfortunately be detained there by his illness. The desire was of course immediately satisfied, and he would not listen to me when I asked him to allow me to remain with him. It was beyond question under such a seizure as he was then afflicted with that he retired to his bed on that mournful night in December, 1863, when he endured his sufferings for the last time.

Some short period after I had left Mr. Thackeray at Norwich in the condition described, I saw him at his house in London, and on his making allusion to those dreadful illnesses which he said were the very bane of his life, I asked if he had ever received the best medical advice. Certainly he had, was his reply: "but what is the use of advice, if you don't follow it?" he continued. "They tell me not to drink, and I *do* drink. They tell me not to smoke, and I *do* smoke. They tell me not to eat, and I *do* eat. In short, I do everything that I am desired *not* to do, and, therefore, what am I to expect?"

As I was brought little in contact with Mr. Thackeray from this time forth, except in the lobby of the Reform Club (where, on occasions when I was waiting for a friend who was a member, I enjoyed the sight of forbidden luxuries), or on the steps of the Garrick, or sauntering along Pall Mall in that *insouciant* manner which was becoming as familiar at the West of London as Johnson's "rolling walk" was in Fleet Street, I shall not weary the reader with any details as to what might, could, would, or should have happened in connection with his every-day life. My sole object has been to place him before the reader precisely as I saw him, and to jot down such things as appeared to have some little historical interest. The most memorable event I can now call to mind, in relation to Mr. Thackeray, is at the same time the most melancholy one, for it brings me to the morning of Christmas-day, 1863, when I chanced to pay a visit to Horace Mayhew, in Old Bond Street. I entered the room cheerfully,

"As fits the merry Christmas-time,"

and proffered the usual good wishes to Mayhew and another friend who was present; but I was surprised to find that my animal spirits met with no response, and that my companions were as depressed as I was inclined to be the reverse. "Have n't you heard?" said Mayhew, looking ominously blank and chop-fallen. "Heard!" I exclaimed; "heard *what?*" "Why, about poor Thackeray?" "No; what about him?" "He 's dead!" "What!" I cried, almost petrified; "*our* Thackeray, the *great* Thackeray?" "Yes," he said, "too true. William Makepeace Thackeray: he died yesterday morning, or on the previous night." This was indeed a piece of news as saddening as it was unexpected, and when it was revealed to me I was dumb with an emotion which it would have been affectation in me to endeavor to disguise. As to Horace Mayhew, he had formed an affection for Thackeray which on that occasion expressed itself in accents of the most bitter grief.

It was soon explained that the lamented writer was found dead in his bed on Christmas-eve, and that the immediate cause of his disease was an effusion of blood on the brain, brought on by one of those violent stomach afflictions to which I have already referred. I could not but remark what a deep gloom the event would cast over many an otherwise happy fireside at that festive period; and I was afterward led to the reflection that the line above quoted would now too painfully bear the *second* reading given to it by the author—

"As fits the *solemn* Christmas-tide."

The line occurs in the last stanza of a little poem called "The End of the Play," with which Mr. Thackeray's Christmas book, "Dr. Birch and his Young Friends," closes; and as its plaintive tone of farewell would seem to be especially in harmony with the author's removal from the scene, I will quote the entire verse: —

"My song, save this, is little worth;
I lay the weary pen aside,
And wish for health and love and mirth,
As fits the solemn Christmas-tide.
As fits the holy Christmas birth
Be this, good friends, our carol still —
Be peace on earth, be peace on earth,
To men of gentle will."

He laid the weary pen aside! If these simple but impressive words may be taken as a foreshadowing of what his feelings might be when called upon to lay it aside for the last time, we may well believe that at that sad moment his thoughts were full of prayer for the earthly peace of all.

The duty of describing in detail the funeral of Mr. Thackeray must be left to his biographer — a character which will, doubtless, ere long be assumed by one who can speak of "greatness greatly;" but as I was present on that mournful occasion I am constrained to allude to it, as affording the last link in the chain of my reminiscences of this conspicuous example of representative men.

It was on the morning of the 30th December that Thackeray was carried to his resting-place in Kensal Green Cemetery. The atmosphere was warm, crisp, and clear; the ground was unusually elastic, and there was a genial glow over the face of nature which almost forbade the idea that the hundreds who were hastening to the burial-place were absorbed by other than cheering thoughts.

"The sun shone bright o'erhead;
Nothing in Nature's aspect intimated
That a great man was dead."

The number of persons present was estimated at about 2,000, and among them were many of the chosen lights of literature and art. Mr. Charles Dickens, Mr. Robert Browning, Mr.

Anthony Trollope, Mr. Mark Lemon, Mr. G. H. Lewes, the historian and critic; Mr. Theodore Martin, poet and satirist; Dr. Russell, of the "Times;" Mr. Frederick Lawrence, the author of "The Life of Fielding:" Mr. Higgins (Jacob Omnium), Mr. Robert Bell, Mr. Millais, R. A., Mr. George Cruikshank, Mr. John Leech, Mr. Shirley Brooks, Mr. Horace Mayhew, Mr. Charles Mathews, Mr. Tom Taylor, Mr. Creswick, R. A., M. Louis Blanc, Mr. John Tenniel, Mr. Edmund Yates — these are a few taken almost at random from the numerous gathering of friends assembled at the cemetery; but the most noteworthy circumstance struck me as being the deep sympathy shown in the event by a very large majority who could have known nothing of Thackeray except from his works.

It was, in truth, a ceremony so full of universal interest that it will be remembered as a tribute of respect to one of the few whose genius could alone command it; and, if I might be allowed for one moment to associate the *living* Thackeray with the scene, I should remark how forcibly it brought to the recollection of many, who saw the hearse enter the grounds, the funeral of Douglas Jerrold, when the noble gray head now laid low was observed towering among the pall-bearers. Indeed the mournful proceeding brought these two great names closely together in my mind; and I am free to confess that, remembering what I had seen of the inherent kindness of each, and recognizing so many faces at Kensal Green, which, six years before, I had marked at the ceremony at Norwood, I could not but regard the coincidence as fraught with both pleasure and pain. So striking, I thought, was the similarity between the circumstances attending the two burials, that it was difficult to dispel the illusion that, although the two men were not bound together in life by the strongest ties of friendship, the same spirit of literary brotherhood which had guided their fortunes on earth seemed to hover at last over their graves.

THE SNOB.

The earliest of Thackeray's literary efforts are associated with Cambridge. It was in the year 1829 that he commenced, in conjunction with a friend and fellow student, to edit a series of humorous papers, published in that city, which bore the title of "The Snob: a Literary and Scientific Journal." The first number appeared on the 9th of April in that year, and the publication was continued weekly. Though affecting to be a periodical, it was not originally intended to publish more than one number; but the project was carried on for eleven weeks, in which period Mr. Lettsom had resigned the entire management to his friend. The contents of each number—which consisted only of four pages of about the size of those of the present volume—were scanty and slight, and consisted entirely of squibs and humorous sketches in verse and prose, many of which, however, show some germs of that spirit of wild fun which afterwards distinguished the "Yellowplush" papers in "Fraser." When completed, the papers bore the following title:—

THE SNOB:

A LITERARY AND SCIENTIFIC JOURNAL.

NOT

"CONDUCTED BY MEMBERS OF THE UNIVERSITY."

Tityre, tu patulæ recubans sub tegmine fagi
Sylvestrem. VIRGIL.

Cambridge:

PUBLISHED BY W. H. SMITH,

ROSE CRESCENT.

1829.

A few specimens of the contents of this curious publication cannot but be interesting to the reader. The first specimen we shall select is a clever skit upon the Cambridge Prize Poem, as follows : —

TIMBUCTOO.

TO THE EDITOR OF THE "SNOB."

SIR, — Though your name be "Snob," I trust you will not refuse this tiny "Poem of a Gownsman," which was unluckily not finished on the day appointed for delivery of the several copies of verses on Timbuctoo. I thought, Sir, it would be a pity that such a poem should be lost to the world ; and conceiving "The Snob" to be the most widely-circulated periodical in Europe, I have taken the liberty of submitting it for insertion or approbation.

I am, Sir, yours, &c. &c. &c.

TIMBUCTOO. — PART I.

The situation.

In Africa (a quarter of the world),
Men's skins are black, their hair is crisp and curl'd,
And somewhere there, unknown to public view,
A mighty city lies, called Timbuctoo.

The natural history.

There stalks the tiger, — there the lion roars,
Who sometimes eats the luckless blackamoors ;
All that he leaves of them the monster throws
To jackals, vultures, dogs, cats, kites, and crows ;
His hunger thus the forest monarch gluts,
And then lies down 'neath trees called cocoa-nuts.

Lines 1 and 2. — See Guthrie's Geography.

The site of Timbuctoo is doubtful ; the Author has neatly expressed this in the poem, at the same time giving us some slight hints relative to its situation.

Line 5. — So Horace : "*leonum arida nutrix*."

Line 8. — Thus Apollo :

ελωρια τευχε κυνεσσιν
Οιωνοισι τε πᾶσι.

Lines 5–10. — How skillfully introduced are the animal and vegetable productions of Africa! It is worthy to remark the various garments in which the Poet hath clothed the lion. He is called, 1st, the "Lion" ; 2d, the "Monster" (for he is very large) ; and 3d, the "Forest Monarch," which undoubtedly he is

The lion hunt.
Quick issue out, with musket, torch, and brand,
The sturdy blackamoors, a dusky band!
The beast is found — pop goes the musketoons —
The lion falls covered with horrid wounds.
Their lives at home.
At home their lives in pleasure always flow,
But many have a different lot to know!
Abroad.
They 're often caught, and sold as slaves, alas!
Reflections on the foregoing.
Thus men from highest joys to sorrow pass.
Yet though thy monarchs and thy nobles boil
Rack and molasses in Jamaica's isle;
Desolate Afric! thou art lovely yet!

Lines 11–14. — The author confesses himself under peculiar obligations to Denham's and Clapperton's Travels, as they suggested to him the spirited description contained in these lines.

Line 13. — "Pop goes the musketoons." A learned friend suggested "Bang" as a stronger expression, but as African gunpowder is notoriously bad, the Author thought "Pop" the better word.

Lines 15–18. — A concise but affecting description is here given of the domestic habits of the people. The infamous manner in which they are entrapped and sold as slaves is described, and the whole ends with an appropriate moral sentiment. The Poem might here finish, but the spirit of the bard penetrates the veil of futurity, and from it cuts off a bright piece for the hitherto unfortunate Africans, as the following beautiful lines amply exemplify.

It may perhaps be remarked that the Author has here "changed his hand." He answers that it was his intention to do so. Before it was his endeavor to be elegant and concise, it is now his wish to be enthusiastic and magnificent. He trusts the Reader will perceive the aptness with which he has changed his style; when he narrated facts he was calm, when he enters on prophecy he is fervid.

The enthusiasm which he feels is beautifully expressed in lines 25 and 26. He thinks he has very successfully imitated in the last six lines the best manner of Mr. Pope; and in lines 12–26, the pathetic elegance of the author of "Australasia and Athens."

The Author cannot conclude without declaring that his aim in writing this Poem will be fully accomplished, if he can infuse into the breasts of Englishmen a sense of the danger in which they lie. Yes — Africa! If he can awaken one particle of sympathy for thy sorrows, of love for thy land, of admiration for thy virtue, he shall sink into the grave with the proud consciousness that he has raised esteem, where before there was contempt, and has kindled the flame of hope on the mouldering ashes of despair!

One heart yet beats which ne'er thee shall forget.
What though thy maidens are a blackish brown,
Does virtue dwell in whiter breasts alone?
Oh no, oh no, oh no, oh no, oh no!
It shall not, must not, cannot, e'er be so.
The day shall come when Albion's self shall feel
Stern Afric's wrath, and writhe 'neath Afric's steel.
I see her tribes the hill of glory mount,
And sell their sugars on their own account;
While round her throne the prostrate nations come,
Sue for her rice, and barter for her rum!

This concludes with a little vignette in the "Titmarsh" manner, representing an Indian smoking a pipe of the type once commonly seen in the shape of a small carved image at the doors of tobacconists' shops. In another paper we find the following pretended

ADVERTISEMENT.

This day is published, price 3*s.* 6*d.*, "An Essay on the Great Toe," together with the nature and properties of Toes in general, with many sagacious inquiries why the Great Toes are bigger than the Little, and why the Little are less than the Great. Proving also that Gout is not the Dropsy, and that a Gentleman may have a swelled Face without a pain in his Back. Also a Postscript to establish that a Chilblain is very unlike a Lock-jaw. Translated from the original Chaldee.

N. B. A few light summer lectures on Phrenology to be disposed of; inquire of Mr. Smith.

A little further we come upon an exercise in Malapropisms,[1] under the form of a letter from Mrs.

RAMSBOTTOM IN CAMBRIDGE.

Radish Ground Buildings. — DEAR SIR, — I was surprised to see my name in Mr. Bull's paper, for I give you my word I have not written a syllabub to him since I came to reside here,

[1] Signed "Dorothea Julia Ramsbottom," after Theodore Hook's Paris Correspondent.

that I might enjoy the satiety of the literary and learned world.

I have the honor of knowing many extinguished persons. I am on terms of the greatest contumacy with the Court of Alderman, who first recommended your weekly dromedary to my notice, knowing that I myself was a great literati. When I am at home, I make Lavy read it to me, as I consider you the censure of the anniversary, and a great upholder of moral destruction.

When I came here, I began reading Mechanics (written by that gentleman whose name you whistle). I thought it would be something like the "Mechanics' Magazine," which my poor dear Ram used to make me read to him, but I found them very foolish. What do I want to know about weights and measures and bull's eyes, when I have left off trading. I have, therefore, begun a course of ugly physics, which are very odd, and written by the Marquis of Spinningtoes.

I think the Library of Trinity College is one of the most admiral objects here. I saw the busks of several gentlemen whose statutes I had seen at Room, and who all received their edification at that College. There was Aristocracy who wrote farces for the Olympic Theatre, and Democracy who was a laughing philosophy.

I forgot to mention that my son George Frederick is entered at St. John's, because I heard that they take most care of their morals at that College. I called on the tutor, who received myself and son very politely, and said he had no doubt my son would be a tripod, and he hoped perspired higher than polly, which I did not like. I am going to give a tea at my house, when I shall be delighted to see yourself and children.

Believe me, dear Sir,

Your most obedient and affectionate,

DOROTHEA JULIA RAMSBOTTOM.

Further still, we have an example of droll errors in orthography similar to those in which Thackeray afterwards learned to revel in the characters of "Yellowplush," and "Jeames of Buckley Square." This is entitled : —

A STATEMENT ON FAX RELATIVE TO THE LATE MURDER.

By D. J. Ramsbottom.

> "Come I to speak in Cæsar's funeral."
> *Milton. Julius Cæsar*, Act III.

On Wednesday, the 3rd of June as I was sitting in my back parlor taking tea, young Frederick Tudge entered the room; I reserved from his disevelled hair and vegetated appearance, that something was praying on his vittles. When I heard from him the cause of his vegetation, I was putrified! I stood transfigured! His father, the editor of "The Snob," had been macerated in the most sanguine manner. The drops of compassion refused my eyes, for I thought of him whom I had lately seen high in health and happiness; that ingenuous indivisable, who often and often when seated alone with me has "made the Table roar," as the poet has it, and whose constant aim in his weakly dromedary, was to delight as well as to reprove. His son Frederick, too young to be acquainted with the art of literal imposition, has commissioned me to excommunicate the circumstances of his death, and call down the anger of the Proctors and Court of Aldermen on the phlogitious perforators of the deed.

It appears he was taking his customary rendezvous by the side of Trumpington Ditch, he was stopped by some men in under-gravy dresses, who put a pitch-plaister on him, which completely developed his nose and eyes, or, as Shakspeare says, "his visible ray." He was then dragged into a field, and the horrid deed was replete! Such are the circumstances of his death; but Mr. Tudge died like Wriggle-us, game to the last; or like Cæsar in that beautiful faction of the poet, with which I have headed my remarks, I mean him who wanted to be Poop of Room, but was killed by two Brutes, and the fascinating hands of a perspiring Senate.

With the most sanguinary hopes that the Anniversary and Town will persecute an inquiry into this dreadful action, I will conclude my repeal to the pathetic reader; and if by such a misrepresentation of fax, I have been enabled to awaken an apathy for the children of the late Mr. Tudge, who are left in the most desultory state, I shall feel the satisfaction of having exorcised my pen in the cause of Malevolence, and soothed the inflictions of indignant Misery.

D. J. Ramsbottom.

P. S. The Publisher requests me to state that the present Number is published from the MS. found in Mr. Tudge's pocket, and one more number will be soon forthcoming, containing his inhuman papers.

Thackeray in Paris.

A recent writer has given some amusing particulars of his Paris life, and his subsequent interest in the city, where he had many friends and was known to a wide circle of readers. "He lived," says this writer, "in Paris 'over the water,' and it is not long since, in strolling about the Latin Quarter with the best of companions, that we visited his lodgings, Thackeray inquiring after those who were already forgotten — unknown. Those who may wish to learn his early Parisian life and associations should turn to the story of 'Philip on his Way through the World.' Many incidents in that narrative are reminiscences of his own youthful literary struggles whilst living modestly in this city. Latterly, fortune and fame enabled the author of 'Vanity Fair' to visit imperial Paris in imperial style, and Mr. Thackeray put up generally at the Hôtel de Bristol, in the Place Vendôme. Never was increase of fortune more gracefully worn or more generously employed. The struggling artist and small man of letters whom he was sure to find at home or abroad, was pretty safe to be assisted if he learned their wants. I know of many a kind act. One morning, on entering Mr. Thackeray's bedroom in Paris, I found him placing some napoleons in a pill-box, on the lid of which was written, 'One to be taken occasionally.' 'What are you doing?' said I. 'Well,' he replied, 'there is an old person here who says she is very ill and in distress, and I strongly suspect that this is the sort of medicine she wants. Dr. Thackeray intends to leave it with her himself. Let us walk out together.' Thackeray used to say that he came to Paris for a holiday, and to revive his recollections of French cooking. But he generally worked here, especially when editing the 'Cornhill Magazine.'"

Thackeray's affection for Paris, however, appears to have been founded upon no relish for the gayeties of the French metropolis, and certainly not upon any liking for French institutions. His papers on this subject are generally criticisms upon political, social, and literary failings of the French, written in a severe spirit which savors more of the confident judgment of youth than of the calm spirit of the citizen of the world. The reactionary rule of Louis Philippe, the Government of July, and the boasted Charter of 1830, were the objects of his especial dislike; nor was he less unsparing in his views of French morals as exemplified in their law courts, and in the novels of such writers as Madame Dudevant. The truth is, that at this period Paris was, in the eyes of the art-student, simply the Paradise of young painters. Possessed of a good fortune — said to have amounted on his coming of age in 1832 to £20,000 — the young Englishman passed his days in the Louvre, his evenings with his French artist acquaintances, of whom his preface to Louis Marvy's sketches gives so pleasant a glimpse; or sometimes in his quiet lodgings in the Quartier Latin, in dashing off for some English or foreign paper his enthusiastic notices of the Paris Exhibition, or a criticism on French writers, or a story of French artist life, or an account of some great *cause célèbre* then stirring the Parisian world. This was doubtless the happiest period of his life. In one of these papers he describes minutely the life of the art-student in Paris, and records his impressions of it at the time.

"To account (he says) for the superiority over England —

which, I think, as regards art, is incontestable — it must be remembered that the painter's trade, in France, is a very good one; better appreciated, better understood, and, generally, far better paid than with us. There are a dozen excellent schools in which a lad may enter here, and, under the eye of a practiced master, learn the apprenticeship of his art at an expense of about ten pounds a year. In England there is no school except the 'Academy,' unless the student can afford to pay a very large sum, and place himself under the tuition of some particular artist. Here, a young man for his ten pounds has all sorts of accessory instruction, models, etc.; and has further, and for nothing, numberless incitements to study his profession which are not to be found in England; the streets are filled with picture shops, the people themselves are pictures walking about; the churches, theatres, eating-houses, concert-rooms, are covered with pictures; Nature itself is inclined more kindly to him, for the sky is a thousand times more bright and beautiful, and the sun shines for the greater part of the year. Add to this incitements more selfish, but quite as powerful: a French artist is paid very handsomely; for five hundred a year is much where all are poor; and has a rank in society rather above his merits than below them, being caressed by hosts and hostesses in places where titles are laughed at, and a baron is thought of no more account than a banker's clerk.

"The life of the young artist here is the easiest, merriest, dirtiest existence possible. He comes to Paris, probably at sixteen, from his province; his parents settle forty pounds a year on him, and pay his master; he establishes himself in the Pays Latin, or in the new quarter of Nôtre Dame de Lorette (which is quite peopled with painters): he arrives at his *atelier* at a tolerably early hour, and labors among a score of companions as merry and poor as himself. Each gentleman has his favorite tobacco-pipe, and the pictures are painted in the midst of a cloud of smoke, and a din of puns and choice French slang, and a roar of choruses, of which no one can form an idea who has not been present at such an assembly."

In another paper he discourses enthusiastically of the French school of painting as exemplified in a picture in the Exhibition by Carel Dujardin, as follows : —

"A horseman is riding up a hill, and giving money to a blowsy beggar-wench. 'O matutini rores auræque salubres!' in what a wonderful way has the artist managed to create you out of a few bladders of paint and pots of varnish. You can see the matutinal dews twinkling in the grass, and feel the fresh, salubrious airs ('the breath of Nature blowing free,' as the Corn-law man sings) blowing free over the heath. Silvery vapors are rising up from the blue lowlands. You can tell the hour of the morning and the time of the year; you can do anything but describe it in words. As with regard to the Poussin above mentioned, one can never pass it without bearing away a certain pleasing, dreaming feeling of awe and musing; the other landscape inspires the spectator infallibly with the most delightful briskness and cheerfulness of spirit. Herein lies the vast privilege of the landscape-painter; he does not address you with one fixed particular subject or expression, but with a thousand never contemplated by himself, and which only arise out of occasion. You may always be looking at a natural landscape as at a fine pictorial imitation of one; it seems eternally producing new thoughts in your bosom, as it does fresh beauties from its own."

Mr. Thackeray was in Paris in March, 1836, at the time of th execution of Fieschi and Lacénaire, upon which subject he wrote some remarks in one of his anonymous papers which it is interesting to compare with the more advanced views in favor of the abolition of the punishment of death which are familiar to the readers of his subsequent article, "On Going to see a Man Hanged." He did not witness the execution either of Fieschi or Lacénaire, though he made unsuccessful attempts to be present at both events.

The day for Fieschi's death was purposely kept secret; and he was executed at a remote quarter of the town. But the scene on the morning when his execution did not take place was never forgotten by the young English artist.

It was carnival time, and the rumor had pretty generally been carried abroad, that the culprit was to die on that day. A friend who accompanied Thackeray came many miles through the mud and dark, in order to be "in at the death." They set out before light, floundering through the muddy Champs Elysées, where were many others upon the same errand. They passed by the Concert of Musard, then held in the Rue St. Honoré; and round this, in the wet, a number of coaches were collected: the ball was just up; and a crowd of people, in hideous masquerade, drunk, tired, dirty, dressed in horrible old frippery and daubed with filthy rouge, were trooping out of the place; tipsy women and men, shrieking, jabbering, gesticulating, as French will do; parties swaggering, staggering forward, arm in arm, reeling to and fro across the street, and yelling songs in chorus. Hundreds of these were bound for the show, and the two friends thought themselves lucky in finding a vehicle to the execution place, at the Barrière d'Enfer. As they crossed the river, and entered the Rue d'Enfer, crowds of students, black workmen, and more drunken devils, from more carnival balls, were filling it; and on the grand place there were thousands of these assembled, looking out for Fieschi and his *cortége*. They waited, but no throat-cutting that morning; no august spectacle of satisfied justice; and the eager spectators were obliged to return, disappointed of the expected breakfast of blood. "It would" (says Mr. Thackeray) "have been a fine scene, that execution, could it but have taken place in the midst of the mad mountebanks and tipsy strumpets who had flocked so far to witness it, wishing to wind up the delights of their carnival by a *bonne-bouche* of a murder."

The other attempt was equally unfortunate. The same friend accompanied him, but they arrived too late on the ground to be present at the execution of Lacénaire and his comate in murder, Avril. But as they came to the spot (a gloomy round space, within the barrier — three roads led to it — and, outside, they saw the wine-shops and restaurateurs of the barrier looking gay and inviting), they only found in the midst of it, a little pool of ice, just partially tinged with red. Two or three idle street boys were dancing and stamping about this pool; and when the Englishmen asked one of them whether the execution had taken place, he began dancing more madly than ever, and shrieked out with a loud fantastical theatrical voice, "Venez tous Messieurs et Dames, voyez ici le sang du monstre Lacénaire, et de son campagnon, le traitre Avril;" and straightway all the other gamins screamed out the words in chorus, and took hands and danced round the little puddle. "Oh, august justice!" exclaimed the young art-student, "your meal was followed by an appropriate grace! Was any man who saw the show deterred, or frightened, or moralized in any way? He had gratified his appetite for blood, and this was all. Remark what a good breakfast you eat after an execution; how pleasant it is to cut jokes after it, and upon it. This merry, pleasant mood, is brought on by the blood-tonic."

The Dignity of Literature.

It was during the publication of "Pendennis" that a criticism in the "Morning Chronicle" and in the "Examiner" newspapers drew from Thackeray the following remarkable letter on the "Dignity of Literature," addressed to the Editor of the former journal: —

"Reform Club, *Jan. 8th*, 1850.

"*To the Editor of the 'Morning Chronicle.'*

"Sir, — In a leading article of your journal of Thursday the 3d instant you commented upon literary pensions and the *status* of literary men in this country, and illustrated your argument by extracts from the story of 'Pendennis,' at present in course of publication. You have received my writings with so much kindness that, if you have occasion to disapprove of them or the author, I can't question your right to blame me, or doubt for a moment the friendliness and honesty of my critic; and however I might dispute the justice of your verdict in my case, I had proposed to submit to it in silence, being indeed very quiet in my conscience with regard to the charge made against me. But another newspaper of high character and repute takes occasion to question the principles advocated in your article of Thursday; arguing in favor of pensions for literary persons, as you argued against them; and the only point upon which the 'Examiner' and the 'Chronicle' appear to agree unluckily regards myself, who am offered up to general reprehension in two leading articles by the two writers: by the latter, for 'fostering a baneful prejudice' against literary men; by the former, for 'stooping to flatter' this prejudice in the public mind, and condescending to caricature (as is too often my habit) my literary fellow-laborers, in order to pay court to 'the non-literary class.' The charges of the 'Examiner' against a man who has never, to his knowledge, been ashamed of his profession, or (except for its dullness) of any single line from his pen — grave as they are, are, I hope, not proven. 'To stoop to flatter' any class is a novel accusation brought against my writings; and as for my scheme 'to pay court to the non-literary class by disparaging my literary fellow-laborers,' it is a design which would exhibit a degree not only of baseness but of folly upon my part, of which I trust I am not capable. The editor of the 'Examiner may, perhaps, occasionally write, like other authors, in a hurry, and not be aware of the conclusions to which some of his sentences may lead. If I stoop to flatter anybody's prejudice for some interested motives of my own, I am no more nor less than a rogue and a cheat: which deductions from the 'Examiner's' premises I will not stoop to contradict, because the premises themselves are simply absurd. I deny that the considerable body of our countrymen described by the 'Examiner' as the 'non-literary class' has the least gratification in witnessing the degradation or disparagement of literary men. Why accuse 'the non-literary class' of being so ungrateful? If the writings of an author give a reader pleasure or profit, surely the latter will have a favorable opinion of the person who so benefits him. What intelligent man, of what political views, would not receive with respect and welcome that writer of the 'Examiner' of whom your paper once said, that 'he made all England laugh and think?' Who would deny to that brilliant wit, that polished satirist, his just tribute of respect and admiration? Does any man who has written a book worth reading — any poet, historian, novelist, man of science — lose reputation by his character for genius or for learning? Does he not, on the contrary, get friends, sympathy, applause — money, perhaps? — all good and pleasant things in themselves, and not ungenerously awarded as they are honestly won. That generous faith in men of letters, that kindly regard in which the whole reading nation holds them, appear to me to be so clearly shown in our country every day, that to question them would be as absurd as, permit me to say for my part, it would be ungrateful. What is it that fills mechanics' institutes in the great provincial towns when literary men are invited to attend their festivals? Has not every literary man of mark his friends and his circle, his hundreds or his tens of thousands of readers? And has not every one had from these constant and affecting testimonials of the esteem in which they hold him? It is of course one writer's lot, from the nature of his subject or of his genius, to command the sympathies or awaken the curiosity of many more readers than shall choose to listen to another author; but surely all get their hearing. The literary profession is not held in disrepute; nobody wants to disparage it; no man loses his social rank, whatever it may be, by practicing it. On the contrary, the pen gives a place in the world to men who had none before — a fair place fairly achieved by their genius; as any other degree of eminence is by any other kind of merit. Literary men need not, as it seems to me, be in the least querulous about their position any more, or want the pity of anybody. The money-prizes which the chief among them get are not so high as those which fall to men of other callings — to bishops, or to judges, or to opera-singers and actors; nor have they received stars and garters as yet, or peerages and governorships of islands, such as fall to the lot of military officers. The rewards of the profession are not to be measured by the money standard: for one man spends a life of learning and labor on a book which does not pay the printer's bill, and another gets a little fortune by a few light volumes. But, putting the money out of the question, I believe that the social estimation of the man of letters is as good as it deserves to be, and as good as that of any other professional man. With respect to the question in debate between you and the 'Examiner' as to the propriety of public rewards and honors for literary men, I don't see why men of letters should not very cheerfully coincide with Mr. 'Examiner' in accepting all the honors, places, and prizes which they can get. The amount of such as will be awarded to them will not, we may be pretty sure, impoverish the country much; and if it is the custom of the State to reward by money, or titles of honor, or stars and garters of any sort, individuals who do the country service, and if individuals are gratified at having 'Sir' or 'My lord' appended to their names, or stars and ribbons hooked on their coats and waistcoats, as men most undoubtedly are, and as their wives, families, and relations are, there can be no reason why men of letters should not have the chance, as well as men of the robe or the sword; or why, if honor and money are good for one profession, they should not be good for another. No man in other callings thinks himself degraded by receiving a reward from his Government; nor, surely, need the literary man be more squeamish about pensions, and ribbons, and titles, than the ambassador, or general, or judge. Every European state but ours rewards its men of letters; the American Government gives them their full share of its small patronage, and if Americans, why not Englishmen? If Pitt Crawley is disappointed at not getting a ribbon on retiring from his diplomatic post at Pumpernickel, if General O'Dowd is pleased to be called Sir Hector O'Dowd, K. C. B., and his wife at being denominated my Lady O'Dowd, are literary men to be the only persons exempt from vanity, and is it to be a sin in them to covet honor? And now, with regard to the charge against myself of fostering baneful prejudices against our calling — to which I no more plead guilty than I should think Fielding would have done if he had been accused of a design to bring the Church into contempt by describing

Parson Trulliber — permit me to say, that before you deliver sentence it would be as well if you had waited to hear the whole of the argument. Who knows what is coming in the future numbers of the work which has incurred your displeasure and the 'Examiner's,' and whether you, in accusing me of prejudice, and the 'Examiner' (alas !) of swindling and flattering the public, have not been premature ? Time and the hour may solve this mystery, for which the candid reader is referred 'to our next.' That I have a prejudice against running into debt, and drunkenness, and disorderly life, and against quackery and falsehood in my profession I own, and that I like to have a laugh at those pretenders in it who write confidential news about fashion and politics for provincial *gobemouches;* but I am not aware of feeling any malice in describing this weakness, or of doing anything wrong in exposing the former vices. Have they never existed amongst literary men ? Have their talents never been urged as a plea for improvidence, and their very faults adduced as a consequence of their genius ? The only moral that I, as a writer, wished to hint in the descriptions against which you protest, was, that it was the duty of a literary man, as well as any other, to practice regularity and sobriety, to love his family, and to pay his tradesmen. Nor is the picture I have drawn 'a caricature which I condescend to,' any more than it is a willful and insidious design on my part to flatter 'the non-literary class.' If it be a caricature, it is the result of a natural perversity of vision, not of an artful desire to mislead : but my attempt was to tell the truth, and I meant to tell it not unkindly. I have seen the bookseller whom Bludyer robbed of his books : I have carried money, and from a noble brother man-of-letters, to some one not unlike Shandon in prison, and have watched the beautiful devotion of his wife in that dreary place. Why are these things not to be described, if they illustrate, as they appear to me to do, that strange and awful struggle of good and wrong which takes place in our hearts and in the world ? It may be that I worked out my moral ill, or it may be possible that the critic of the 'Examiner' fails in apprehension. My efforts as an artist come perfectly within his province as a censor; but when Mr. 'Examiner' says of a gentleman that he is 'stooping to flatter a public prejudice,' which public prejudice does not exist, I submit that he makes a charge which is as absurd as it is unjust, and am thankful that it repels itself. And, instead of accusing the public of persecuting and disparaging us as a class, it seems to me that men of letters had best silently assume that they are as good as any other gentlemen, nor raise piteous controversies upon a question which all people of sense must take to be settled. If I sit at your table, I suppose that I am my neighbor's equal as that he is mine. If I begin straightway with a protest of 'Sir, I am a literary man, but I would have you to know I am as good as you,' which of us is it that questions the dignity of the literary profession — my neighbor who would like to eat his soup in quiet, or the man of letters who commences the argument? And I hope that a comic writer, because he describes one author as improvident and another as a parasite, may not only be guiltless of a desire to vilify his profession, but may really have its honor at heart. If there are no spendthrifts or parasites amongst us, the satire becomes unjust; but if such exist, or have existed, they are as good subjects for comedy as men of other callings. I never heard that the Bar felt itself aggrieved because 'Punch' chose to describe Mr. Dunup's notorious state of insolvency, or that the picture of Stiggins in 'Pickwick' was intended as an insult to all Dissenters, or that all the attorneys in the empire were indignant at the famous history of the firm of 'Quirk, Gammon, and Snap.' Are we to be passed over because we are faultless, or because we cannot afford to be laughed at? And if every character in a story is to represent a class, not an individual — if every bad figure is to have its obliged contrast of a good one, and a balance of vice and virtue is to be struck —novels, I think, would become impossible, as they would be intolerably stupid and unnatural, and there would be a lamentable end of writers and readers of such compositions.

"Believe me, Sir, to be your very faithful servant,

"W. M. Thackeray."

Personal Appearance of Thackeray.

Who that has seen will ever forget the commanding figure and the stately head? Sauntering — usually a solitary man — through the hall of the Reform Club, or in the quietudes of the Athenæum, making up his mind to find a corner to work for an hour or so on the small sheets of paper in his pocket, in a hand as neat as Peter Cunningham's, or Leigh Hunt's;[1] gazing dreamily, and often with a sad and weary look, out of window; moving slowly westward home to dinner on a summer's evening; or making a strange presence, as obviously not belonging to the place, in Fleet Street, on his way to Whitefriars or Cornhill; who that knew him does not remember dear Old Thackeray, as his familiars lovingly called him, in some or all of these moods and places? In Thackeray as in Dickens, there was a strong and impressive individuality. No two men could be less alike, in person or mind, than these two writers who shared the world's favor together; and yet there was an equality and identity in their impressiveness. Dickens's strength was quick, alert, and with the glow of health in it; it seemed to proceed like that of a mighty engine from an inward fire. Thackeray's was calm, majestic by its ease and extent, as the force of a splendid stream. Hawthorne's figure and air has been described as "modestly grand:" and the observation, it occurs to me, applies exactly to Thackeray. Indeed I have often been struck with the idea that the two men must have affected society much in the same way, and by the same mental and physical qualities. Like Hawthorne, Thackeray

"Wandered lonely as a cloud,"

— a cloud, it should be noted and remembered, with a silver lining. In their solitude, when suddenly observed, both had a sad, a grave aspect: and each was "marvelously moved

[1] Shortly before his death he spent a morning in the reading-room of the British Museum, and there by accident left upon a table a page of the MS. of the story he had in hand. The paper being found, the clearness and roundness of the writing at once suggested the owner to the attendant, and the precious, missing leaf was forwarded to Kensington.

to fun" on occasions. In both the boy appeared easily; and this was a quality of Dickens's genius, as it was of my father's. I should like to see pictures of Thackeray holding a skein of silk for a child upon his broad hands; of Dickens playing at leap-frog or rounders: of Hawthorne lying in the grass listening to the birds, and ducking lest the passers by should interrupt him; and of Douglas Jerrold taking part in basting the bear in his Kentish orchard. Mr. Fields's description of Hawthorne's fun at sea, and of his grand solitary figure under the stars at night, might stand for portraiture of Thackeray.

If Thackeray cast upon the outer world an austere — almost contemptuous look — and walked the streets and paced the clubs self-contained, solitary, — it was because he was an observer of human nature, indeed of all nature. You stand away to examine a picture. He who goes to observe the Downs on a Derby day does not take three sticks at Aunt Sally. When Thackeray observed a child at play, he was touched by the natural flow of its movements and the natural philosophy underlying its prattle. Dickens put himself under the glossy plumes of the raven in the happy family, and dwelt unctuously on the juiciness of the youngster's exposed calves. The difference, I have thought, having often come upon both at busy points of observation, was shown in their attitude towards the world when in the thick of it. Thackeray sailed majestically along, one hand thrust in his pocket, a cultivated, fastidious, high-bred man, deep-hearted withal. Dickens had a swifter headway, a more combative and a compacter air, and bore down with his bright eye that had (to use Doré's phrase to me applied to his own retentive vision) plenty of collodion in it, upon every human countenance, every beggar's limp, or groundling's daub of dirt. Brave and loyal workers both, who have laid the world under immeasurable debts of gratitude to them; they held along opposite sides of the way, and at each passing man and woman gazed, albeit they knew them not, feeling that there were no ordinary men abroad that day.

It was with Thackeray as with Hawthorne. The grand, sad

mask could pucker in a moment, and break into hearty fun and laughter. A friend went laughing into the Reform Club one afternoon; he had just met Thackeray at the door of the Athenæum Club. He had had a dispute with his cabman about the fare, which he had just proposed to settle by a toss. If Thackeray won, the cabman was to receive two shillings, and if the toss went against the author of "Vanity Fair" the cabman was to receive one shilling. Fortune was with the novelist; and he dwelt delightfully afterwards on the gentlemanly manner in which the driver took his defeat. Yet there were times, and many, when Thackeray could not break through his outward austerity, even when passing an intimate friend in the street. I and a mutual friend met him one afternoon in Fleet Street, ambling to Whitefriars on his cob, and a very extraordinary figure he made. He caught sight of us, and my companion was about to grasp his hand, but he just touched his hat with his finger, and without opening his lips or relaxing the solemn cast of his features, he passed on. My companion stamped his foot upon the pavement and cried, "Who would think that we were up till four o'clock this morning together, and that he sang his 'Reverend Dr. Luther,' and was the liveliest of us."

But Thackeray was a sick man, as well as a hard-worked one. He was threatened by several disorders of long continuance; and against which he stoutly fought, turning his noble placid face bravely upon the world — this "great Achilles whom we knew," and who was most loved by those who knew him best. Indeed by the outer world — by those with whom he came in contact for the first time — he was not loved, and not often liked. His address was as polished as a steel mirror, and as cold. In the "Hoggarty Diamond," in that exquisite chapter given to Mr. Titmarsh's drive with Lady Drum, Mr. Samuel observes: "For though I am but a poor fellow, and hear people cry out how vulgar it is to eat peas with a knife, or ask three times for cheese, and such like points of ceremony, there 's something, I think, much more vulgar than all this, and that is insolence to one's inferiors. I hate the chap that uses it, as I scorn him of humble rank that affects to be of the fashion; and so I determined to let Mr. Preston know a piece of my mind." And Mr. Preston knew it accordingly. In this passage there is the key-note of the wordly side of Thackeray's character. He was beloved by his inferiors, and reserved his hottest scorn for those pretenders who, buffeted and cold-shouldered by those in whose society they aspire to mix, take their revenge upon their dependents.

Testimonies of love, of friendship, of admiration, in records of kindly acts, in anecdotes of tender heart, in passages from his works illustrating passages of his life, filled the papers at that mournful Christmas-time when he died. The instances of his kindly and unostentatious help to many of his young literary friends might be given by the score. I can remember many that came under my own observation. I was one morning at Horace Mayhew's chambers in Regent Street when Thackeray knocked at the door, and cried from without — "It 's no use, Porry Mayhew: open the door."

"It 's dear old Thackeray," said Mayhew, instinctively putting chairs and table in order to do honor to the friend of whom he never spoke without pride, and without adding, — "I know dear good Thackeray is very fond of me."

Thackeray came in, saying cheerily — "Well, young gentlemen, you 'll admit an old fogy."

He always spoke of himself as an old man. Between him and Mayhew there were not many years. He took up the papers lying about, talked the gossip of the day, and then suddenly said — with his hat in his hand — "I was going away without doing part of the business of my visit. You spoke the other day at the dinner (the "Punch" weekly-meeting) of poor George. Somebody — most unaccountably — has returned me a five pound note I lent him a long time ago. I did n't expect it: — so just hand it to George: and tell him, when his pocket will bear it, to pass it on to some poor fellow of his acquaintance. By-bye." A nod and he was gone.

This was, we all agreed, very like "dear old Thackeray.

Thackeray — Yates — Dickens.

The year 1858 was marked by an unfortunate episode the facts of which cannot be omitted from this narrative, because though trifling in their origin, they finally led to a temporary estrangement between Mr. Thackeray and his great brother novelist Mr. Dickens, with whom he had hitherto had only relations of the most friendly character. On the 12th of June in that year an article had appeared in a periodical called "Town Talk," which professed to give an account of Mr. Thackeray — his appearance, his career, and his success. The article was coarse and offensive in tone, but it was notorious that the periodical was edited by a clever writer of the day, well known to Mr. Thackeray as a brother member of a club to which he belonged. As such, the subject of the attack felt himself compelled to take notice of it. In order to understand the resentment displayed by the latter at this unprovoked attack, it is necessary to quote the following passage from the article: —

His Appearance.

"Mr. Thackeray is forty-six years old, though from the silvery whiteness of his hair he appears somewhat older. He is very tall, standing upwards of six feet two inches; and as he walks erect, his height makes him conspicuous in every assembly. His face is bloodless, and not particularly expressive, but remarkable for the fracture of the bridge of the nose, the result of an accident in youth. He wears a small gray whisker, but otherwise is clean shaven. No one meeting him could fail to recognize in him a gentleman: his bearing is cold and uninviting, his style of conversation either openly cynical, or affectedly good-natured and benevolent; his *bonhommie* is forced, his wit biting, his pride easily touched — but his appearance is invariably that of the cool, *suave*, well-bred gentleman, who, whatever may be rankling within, suffers no surface display of his emotion.

HIS SUCCESS,

"Commencing with 'Vanity Fair,' culminated with his 'Lectures on the English Humorists of the Eighteenth Century,' which were attended by all the court and fashion of London. The prices were extravagant, the lecturer's adulation of birth and position was extravagant, the success was extravagant. No one succeeds better than Mr. Thackeray in cutting his coat according to his cloth: here he flattered the aristocracy, but when he crossed the Atlantic, George Washington became the idol of his worship, the 'Four Georges' the objects of his bitterest attacks. These last-named lectures have been dead failures in England, though as literary compositions they are most excellent. Our own opinion is, that his success is on the wane; his writings never were understood or appreciated even by the middle classes; the aristocracy have been alienated by his American onslaught on their body, and the educated and refined are not sufficiently numerous to constitute an audience; moreover, there is a want of heart in all he writes, which is not to be balanced by the most brilliant sarcasm, and the most perfect knowledge of the workings of the human heart."

Two days later Mr. Thackeray addressed the assumed writer of this article, in the following letter: —

"36 ONSLOW SQUARE, S. W., *June* 14.

"SIR, — I have received two numbers of a little paper called 'Town Talk,' containing notices respecting myself, of which, as I learn from the best authority, you are the writer.

"In the first article of 'Literary Talk' you think fit to publish an incorrect account of my private dealings with my publishers.

"In this week's number appears a so-called 'Sketch' containing a description of my manners, person, and conversation, and an account of my literary works, which of course you are at liberty to praise or condemn as a literary critic.

"But you state, with regard to my conversation, that it is

either 'frankly cynical or affectedly benevolent and good-natured;' and of my works (Lectures), that in some I showed 'an extravagant adulation of rank and position,' which in other lectures ('as I know how to cut my coat according to my cloth') became the object of my bitterest attack.

"As I understand your phrases, you impute insincerity to me when I speak good-naturedly in private; assign dishonorable motives to me for sentiments which I have delivered in public, and charge me with advancing statements which I have never delivered at all.

"Had your remarks been written by a person unknown to me, I should have noticed them no more than other calumnies; but as we have shaken hands more than once, and met hitherto on friendly terms (you may ask one of your employers, Mr. ——, of ——, whether I did not speak of you very lately in the most friendly manner), I am obliged to take notice of articles which I consider to be not offensive and unfriendly merely, but slanderous and untrue.

"We meet at a club, where, before you were born, I believe, I and other gentleman have been in the habit of talking without any idea that our conversation would supply paragraphs for professional vendors of 'Literary Talk;' and I don't remember that out of that club I have ever exchanged six words with you. Allow me to inform you that the talk which you have heard there is not intended for newspaper remark; and to beg — as I have a right to do — that you will refrain from printing comments upon my private conversations; that you will forego discussions, however blundering, upon my private affairs; and that you will henceforth please to consider any question of my personal truth and sincerity as quite out of the province of your criticism. I am, etc.,

"W. M. THACKERAY."

Subsequently Mr. Thackeray "rather (he said) than have any further correspondence with the writer of the character," determined to submit the letters which had passed between them to the committee of the club, for that body to decide whether the practice of publishing such articles would not be "fatal to the comfort of the club," and "intolerable in a society of gentlemen." The committee accordingly met, and decided that the writer of the attack complained of was bound to make an ample apology, or to retire from the club. The latter contested the right of the committee to interfere. Suits at law and proceedings in chancery against the committee were threatened, when Mr. Dickens, who was also a member of the club, interfered with the following letter: —

"TAVISTOCK HOUSE, TAVISTOCK SQUARE, LONDON, W. C.
"*Wednesday, 24th November*, 1858.

"MY DEAR THACKERAY, — Without a word of prelude, I wish this note to revert to a subject on which I said six words to you at the Athenæum when I last saw you.

"Coming home from my country work, I find Mr. Edwin James's opinion taken on this painful question of the Garrick and Mr. Edmund Yates. I find it strong on the illegality of the Garrick proceeding. Not to complicate this note or give it a formal appearance, I forbear from copying the opinion; but I have asked to see it, and I have it, and I want to make no secret from you of a word of it.

"I find Mr. Edwin James retained on the one side; I hear and read of the Attorney-general being retained on the other. Let me, in this state of things, ask you a plain question.

"Can any conference be held between me, as representing Mr. Yates, and an appointed friend of yours, as representing you, with the hope and purpose of some quiet accommodation of this deplorable matter, which will satisfy the feelings of all concerned?

"It is right that, in putting this to you, I should tell you that Mr. Yates, when you first wrote to him, brought your letter to me. He had recently done me a manly service I can never forget, in some private distress of mine (generally within your knowledge), and he naturally thought of me as his friend in an emergency. I told him that his article was not to be defended; but I confirmed him in his opinion that it was not reasonably possible for him to set right what was amiss, on the receipt of a letter couched in the very strong terms you had employed. When you appealed to the Garrick committee and they called their General Meeting, I said at that meeting that you and I had been on good terms for many years, and that I was very sorry to find myself opposed to you; but that I was clear that the committee had nothing on earth to do with it, and that in the strength of my conviction I should go against them.

"If this mediation that I have suggested can take place, I shall be heartily glad to do my best in it — and God knows in no hostile spirit towards any one, least of all to you. If it cannot take place, the thing is at least no worse than it was; and you will burn this letter, and I will burn your answer.

"Yours faithfully, CHARLES DICKENS.

"W. M. Thackeray, Esq."

To this Mr. Thackeray replied: —

"36 ONSLOW SQUARE, 26th *November*, 1858

"DEAR DICKENS, — I grieve to gather from your letter that you were Mr. Yates's adviser in the dispute between me and him. His letter was the cause of my appeal to the Garrick Club for protection from insults against which I had no other remedy.

"I placed my grievance before the committee of the club as the only place where I have been accustomed to meet Mr. Yates. They gave their opinion of his conduct and of the reparation which lay in his power. Not satisfied with their sentence, Mr. Yates called for a General Meeting; and, the meeting which he had called having declared against him, he declines the jurisdiction which he had asked for, and says he will have recourse to lawyers.

"You say that Mr. Edwin James is strongly of opinion that the conduct of the club is illegal. On this point I can give no sort of judgment: nor can I conceive that the club will be frightened, by the opinion of any lawyer, out of their own sense of the justice and honor which ought to obtain among gentlemen.

"Ever since I submitted my case to the club, I have had, and can have, no part in the dispute. It is for them to judge if any reconcilement is possible with your friend. I subjoin the copy of a letter which I wrote to the committee, and refer you to them for the issue.

"Yours, etc., W. M. THACKERAY.

"C. Dickens, Esq."

The inclosure referred to was as follows: —

"ONSLOW SQUARE, *Nov.* 28, 1858

"GENTLEMEN, — I have this day received a communication from Mr. Charles Dickens, relative to the dispute which has been so long pending, in which he says: —

"'Can any conference be held between me as representing Mr. Yates, and any appointed friend of yours, as representing you, in the hope and purpose of some quiet accommodation of this deplorable matter, which will satisfy the feelings of all parties?'

"I have written to Mr. Dickens to say, that since the commencement of this business, I have placed myself entirely in the hands of the committee of the Garrick, and am still as ever prepared to abide by any decision at which they may arrive on the subject. I conceive I cannot, if I would, make the dispute once more personal, or remove it out of the court to which I submitted it for arbitration.

"If you can devise any peaceful means for ending it, no one will be better pleased than

"Your obliged faithful servant,

"W. M. THACKERAY.

"The Committee of the Garrick Club."

It would be in vain to attempt to conceal that this painful affair left a coolness between Mr. Thackeray and his brother novelist. Mr. Thackeray, smarting under the elaborate and unjust attack, portions of which were copied and widely circulated in other journals, could not but regard the friend and adviser of his critic as in some degree associated with it; and Mr. Dickens, on the other hand, naturally hurt at finding his offer of arbitration rejected, gave the letters to the original author of the trouble for publication, with the remark: "As the receiver of my letter did not respect the confidence in which it addressed him, there can be none left for you to violate. I send you what I wrote to Mr. Thackeray, and what he wrote to me, and you are at perfect liberty to print the two." Thus, for a while, ended this painful affair. Readers of Disraeli's "Quarrels of Authors" will miss in it those sterner features of the dissensions between literary men as they were conducted in the old times; but none can contemplate this difference between the two great masters of fiction of our day with other than feelings of regret for the causes which led to it.

It is pleasing, however, to learn that the differences between them were ended before Mr. Thackeray's death. Singularly enough, this happy circumstance occurred only a few days before the time when it would have been too late. The two great authors met by accident in the lobby of a club. They suddenly turned and saw each other, and the unrestrained impulse of both was to hold out the hand of forgiveness and fellowship. With that hearty grasp the difference which estranged them ceased forever.

Robert Bell's Watch.

Louis Blanc, the historian of the French Revolution, has recently related in a French newspaper the following story: "A few years ago the London papers announced that a Frenchman, whose name I need not give you [M. Louis Blanc himself], was going to deliver in English what is here called a lecture. Foremost among those who were moved by a feeling of delicate kindness and hospitable curiosity to encourage the lecturer with their presence, was Thackeray. When the lecture was over, the manager of the literary institution where it was delivered, for some reason or other, recommended the company to take care of their pockets in the crowd at the doors — a hint which was not particularly to the taste of a highly respectable and even distinguished audience. Some even protested, and none more warmly than an unknown person, very well dressed, sitting next to Mr. Robert Bell. Not content with speaking, this unknown person gesticulated in a singularly animated manner. 'Is n't such a suggestion indecent, sir — insulting?' said he to Mr. Bell. 'What does he take us for?' etc., etc. After giving vent to his indignation in this way for some moments, the susceptible stranger disappeared, and when Mr. Robert Bell, who wanted to know how long the lecture had lasted, put his hand to his watch-pocket, behold! his watch had disappeared likewise. Thackeray, to whom his excellent friend mentioned the mishap, invited Robert Bell to dinner a day or two after. When the day came, Robert Bell took his seat at his friend's table, round which a joyous company of wits were gathered, and soon found himself encircled by a rattling fire of banter about an article of his which had just appeared in the 'Cornhill Magazine,' then conducted by Thackeray; an article remarkable in all respects, and which had attracted universal notice, as a faithful, serious, and philosophical account of some effects of *Spiritualism* which the author had witnessed at a *séance* given by Mr. Home. Mr. Robert Bell is an admirable *causeur;* his talk is a happy mixture of an Englishman's good sense and an Irishman's *verve.* So his questioners found their match in brilliant fence. Next day a mysterious messenger arrived at Mr. Robert Bell's, and handed to him, without saying who had sent it, a box containing a note, worded, as nearly as I recollect, as follows: 'The Spirits present their compliments to Mr. Robert Bell, and as a mark of their gratitude to him, they have the honor to return him the watch that was stolen from him.' And a watch it really was that the box contained, but a watch far finer and richer than the one which had disappeared. Mr. Robert Bell at once thought of Thackeray, and wrote to him without further explanation: 'I don't know if it is to you, but it is very like you.' Thackeray in reply sent a caricature portrait of himself, drawn by his own hand, and representing a winged spirit in a flowing robe, and spectacles on nose. Thackeray had in early life taken to painting, and perhaps if he had pursued his first vocation, he might have come in time to handle the brush as well as he afterwards handled the pen. At any rate the drawing in question as I can bear witness, was one to bring tears into your eyes for laughing. It was accompanied by a note as follows: 'The Spirit Gabriel presents his compliments to Mr. Robert Bell, and takes the liberty to communicate to him the portrait of the person who stole the watch.' Now, is not this bit of a story charming? What grace! what delicacy! what humor in this inspiration of a friend who, to punish his friend for having done the Spirits the honor to speak of them, sends him with a smile a magnificent present. Honorable to Thackeray, this anecdote is equally so to Robert Bell, who could inspire such feelings in such a man. And this is why I feel a double pleasure in relating it."

Thackeray's Last Illness.

His hand had been missed in the last two numbers of the "Cornhill Magazine," but only because he had been engaged in laying the foundation of another of those continuous works of fiction which his readers so eagerly expected. In the then current number of the "Cornhill Magazine," the customary orange-colored fly-leaf had announced that "a new serial story" by him would be commenced early in the new year; but the promise had scarcely gone abroad when we learnt that the hand which had penned its opening chapters, in the full prospect of a happy ending, could never again add line or word to that long range of writings which must always remain one of the best evidences of the strength and beauty of our English speech.

On the Tuesday preceding he had followed to the grave his relative, Lady Rodd, widow of Vice-admiral Sir John Tremayne Rodd, K. C. B., who was the daughter of Major James Rennell, F. R. S., Surveyor-general of Bengal, by the daughter of the Rev. Dr. Thackeray, Head Master of Harrow School. Only the day before this, according to a newspaper account, he had been congratulating himself on having finished four numbers of a new novel; he had the manuscript in his pocket, and with a boyish frankness showed the last pages to a friend, asking him to read them and see what he could make of them. When he had completed four numbers more he said he would subject himself to the skill of a very clever surgeon, and be no more an invalid. Only two days before he had been seen at his club in high spirits; but with all his high spirits, he did not seem well; he complained of illness; but he was often ill, and he laughed off his present attack. He said that he was about to undergo some treatment which would work a perfect cure in his system, and so he made light of his malady. He was suffering from two distinct complaints, one of which had now wrought his death. More than a dozen years before, while he was writing "Pendennis," the publication of that work was stopped by his serious illness. He was brought to death's door, and he was saved from death by Dr. Elliotson, to whom, in gratitude, he dedicated the novel when he lived to finish it. But ever since that ailment he had been subject every month or six weeks to attacks of sickness, attended with violent retching. He was congratulating himself, just before his death, on the failure of his old enemy to return, and then he checked himself, as if he ought not to be too sure of a release from his plague. On the morning of Wednesday, the 23d of December, the complaint returned, and he was in great suffering all day. He was no better in the evening, and his valet, Charles Sargent, left him at eleven o'clock on Wednesday night, Mr. Thackeray wishing him "Good-night" as he went out of the room. At nine o'clock on the following morning the valet entering his master's chamber as usual, found him lying on his back quite still, with his arms spread over the coverlet, but he took no notice, as he was accustomed to see his master thus after one of his stomach attacks. He brought some coffee and set it down beside the bed, and it was only when he returned after an interval and found that the cup had not been tasted, that a sudden alarm seized him, and he discovered that his master was dead. About midnight Mr. Thackeray's mother, who slept overhead, had heard him get up and walk about his room; but she was not alarmed, as this was a habit of her son when unwell. It is supposed that he had, in fact, been seized at this time, and that the violence of the attack had brought on the effusion on the brain — which, as the *post-mortem* examination showed, was the immediate cause of death. His medical attendants attributed his death to effusion on the brain, and added that he had a very large brain, weighing no less than 58½ oz. He thus died of the complaint which seemed to trouble him least.

Shirley Brooks on Thackeray.

Born a gentleman, educated at a university, and very soon induced to devote himself to authorship, an occupation which, after a determined but not disagreeable struggle, gave him fame and prosperity — Mr. Thackeray underwent few of the adventures which he has described so well, or others of a rougher order. Nor did his well-regulated mind permit him to indulge in the passions, follies, or tentative efforts which have made the lives of so many men hard living but agreeable reading. Sir Walter Scott's history as an author is varied by the story of a mystery more wonderfully kept than that in any of the sensation tales of our day, and by the story of a grand speculation which brought about a ruin more nobly repaired than ever was similar imprudence atoned for. Byron's life was full of real romance, vulgarized into mock romance by the vanity and mystifying tendencies of the man, and by the malevolent propensities of those who refused to see the diamond because it was in brass and backed with tinsel. In the story of Burns we have a constant and painful struggle of genius with frailty, and are everywhere reminded, as in the noble lines of Marlowe,

> "How angels, in their crystal armor, fight
> A doubtful battle with our tempted thoughts."

And we doubt not that when the lives of many men of the present day, who have attained much literary eminence, though far less than Thackeray, come to the press, it will be seen that living authors, like their betters, "have had buffets."

But in Thackeray's career, so far as the world can ever know it, there is little of which a biographer can make points. The story of his inner life and troubles would doubtless have been one of deep interest. The loss of fortune, and a still severer trial to his loving nature — a trial to which this is our first and last reference — must have given him hours and hours of care and sorrow; and, had he chosen to place these on record, and (after the fashion of sundry French and English egotistical psychologists) to lay bare his own soul to the world, we might have had an autobiography inferior to none in that special interest which self-depiction, performed by a master's hand, must ever offer. But he has not done this, and none can presume to supply what he has chosen to withhold. It was not that he shunned the world's eye — we all feel at this moment how endeared he was to us by his delightful habit of treating us all as his friends, and of confiding to us his "little miseries," telling us how discourteous were some of the small enemies who attacked him, and how unreasonable were the small friends who besieged him. He was of much too healthy a mind to fear to walk about in his habit as he lived in private, and he never shrouded himself in mysteries, nor broke upon us, at stated seasons, in a blaze of glory. Simple, natural, and a gentleman, he was ever as frank as those who live in good society are usually found. But his great griefs he kept to himself, and would have instantly recoiled from the idea of making money or fame by a revelation of the pulsations of a troubled heart. Hence, his outside life having been without adventure, and his inner life a secret between his Maker and himself, his biographer has little to tell save what all know.

The "grand county" may add his name to the roll of great, and brave, and good men who have come from Yorkshire. His father was in the civil service of the East India Company; and his mother, who has lived to behold a people in sorrow for the son who was so devoted to her, is understood to claim a descent of equally sturdy English character from the real old English who inhabit the principality. So he is England's by every right of pedigree. His grandfather was a clergyman of the Established Church. William Makepeace Thackeray was born in Calcutta in the year 1811, and soon came to this country. He was a Charterhouse boy and a Cambridge man. His last public appearance was at the Charterhouse dinner, and he gave the time-honored Latin toast (which prays for prosperity to the great foundation) with a heartiness which was sadly remembered by some who heard him, and who stood by his open grave a few days later. He has not made much formal use of his college experiences, but they crop up, ever and anon, in his writings; and in that delightful "Shabby Genteel Story," the foundation upon which, years after, he based the history of "Philip," we find some early sketches of disreputable collegians. But he knew good men and true while at Cambridge, and preserved their friendship till the hour when friendship is ended.

Thackeray's own inclination was for the life of an artist. To his last day he was an earnest and devoted lover of art and of its professors; and it is remarkable that, large as was the number of distinguished men of his own calling who came round his grave, the assemblage of first-rate artists was almost as large. There stood Millais and Marochetti, and Redgrave; Creswick, O'Neil, and Cruikshank; Leech, and Teniel, and Doyle; Munro, Du Maurier, Walker, and Phillips, and others whose faces we saw as faces are seen at such a moment, whose presence we recognize when names do not always arise to the mind. He had ever the largest praise for the artist who had made a reputation, the kindest word for him who was struggling on an upward course, and the most open hand for the artist who was neither successful nor advancing. Intending to educate himself for painting, he travelled much, and, as happens to many men, he was really educating himself in the finest and wisest manner for another art than that which he thought he was studying. And upon this path he soon entered, and trod it to the last. He was fortunate, we think, in not beginning authorship too young. He had not, as Douglas Jerrold said, "to take down the shutters before there was anything in the shop windows." He had been well educated, had moved in refined society, had seen much of the world, and had his mind ennobled and enriched by the study of art, where she shows proudest, before he took pen in hand. Hence, an observer of style will see that even in his earliest writings there is an absence of strain and flutter, and a composed and reticent tone. He knew that he had plenty to say, and hence he did not find it necessary to beat out his gold into the thinnest leaf; he knew that what he said was worth hearing, hence he had no recourse to devices or affectations to attract attention; and he knew that he was able to tell his story well, and hence he told it in his own manner, and calmly waited its acceptance by the hearers. We do not imply any censure upon those who have not possessed his advantages, and who have had to learn to rid themselves, one by one, of the blemishes from which Thackeray was so singularly free. It is greatly to a writer's praise that he has taught himself what Thackeray knew at starting. We merely dwell with pleasant memory upon the finish and composure of his early style. It strengthened with his strength, and, long before the end, had been universally recognized as the purest and best English of the day —

"Strong, without rage: without o'erflowing, full."

Henceforth the story of his life is little more than a recital of the dates of his works. Before he became famous he wrote for many of the journals; and a tribute, as graceful as unexpected, from the editor of the "Examiner," has revealed the fact that the brilliant pen of Thackeray pointed many of the epigrammatic articles for which that journal obtained a reputation which it has now regained. In "Fraser's Magazine," however, he found the amplest range for his powers of sarcasm and of humor; and under the name of Michael Angelo Titmarsh (a characteristic blending of grand and little for satiric purpose) he published some of the very best of his minor works — minor only in the sense that they are of smaller extent than his grand novels, as an exquisite cameo is minor beside a finished statue, not beside a stone mason's giant. "The Great Hoggarty Diamond" is one of the most remarkable of these tales, and through all its humor comes the lesson he ever taught, — that of manliness and hopefulness. The "Shabby Genteel Story" was also in "Fraser;" and who will ever forget that dinner at Margate, and the duel with the painter, and the fat lady getting up in a hurry to rescue her red-bearded, valiant cockney? A powerful paper, in which he described the execution of Courvoisier, and denounced the system of public executions, was another of his contributions; and we have, unfortunately, no space to go through the list, very pleasant as it would be to note, in the spirit in which talks to a friend of the good deeds of a lost friend, the delightful papers which used to make "Fraser" a work to be eagerly scrambled for in public places by those who had imperative claims on their half-crowns, and therefore read no magazines in luxurious privacy.

In a good day for himself, the journal, and the world, Thackeray joined "Punch." Here he had more ample play for all his faculties than had been ever offered him. An epigram in two lines, a sketch in two pages, a head-piece, a tail-piece, a caricature, a pregnant initial, a jovial song (are we thinking of the "Mahogany Tree"?), an Irish chant of ridiculous treason (say the "Limerick Tragedy"), a versified fable for the instruction of Lords and Princes ("Silly Little Finches"), a tale in many chapters ("Jeames's History"), or a series of essays ("The Snob Papers"), — all were welcome and welcomed. And as companions at the hospitable board of council, where such things were conceived, suggested, reviewed, and admired, he sat with two who have preceded him to the world of shadows, and with some who live to mourn him. Douglas Jerrold and Gilbert A'Becket were his neighbors at those feasts, and none appreciated more keenly than Thackeray the magical quickness and sparkle of the wit's repartees, or the ever-ready, shrewd, and kindly talk of the humorist. Others who were of the happy party, and who read these lines, will silently testify to their truth, and add that for each and for all who sat with Thackeray at that board there was always the quaint greeting that dignified the friend with some American military title, the instant and intensely compact gratulation upon any public success or private good fortune, the eagerness to give information; the electric readiness to catch the knavish speech that sleeps in the foolish ear but never had a wink in Thackeray's ; the kindly retort that seemed meant but to show you that you had spoken well ; and then, better than all word-pleasantry, there were the ever-beaming kindness, the lofty moral, the lowly charity, and the noble heart that was so true to the noble brain. This is a sketch — and a very inadequate one — from private life ; and yet we do not think that any one who reads it will blame the writer. As Thackeray is here described, he was, as a hundred friends will testify, whenever he felt himself "at home," and it is because some wretched talk of his supposed "cynicism" has got abroad, and because such talk has come from those who have known scarcely at all, that it is well for once and for all to say that William Thackeray was one of the cheerfullest and cheeriest of men who ever gladdened the heart of a friend.

He went back to the East, but not very far, and recorded his travels in the "Notes of a Journey from Cornhill to Cairo." They are full of humor and wisdom, and the kind heart is always speaking out. The pretty verses on the dawn at sea, suggest thoughts which it would now be sacrilege to print; but we may remember the indignant protest against the acceptance by Christian England of an ally who had actually ordered the murder of a baby, and the semi-serious strain in which Oriental brutality is exposed in the story of the Pacha who, while talking with the Oxford tutor, exported to teach the little infidels, was bothered by a fellah, and then and there, taking out a pistol, "shot that fellah dead, so that he never bothered any more." The varnish which sentimentalists lay over foulness never had a chance with Thackeray. Then there are the tremendous adventures of that Irish Indian Major, which make the tale the most ludicrous book since Munchausen, with the addition of being intensely interesting, in spite of the elephantine exaggeration. "Our Street" is a gallery of social portraits, drawn with a master's facility; and the "Rose and the Ring" has made the author the children's friend, as, indeed, he deserved to be held, for the love of children runs like a silver thread through every story he ever wrote. We believe that he never thoroughly hated Becky Sharp except when she kept her boy in the kitchen, kissed him before company, and slapped his face outside the door. Thackeray never sends the children to the nursery, never seems to find them in the way; and is always completing people's happiness by giving them a baby, or a "toddler," to bring sunshine into the house. The little girl in Gray's chambers, when the wonderful dinner is given by the poor young barrister and his pretty wife, to the great, rich Goldmore, is the most prominent feature in the picture. What does the author of the "Curate's Walk" say about children, and do for them in that most delightful sketch, than which Steele never wrote anything better? He was always rejoicing with the young, this cynic, — both in the pen and in the flesh. Many sentimentalists do neither the one thing nor the other, and yet talk of cynicism as a thing apart from their beautiful natures.

"Vanity Fair," "Pendennis," "Esmond," "The Virginians." There is the Thackeray Quadrilateral, which will defend his name and fame against all comers. It may be that one fortress mounts more guns than another — that is matter of opinion. When one gives way we shall be ready to consider whether the engineer neglected any part of his work, but not till then. There, guarded to all time worth speaking of, is the reputation of William Thackeray. Of these strongholds we need say no more. He was erecting a fifth when called away. It was not needed for the safety of his fame, but would that it had arisen.

There is another point of view from which we must regard him; and few who have actually looked at him, in the body, from that point, but will feel a melancholy satisfaction that they have had such opportunity. Mr. Thackeray's powers as a lecturer was simply proved by results. He lectured in England and America, and was rewarded with a fortune. But those who think that it was easily earned knew little of the *limæ labor* which he bestowed upon the carefully-phrased and eloquent lectures; and, we may add, knew little of his own unaffected distaste for public speaking. But he had resolved that his lectures should make a provision for those who were dearer to him than life; and it was not in his nature to give way either to indolence or to timidity. He elaborated his discourses, and they became rich by his workmanship; he delivered them, and he became rich by the popularity they acquired. Those on the "Humorists of the Eighteenth Century," will probably be more acceptable than "The Four Georges"; but the lecturer had acquired far more power of utterance and of effective delivery when he addressed himself to the latter than he originally possessed; and few who heard the chapter of kings will forget the telling, clean-cut precision with which the innumerable points and epigrams were brought out, or the artistic easiness with which you were led, half carelessly, up to a rocket that the next moment soared away with a train of sparkles that set you staring in pleasant surprise.

"Everybody should try to get into Parliament," said a clever man who kept out of it. Mr. Thackeray thought, in 1857, that he would try. We suppose that somebody at the Reform Club had told him that the legitimate expenses would not be much, and he certainly never meant to pay any others. Oxford — the city — had a vacancy, and Mr. Thackeray offered himself on liberal principles. It is to the honor of Oxford city that so many men were found to vote for a gentleman who had no claim but his literary genius, who did not bribe, who had no influence to procure places for the sons of voters, who was not a successful orator, and who had no past political services to appeal to, except that with the very sharpest pen in England he had been for nearly a quarter of a century stabbing at all inhumanities, follies, and barbarisms. Although an able and well-known man, Mr. Cardwell, who had claims on the electors and had official position, was started against him, Mr. Thackeray was beaten by a small majority only —

1085 to 1018. He took his defeat as he took all the chances of life, gallantly, and like a gentleman, told the electors that they had chosen the best man, and when he lectured next night brought out a shout by beginning, gravely, "I happened yesterday to be in an ancient city, called Oxford, of which some of you may have heard." We could not regret the failure, except in so far as he was disappointed; for he would have obtained some capital political sketches in Parliament, at the expense of his health, comfort, and leisure. The nation, we thought, had clubfuls of men who can sit up all night, vote for "the ballot and liberal measures generally," and deliver extra Parliamentary utterances of more or less dullness; but she had nobody to draw another Becky Sharp or the Marquis of Steyne. Mentioning which thought to the person most concerned, we were answered with a merry "Qui fit, Mæcenas, ut nemo — yes, *sir*," — the last word given with American accent, often adopted by him in no unkind memory of the States. Let us add that Mr. Cardwell, addressing the electors of Oxford, since the melancholy Christmas Eve, has spoken of the departed as became Mr. Cardwell, and as if he felt it an honor to have had such a man as antagonist.

Mr. Thackeray as editor of the "Cornhill Magazine," must have been dreadfully bored, and did not tell us in those "Roundabout Papers" one tenth of his troubles. He ought never to have given time, trouble, or anything but his name to a periodical work; and we may believe that the proprietors did all in their power to prevent his being worried and disturbed in his lawful labors. But it is not permitted in England to deal in England with volunteer contributors to anything as the Pacha dealt with the fellah; and unless they are shot they will write to you, send parcels to you, send angry friends to you, call on you when you are at dinner, abuse you through the press, waylay you in the street, and leave word in their wills that their executors are to avenge them upon you. Thackeray had to undergo a great deal of this, and he had not the sternness which might have saved him some, at least, of the worry. He *would* read applicants' notes; he would even correspond with hopeless and helpless creatures who had no right to touch pen and ink; he would even — it was utterly subversive of all editorial authority — send a charity bank-note to a very poor scribbler who pleaded starvation, and who, two months afterwards, wrote him an abusive letter for not inserting the contribution "on which he had paid half the price on account." We got some agreeable papers out of his troubles in this way, but they were too dearly purchased; and we ourselves were very glad to hear that he was relieved from editorship, though, in effect, that made little difference to the volunteer contributors, who wrote that if he used his great influence, they were sure their papers would be printed, and so on.

And this last record seems to bring us to the very last and saddest of all. This memoir, if it deserve the name, has been but a jotting down of details within the knowledge of all, of a few personal recollections common to a host of friends, and of a few pleasant memories of books which have afforded pleasant memories to millions. The writer of these lines has made no attempt to forestall a more elaborate or more worthy record, which will probably be heard of ere long. It only remains for him to add that the last time he saw William Thackeray was on Wednesday the 16th of December. They were next neighbors at a dinner where all were intimate friends. Thackeray was in his usual spirits, which were never boisterous but always cheerful, and he had pleasant words for all present. Especially was he pretending to incite one very old friend to give a party of an excessively gay description in order, as he said, that we might fancy ourselves all young again. He had something to say of the "circumstances" touching which the National Shakspeare Committee had passed a vote of "regret," and which Mr. Lucas has indignantly declared will cause posterity to "point with scorn" at that passage in the committee's history. They did not ruffle Thackeray, however they may have incensed his friends; and it is not needful, at least at present, to reproduce his smiling judgment on those whom it concerned. On that evening he enjoyed himself much in his own quiet way, and contributed generally to the enjoyment of those who were something less quiet; and a question arising about a subscription in aid of a disabled artist, he instantly offered to increase, if necessary, a sum he had previously promised. The writer's very last recollection of the cynic, therefore, is in connection with an unasked act of Christian kindness. On the following Monday he attended the funeral of a lady, who was interred in Kensal Green Cemetery. On the Tuesday he came to his favorite club, — the Garrick, — and asked a seat at the table of two friends, who, of course, welcomed him as all welcomed Thackeray. It will not be deemed too minute a record by any of the hundreds who personally loved him to note where he sat for the last time in that club. There is in the dining-room on the first floor a nook near the reading-room. The principal picture hanging in that nook, and fronting you as you approach it, is the celebrated one from "The Clandestine Marriage," with Lord Ogleby, Canton, and Brush. Opposite to that Thackeray took his seat and dined with his friends. He was afterwards in the smoke-room, a place in which he delighted. The Garrick Club will remove in a few months, and all these details will be nothing to its new members, but much to many of its old ones. His place there will know him and them no more. On Wednesday he was out several times, and was seen in Palace-gardens "reading a book." Before the dawn of Thursday he was where there is no night! May we meet him there!

JAMES HANNAY ON THACKERAY.

By birth Mr. Thackeray belonged to the upper middle class, — a section of our curiously divided society which contains many cadets of old families, and forms a link between the aristocracy and the general bulk of the liberal professions. He used sometimes to say that "it takes three generations to make a gentleman;" and though this was not a maxim which he would have applied strictly in the case of another man, he was far from insensible to the advantage in himself. He was descended from an old Saxon stock long settled in Yorkshire. His great-grandfather was Dr. Thackeray, of Harrow, who went to Cambridge in 1710, an excellent scholar and clever man, who partly educated Sir William Jones, and whose epitaph was written by his pupil Dr. Parr. The son of the Doctor married a Miss Webb, of the old English family to which the Brigadier Webb, of Marlborough's wars, belonged, — whose portrait is drawn with something of the geniality of kinsmanship in "Esmond." This Thackeray, we believe, was the first of the race to settle in India; where his son also sought his fortunes; and where his grandson the novelist was born — at Calcutta — in 1811. There are numerous descendants of the scholarly old Headmaster of Harrow scattered over the English Church and in the Indian Service, and traces of the influence of family connections are found all through the books of the man who has made his name famous. The feudal feeling of Scott — which in any case is Scotch rather than English — Thackeray did not share. Heraldry to him had only the quaint interest and prettiness of old china. But it is impossible to appreciate either his philosophy, his style, or his literary position, without remembering that he was a well-born, well-bred, and well-educated gentleman.

Like other English children born in India, young Thackeray was sent home early, and the voyage — during which he had an eager and wondering peep at the great Napoleon in his island prison, — was among his earliest recollections. He received his education at Charterhouse — the well-known Greyfriars of his stories, — an ancient and famous public school. He somewhere talks of the "monkish seclusion" of his school-days, and in his critical and questioning moods he has sufficiently proved that he knew the weak points of the old educational system. But he never lost an opportunity of showing his respect for Charterhouse, and he was perfectly aware how much he owed to it. In after-life, he let most of his Greek slip away; but his acquaintance with the Latin language, and especially the Latin poets, was eminently respectable, and exercised a profound influence over his genius and his diction. The "Odes of Horace" he knew intimately well, and there are subtle indications of the knowledge — the smell of Italian violets hidden in the green of his prose — only to be truly enjoyed by Horatians. A quotation from Horace was one of the favorite forms in which he used to embody his jokes. If you bored him with genealogy, he would begin —

"Quantum distet ab Inacho,"

which was quite a sufficient hint; and when a low fellow in London hanged himself, he observed that it was a "dignus vindice NODUS." Latin writers, French writers, and English eighteenth century men were the three sources at which his genius fed, and on which it was nourished.

From Charterhouse he went to Cambridge, which he left without taking a degree; and he entered on life with health, strength, a noble figure, an excellent genius, and twenty thousand pounds, — the last of which blessings was the first (owing, it is said, to unfortunate speculations) to leave him. But this loss was not complete, till he had had the full benefit of a good culture and a good experience. He travelled over Europe, and resided in its capitals, while his mind was young and fresh, and laid in those stores of observation to which we owe sketches with which everybody is familiar. He had an interview with Goethe at Weimar, his description of which may be seen in the "Life of Goethe" by Mr. Lewes; and he studied art at Rome. If he had had his choice, he would rather have been famous as an artist than as a writer; but it was destined that he should paint in colors which will never crack and never need restoration. All his artist experience did him just as much good in literature as it could have in any other way; and, in travelling through Europe to see pictures, he learned not them only, but men, manners, and languages. He read German; he knew French well and spoke it elegantly; and in market-places, *salons*, hotels, museums, studios, the sketch-book of his mind was always filling itself. Paris was one of his most important head-quarters in every way, and to his stay there the world owes perhaps the best of his poems — the "Chronicle of the Drum." His poetic vein was curiously original. He was not *essentially poetical*, as

Tennyson, for instance, is. Poetry was not the predominant mood of his mind, or the intellectual law by which the objects of his thought and observation were arranged and classified. But *inside* his fine sagacious common-sense understanding, there was, so to speak, a pool of poetry, — like the *impluvium* in the hall of a Roman house, which gave an air of coolness and freshness and nature to the solid marble columns and tessellated floor. The highest products of this part of his mind were the "Chronicle" above mentioned, the "Bouillebaisse," the lines on Charles Buller's death at the end of one of his "Christmas Books," and the "Ho, pretty page with dimpled chin" of another of them. A song or two in his novels, and some passages in which rural scenery is quietly and casually described, might also be specified. But all this is chiefly valuable as showing that his nature was *complete*, and that there wanted not in his genius that softer and more sensitive side natural to one whose observation was so subtle and his heart so kind. He was essentially rather moralist and humorist, — thinker and wit, — than poet; and he was too manly to *overwork* his poetic vein as a man may legitimately work his mere understanding. This honorable self-restraint, this decent reticence, so natural to English gentlemen, was by some writers of the Gushing School mistaken for hardness. The Gusher is always for plenty of sentimentalism; — for showing his heart on his sleeve, after having previously inflated the vessels of that organ with wind to make it look bigger; and he sheds "blinding tears," — as the lower animals perform all the properly secret operations of nature, — in public. This kind of thing was not in Thackeray's way, and wide as his sympathies were, he despised it. "I shall not try to describe her grief," he makes Sam Titmarsh say in the "Hoggarty Diamond, "for such things are sacred and secret; and a man has no business to place them on record for all the world to read." Few of his sentences are more characteristic.

Thackeray was still young and opulent when he began to make the acquaintance of London men of letters. Certain it is, that he lent — or in plainer English, gave — five hundred pounds to poor old Maginn, when he was beaten in the battle of life, and like other beaten soldiers made a prisoner — in the Fleet. With the generation going out, — that of Lamb and Coleridge, — he had, we believe, no personal acquaintance. Sydney Smith he met at a later time; and he remembered with satisfaction that something which he wrote about Hood gave pleasure to that delicate humorist and poet in his last days. But his first friends were the Fraserians, of whom Father Prout, — always his intimate, — and Carlyle, — always one of his most appreciating friends, — survive. From reminiscences of the wilder lights in the "Fraser" constellation were drawn the pictures of the queer fellows connected with literature in "Pendennis," — Captain Shandon, — the ferocious Bludyer, — stout old Tom Serjeant, — and so forth. Magazines in those days were more brilliant than they are now, when they are haunted by the fear of shocking the Fogy element in their circulation; and the effect of their greater freedom is seen in the buoyant, riant, and unrestrained comedy of Thackeray's own earlier "Fraser" articles. "I suppose we all begin by being too savage," is the phrase of a letter which he wrote in 1849; "*I know one who did.*" He was alluding here to the "Yellowplush Papers" in particular, where living men were very freely handled. This old, wild satiric spirit it was which made him interrupt even the early chapters of "Vanity Fair," by introducing a parody, which he could not resist, of some contemporary novelists. In the last fifteen years of his life he wrote under greater restraint, and with a sense of his graver responsibilities as one of the leading men of letters of the country. But his satire was never at any time malignant; and the fine freedom of his early writing developed his genius as the scenes of the arena developed the athlete. He was writing for twelve or thirteen years, as a professional author, before "Vanity Fair" made him really known to the world at large. The best works of that epoch will be found in the "Miscellanies," published by Bradbury & Evans in 1857. But there is much of his writing buried in periodicals, some of which have been long dead. He was connected with at least one failure, the "Parthenon," — an ill-omened name borne after a long interval by another journal quite recently defunct. He certainly contributed some things to the "Times," during Barnes's editorship, — an article on Fielding amongst them; though not, we should think, leading articles, — a kind of work for which he had no relish, and for which he believed himself to have no turn. "Fraser" was the organ with which he was most successfully connected till the days of his "Punch" engagement. It was indeed as a magazinist that he educated himself for a novelist. With a playful reference to his early and never-forgotten ambition to be an artist, he called himself Michael Angelo Titmarsh, and published under that name, not only articles but books. The "Paris Sketchbook," the "Second Funeral of Napoleon" (comprising the "Chronicle of a Drum"), the "Fatal Boots," the "Hoggarty Diamond," the "Irish Sketchbook," the "Journey from Cornhill to Grand Cairo," sufficiently attest his activity during the years which preceded the great epoch of "Vanity Fair." These books are full of sense, and wit, and humor, and it seems extraordinary that their author should have been within a year or two of forty before he was really famous. Their very truthfulness, however, — the easy quiet of their best philosophy, — the slyness of their choicest irony, — the gentlemanly taste of their heartiest *abandon*, — all this was *caviare* to the vulgar, including the vulgar of the critical press. The offer of "Vanity Fair" was declined by one publisher; and good judges said that a necessary impulse was given to its appreciation, by an article during its progress, in the "Edinburgh Review." It was still the fashion, as far as it was fashionable to speak of Thackeray at all, to treat him as a satirist. An admirable satirist he had, indeed, just proved himself in the "Snob Papers" — a series that stands high above anything ever given to the world in "Punch," excepting Hood's "Song of the Shirt." Nor was Thackeray ever ashamed of the title of satirist, knowing by what great men it had been borne before him, and how much honest work there was in the world for satire to do. But that he was a satirist only, he had proved, long before the "Snob Papers," to be absurd. Anybody who can read, for instance, the story of Sam Titmarsh's sufferings and the loss of his child, after the Diddlesex catastrophe, in the "Hoggarty Diamond," without seeing that the writer's tenderness and power of representing tenderness were exquisitely deep and exquisitely real, may conclude himself disqualified by nature for having an opinion on literary matters. There are few whose judgment on such things is much worth, — but his is certainly worth nothing.

When Thackeray wrote "Vanity Fair," in 1846, '7, '8, he was living in Young Street, Kensington, — a street on your left hand, before you come to the church; and here, in 1848, the author of this sketch had first the pleasure of seeing him, of being received at his table, and of knowing how essentially a kind, humane, and perfectly honest man he was. "Vanity Fair" was then unfinished, but its success was made, and he spoke frankly and genially of his work, and his career. "Vanity Fair" always, we think, ranked in his own mind as best in *story* of his greater books; and he once pointed out to us the very house in Russell Square where his imaginary Sedleys lived, — a curious proof of the reality his creations had for his mind. The man and the books were equally real and true; and it was natural that he should speak without hesitation of his books, if you wished it; though as a man of the world and a polished gentleman who knew the world thoroughly, literature to him only took its turn among other topics. From this point of view, his relation to it was a good deal like that of Scott. According to Lockhart, people were wrong in saying that Sir Walter declined at all markedly to talk about Literature, and yet his main interest was in active life. Just so, Thackeray was not bookish, and yet turned readily to the subject of books if invited. His reading was undoubtedly large in Memoirs, Modern History, Biography, Poetry, Essays, and Fiction — and, taken in conjunction with his scholarship, probably placed him, as a man of letters, above any other novelist except Sir Bulwer Lytton. Here is a characteristic fragment from one of his letters, written in August 1854, and now before us: "I hate Juvenal," he says; "I mean I think him a truculent brute, and I love Horace better than you do, and rate Churchill much lower; and as for Swift, you haven't made me alter my opinion. I admire, or rather admit, his power as much as you do; but I don't admire that kind of power so much as I did fifteen years ago, or twenty shall we say. Love is a higher intellectual exercise than Hatred: and when you get one or two more of those young ones you write so pleasantly about, you 'll come over to the side of the kind wags, I think, rather than the cruel ones." Passages like this, — which men who knew him will not need to have quoted to them, — have a double value for the world at large. They not only show a familiar command of writers whom it is by no means easy to know well, — but they show what the real philosophy was of a man whom the envious represented to the ignorant as a cynic and a scoffer. Why, his favorite authors were just those whose influence he thought had been beneficial to the cause of virtue and charity. "I take off my hat to Joseph Addison," he would say, after an energetic testimony to his good effect on English life. He was, in fact, even greater as a moralist than as a mere *describer* of manners; and his very hatred of quackery and meanness was proved to be real by his simplicity, humanity, and kindliness of character. In private, this great satirist, whose aspect in a crowd was often one of austere politeness and reserve, unbent into a familiar *naïveté* which somehow one seldom finds in the demonstratively genial. And this was the more charming and precious that it rested on a basis of severe and profound reflection, before the glance of which all that was dark and serious in man's life and prospects lay open. The gravity of that white head, with its noble brow, and thoughtful face full of feeling and meaning, enhanced the piquancy of his playfulness, and of the little personal revelations which came with such a grace from the depths of his kindly nature. When we congratulated him, many years ago, on the touch in "Vanity

Fair" in which Becky "*admires*" her husband when he is giving Lord Steyne the chastisement which ruins *her* for life, "Well," he said, — "when I wrote the sentence, I slapped my fist on the table, and said '*that* is a touch of genius!'" The incident is a trifle, but it will reveal, we suspect, an element of fervor, as well as a heartiness of frankness in recording the fervor, both equally at variance with the vulgar conception of him. This frankness and *bonhommie* made him delightful in a *tête-a-tête*, and gave a pleasant human flavor to talk full of sense, and wisdom, and experience, and lighted up by the gayety of the true London man of the world. Though he said witty things, now and then, he was not a wit in the sense in which Jerrold was, and he complained, sometimes, that his best things occurred to him after the occasion had gone by! He shone most, — as in his books, — in little subtle remarks on life, and little descriptive sketches suggested by the talk. We remember in particular, one evening, after a dinner party at his house, a fancy picture he drew of Shakespeare during his last years at Stratford, sitting out in the summer afternoon watching the people, which all who heard it, brief as it was, thought equal to the best things in his Lectures. But it was not for this sort of talent, — rarely exerted by him, — that people admired his conversation. They admired, above all, the broad sagacity, sharp insight, large and tolerant liberality, which marked him as one who was a sage as well as a story-teller, and whose stories were valuable because he was a sage. Another point of likeness to him in Scott was that he never overvalued story-telling, or forgot that there were nobler things in Literature than the purest creations of which the object was amusement. "I would give half my fame," wrote Scott, "if by so doing I could place the other half on a solid basis of science and learning." "Now is the time," wrote Thackeray, to a young friend in 1849, "to lay in stock. I wish I had had five years' reading before I took to our trade." How heartily we have heard him praise Sir Bulwer Lytton for the good example he set by being "thoroughly *literate!*" We are not going to trench here on any such ground as Thackeray's judgments about his contemporaries. But we may notice an excellent point bearing on these. If he heard a young fellow expressing great admiration for one of them he encouraged him in it. When somebody was mentioned as worshipping an eminent man just dead, — "I am glad," said Thackeray, "that he worships anybody."

After "Vanity Fair," Thackeray's fame steadily increased. "Pendennis" appeared during 1849 and 1850, and though it was generally considered inferior in mere plot to its predecessor, no inferiority was perceived in the essential qualities of character, thought, humor, and style. The announcement in the summer of 1851 that he was about to lecture on the English Humorists gave a thrill of pleasure to intellectual London; and when he rose in Willis's Rooms to commence the course with Swift, all that was most brilliant in the Capital was assembled to hear him. Amidst a throng of nobles, and beauties, and men of fashion, were Carlyle, and Macaulay, — Hallam with his venerable head, — and Charlotte Brontë, whose own fame was just at its height, and who saw in the lecturer her ideal of an elevated and high-minded master of literary art. The lectures were thoroughly appreciated. Everybody was delighted to see the great masters of English of a past age brought to life again in their habits as they lived, and endowed with the warm human reality of the lecturer's Dobbins, and Warringtons, and Pendennises. It was this power, and not the literary criticism, which constituted the value of Thackeray's lectures, and will secure their place in the biographical literature of the country.

Towards the close of 1852, "Esmond" appeared, and Thackeray sailed for America.[1] "Esmond" constituted a new epoch in his career. By this time his celebrity, and the impression made by his distinct and peculiar genius, — so different from that of the common sentimental schools, — had provoked a certain amount of reaction. Cads who disliked him as a gentleman, — Mechanics' Institute men who dis-

[1] He recalled the present writer from a tour in Scotland in October, and placed the MS. of the *Humorists* in his hands to edit and annotate during his absence.

liked him as a scholar, — Radicals who knew that he associated with the aristocracy, — and the numerous weaklings to whom his severe truth and perfect honesty of art seemed horrible after the riotous animal spirits, jolly caricature, and lachrymose softness of the style which he was putting out of fashion, — this crew, we say, was by no means satisfied with the undoubted fact that Thackeray was becoming the favorite writer of the cultivated classes. They accordingly began to call his honesty cynicism, and his accuracy reporting. They forgot that tears are pure in proportion to the depth from which they come, and not to the quantity in which they flow, and that the tenderness of a writer is to be estimated by the *quality* of his pathos. They also forgot that as what they called hardness was mere fidelity to truth, so what they called stenographic detail was mere finish of art. The richer imaginativeness of "Esmond," and the freer play of feeling in which the author allowed himself to indulge when dealing with a past age, came in good time to rebuke cavillers, and prove that Thackeray's mind w ıs rich as well as wide. "Esmond," we take it, is the favorite novel of his choicest admirers. He takes certain liberties with history in it. For instance, the Duke of Hamilton, whom he represents as about to marry Beatrix when he is cut off in a duel, left a widow, spoken of by Swift in the "Journal to Stella." But as Scott makes Leicester quote the "Midsummer Night's Dream" in "Kenilworth," when Shakespeare was about twelve or thirteen years of age, this may be excused.

It is a pity that Thackeray did not write expressly on America, for we think that he would have written the most impartial English book to which that country has yet given rise. When he returned from this first visit, he was a good deal away from town. "Since my return from America," he writes in August 1854, "I have hardly been in London at all, and when here, in such a skurry of business and pleasure as never to call a day my own scarcely." The passage is significant. Few lives were more engrossed than his, discharging, as he did, at once the duties of a man of letters and a man of fashion. He dined out a great deal during the season. He went to the theatres. He belonged to three clubs — the Athenæum, Reform, and Garrick — to say nothing of minor associations for the promotion of good fellowship. With less of this wear and tear, we should have had more work from him, — should have had, perhaps, the History which long dwelt in his imagination as one of the creations of the future. As it is, he achieved a great deal during the last eight or ten years of his life. Two such elaborate novels as the "Newcomes" and "Virginians," a second trip to America, and a ramble over Great Britain, with a new set of Lectures on the "Four Georges," — not to mention a contested election, and what he did for the "Cornhill," established on the strength of his name, and for a time directly conducted by him, — these were great doings for a man who, though naturally robust, was plagued and menaced by more than one vexatious disorder of long continuance. And he did them greatly, — going into the world gayly and busily to the last, and always finding time for such holy little offices of personal kindness and charity as gave him — we believe and know — more real pleasure than all his large share of the world's applause. He was much gratified by the success of the "Four Georges" (a series which superseded an earlier scheme for as many discourses on "Men of the World") in Scotland. "I have had three per cent. of the whole population here," he wrote from Edinburgh, in November, 1856. "If I could but get three per cent. of London!" He thoroughly appreciated the attention and hospitality which he met with during these lecturing tours. And if, as would sometimes happen, a local notability's adoration became obtrusive, or such a person thrust his obsequious veneration upon him beyond the limits of the becoming, his forbearance was all the more respectable on account of his sensitiveness.

Latterly he had built himself a handsome house in Kensington, to which he moved from Onslow Square, Brompton, — his residence after leaving the Young Street in which he wrote "Vanity Fair." It was a dwelling worthy of one who really represented literature in the great world, and who, planting himself on his books, yet sustained the character of his profession with all the dignity of a gentleman. A friend who called on him there from Edinburgh, in the summer of 1862, knowing of old his love of the Venusian, playfully reminded him what Horace says of those who, regardless of their sepulchre, employ themselves in building houses: —

"Sepulchri
Immemor, struis domos."

"Nay," said he, "I am *memor sepulchri*, for this house will always let for so many hundreds (mentioning the sum) a year." How distant, then, seemed the event which has just happened, and with which the mind obstinately refuses to familiarize itself, though it stares at one from a thousand broadsheets! Well, indeed, might his passing-bell make itself heard through all the myriad joy-bells of the English Christmas! It is long since England has lost such a son; it will be long before she has such another to lose. He was indeed emphatically English, — English as distinct from Scotch, — no less than English as distinct from Continental, — a different type of great man from Scott, and a different type of great man from Balzac. The highest purely English novelist since Fielding, he combined Addison's love of virtue with Johnson's hatred of cant, — Horace Walpole's lynx-like eye for the mean and the ridiculous, with the gentleness and wide charity for mankind as a whole, of Goldsmith. *Non omnis mortuus est.* He will be remembered in his due succession with these men for ages to come, as long as the hymn of praise rises in the old Abbey of Westminster,[1] and wherever the English tongue is native to men, from the banks of the Ganges to those of the Mississippi.[2] This humble tribute to his illustrious and beloved memory comes from one whom he loaded with benefits, and to whom it will always throw something of sadness over the great city where he first knew him, that it contains his too early grave.

[1] "Dum Capitolium
Scandet cum tacita virgine Pontifex."

[2] "Dicar qua violens obstrepit Aufidus," &c.

In Memoriam.

It has been desired by some of the personal friends of the great writer who established the "Cornhill Magazine," that its brief record of his having been stricken from among men should be written by the old comrade and brother in arms who pens these lines, and of whom he often wrote himself, and always with the warmest generosity.

I saw him first, nearly twenty-eight years ago, when he proposed to become the illustrator of my earliest book. I saw him last, shortly before Christmas, at the Athenæum Club, when he told me that he had been in bed three days — that, after these attacks, he was troubled with cold shiverings, "which quite took the power of work out of him" — and that he had it in his mind to try a new remedy which he laughingly described. He was very cheerful, and looked very bright. In the night of that day week he died.

The long interval between those two periods is marked in my remembrance of him by many occasions when he was supremely humorous, when he was irresistibly extravagant, when he was softened and serious, when he was charming with children. But by none do I recall him more tenderly than by two or three that start out of the crowd, when he unexpectedly presented himself in my room, announcing how that some passage in a certain book had made him cry yesterday, and how that he had come to dinner, "because he could n't help it," and must talk such passage over. No one can ever have seen him more genial, natural, cordial, fresh, and honestly impulsive, than I have seen him at those times. No one can be surer than I, of the greatness and goodness of the heart that then disclosed itself.

We had our differences of opinion. I thought that he too much feigned a want of earnestness, and that he made a pretense of undervaluing his art, which was not good for the art that he held in trust. But when we fell upon these topics, it was never very gravely, and I have a lively image of him in my mind, twisting both his hands in his hair, and stamping about, laughing, to make an end of the discussion.

When we were associated in remembrance of the late Mr.

Douglas Jerrold, he delivered a public lecture in London, in the course of which he read his very best contribution to "Punch," describing the grown-up cares of a poor family of young children. No one hearing him could have doubted his natural gentleness, or his thoroughly unaffected manly sympathy with the weak and lowly. He read the paper most pathetically, and with a simplicity of tenderness that certainly moved one of his audience to tears. This was presently after his standing for Oxford, from which place he had dispatched his agent to me, with a droll note (to which he afterward added a verbal postscript), urging me to "come down and make a speech, and tell them who he was, for he doubted whether more than two of the electors had ever heard of him, and he thought there might be as many as six or eight who had heard of me." He introduced the lecture just mentioned, with a reference to his late electioneering failure, which was full of good sense, good spirits, and good humor.

He had a particular delight in boys, and an excellent way with them. I remember his once asking me with fantastic gravity, when he had been to Eton where my eldest son then was, whether I felt as he did in regard of never seeing a boy without wanting instantly to give him a sovereign? I thought of this when I looked down into his grave, after he was laid there, for I looked down into it over the shoulder of a boy to whom he had been kind.

These are slight remembrances; but it is to little familiar things suggestive of the voice, look, manner, never, nevermore to be encountered on this earth, that the mind first turns in a bereavement. And greater things that are known of him, in the way of his warm affections, his quiet endurance, his unselfish thoughtfulness for others, and his munificent hand, may not be told.

If, in the reckless vivacity of his youth, his satirical pen had ever gone astray or done amiss, he had caused it to prefer its own petition for forgiveness, long before: —

> I've writ the foolish fancy of his brain;
> The aimless jest that, striking, hath caused pain,
> The idle word that he'd wish back again.

In no pages should I take it upon myself at this time to discourse of his books, of his refined knowledge of character, of his subtle acquaintance with the weaknesses of human nature, of his delightful playfulness as an essayist, of his quaint and touching ballads, of his mastery over the English language. Least of all, in these pages, enriched by his brilliant qualities from the first of the series, and beforehand accepted by the Public through the strength of his great name.

But, on the table before me, there lies all that he had written of his latest and last story. That it would be very sad to any one — that it is inexpressibly so to a writer — in its evidences of matured designs never to be accomplished, of intentions begun to be executed and destined never to be completed, of careful preparation for long roads of thought that he was never to traverse, and for shining goals that he was never to reach, will be readily believed. The pain, however, that I have felt in perusing it, has not been deeper than the conviction that he was in the healthiest vigor of his powers when he wrought on this last labor. In respect of earnest feeling, far-seeing purpose, character, incident, and a certain loving picturesqueness blending the whole, I believe it to be much the best of all his works. That he fully meant it to be so, that he had become strongly attached to it, and that he bestowed great pains upon it, I trace in almost every page. It contains one picture which must have cost him extreme distress, and which is a master-piece. There are two children in it, touched with a hand as loving and tender as ever a father caressed his little child with. There is some young love, as pure and innocent and pretty as the truth. And it is very remarkable that, by reason of the singular construction of the story, more than one main incident usually belonging to the end of such a fiction is anticipated in the beginning, and thus there is an approach to completeness in the fragment, as to the satisfaction of the reader's mind concerning the most interesting persons, which could hardly have been better attained if the writer's breaking-off had been foreseen.

The last line he wrote, and the last proof he corrected, are among these papers through which I have so sorrowfully made my way. The condition of the little pages of manuscript where Death stopped his hand, shows that he had carried them about, and often taken them out of his pocket here and there, for patient revision and interlineation. The last words he corrected in print, were, "And my heart throbbed with an exquisite bliss." God grant that on that Christmas Eve when he laid his head back on his pillow and threw up his arms as he had been wont to do when very weary, some consciousness of duty done and Christian hope throughout life humbly cherished, may have caused his own heart so to throb, when he passed away to his Redeemer's rest!

He was found peacefully lying as above described, composed, undisturbed, and to all appearance asleep, on the twenty-fourth of December, 1863. He was only in his fifty-third year; so young a man, that the mother who blessed him in his first sleep blessed him in his last. Twenty years before, he had written, after being in a white squall, —

> And when, its force expended,
> The harmless storm was ended,
> And, as the sunrise splendid
> Came blushing o'er the sea;
> I thought, as day was breaking,
> My little girls were waking,
> And smiling, and making
> A prayer at home for me

Those little girls had grown to be women when the mournful day broke that saw their father lying dead. In those twenty years of companionship with him, they had learned much from him; and one of them has a literary course before her worthy of her famous name.

On the bright wintry day, the last but one of the old year, he was laid in his grave at Kensal Green, there to mingle the dust to which the mortal part of him had returned, with that of a third child, lost in her infancy, years ago. The heads of a great concourse of his fellow-workers in the Arts were bowed around his tomb.

OBITUARY POEMS.

WILLIAM MAKEPEACE THACKERAY.

He was a cynic: by his life all wrought
  Of generous acts, mild words, and gentle ways;
His heart wide open to all kindly thought,
  His hand so quick to give, his tongue to praise.

He was a cynic: you might read it writ
  In that broad brow, crowned with its silver hair:
In those blue eyes, with childlike candor lit,
  In that sweet smile his lips were wont to wear.

He was a cynic: by the love that clung
  About him from his children, friends, and kin:
By the sharp pain, light pen and gossip tongue
  Wrought in him, chafing the soft heart within.

He was a cynic: let his books confess
  His *Dobbin's* silent love; or yet more rare
His *Newcome's* chivalry and simpleness;
  His *Little Sister's* life of loving care.

And if his acts, affections, works, and ways
  Stamp not upon the man the cynic's sneer,
From life to death, O Public, turn your gaze,—
  The last scene of a cynical career!

These uninvited crowds, this hush that lies,
  Unbroken, till the solemn hush of prayer
From many hundred reverent voices rise,
  Into the sunny stillness of the air.

These tears, in eyes but little used to tears,
  These sobs, from manly lips, hard set and grim,
Of friends, to whom his life lay bare for years,
  Of strangers, who but knew his books, not him.

A cynic? Yes, if 't is the cynic's part
  To track the serpent's trail, with saddened eye,
To mark how good and ill divide the heart,
  How lives in checkered shade and sunshine lie ·

How e'en the best unto the worst is knit
  By brotherhood of weakness, sin, and care;
How, even in the worst, sparks may be lit
  To show all is not utter darkness there.

Through Vanity's bright flaunting fair he walked,
  Making the puppets dance, the jugglers play;
Saw Virtue tripping, honest effort balked,
  And sharpened wit on roguery's downward way;

And told us what he saw; and if he smiled
  His smile had more of sadness than of mirth —
But more of love than either. Undefiled,
  Gentle, alike by accident of birth,

And gift of courtesy and grace of love,
  When shall his friends find such another friend?
For them, and for his children, God above
  Has comfort. Let us bow: God knows the end.

WILLIAM MAKEPEACE THACKERAY.

A heart beneath a cynic's cloak,
  Tender as true, and good as strong;
A voice that like a sabre's stroke,
  Smote down the gilded shield of wrong;
A stanch right hand, and full of might,
  That never dealt the unfair blow —
That even in the thickest fight
  Could pause, and spare a fallen foe.
A giant genius, wit unblamed,
  A scholar's intellect refined,
A kindly spirit, half ashamed
  To own how well it loved mankind.

This was our general. Many a year,
  Unsullied, free from rents or flaws,
Our standard did he o'er us rear,
  And gathered glory for our cause.
He never showed the wounds he bore —
  None knew how deep — within his breast,
And now the long, fierce battle o'er,
  His gallant spirit is at rest.
O brother soldiers of the pen!
  Whose words are faint, whose eyes are dim,
Vow by his grave to be true men,
  And in life's warfare copy him.

Historical Contrast.

May 1701, December 1863.

When one whose nervous English verse
  Public and party hate defied,
Who bore and bandied many a curse
  Of angry times — when Dryden died,

Our royal Abbey's Bishop-Dean
  Waited for no suggestive prayer,
But, ere one day closed o'er the scene,
  Craved, as a boon, to lay him there.

The wayward faith, the faulty life,
  Vanished before a Nation's pain;
"Panther" and "Hind" forgot their strife,
  And rival statesmen thronged the fane.

O gentle Censor of our age!
  Prime master of our ampler tongue!
Whose word of wit and generous page
  Were never wrath, except with Wrong.

Fielding — without the manners' dross,
  Scott — with a spirit's larger room,

What Prelate deems thy grave his loss?
  What Halifax erects thy tomb?

But, maybe, He — who so could draw
  The hidden Great — the humble Wise,
Yielding with them to God's good law
  Makes the Pantheon where he lies.

WILLIAM MAKEPEACE THACKERAY.

Now that his noble form is clay,
One word for good old Thackeray,
One word for gentle Thackeray,
Spite of his disbelieving eye,
True Thackeray — a man who would not lie.

Among his fellows he was peer
For any gentleman that ever was;
And if the lordling stood in fear
Of the rebuke of that satiric pen,
Or if the good man sometimes gave a tear,
They both were moved by equal cause,
They loved and hated him with honest cause;
'T was Nature's truth that touched the men.

O nights of Addison and Steele,
And Swift, and all those men, return!
Oh, for some writer now to make me feel!
Oh, for some talker that can bid me burn,
Like him, with his majestic power
Of pathos, mixed with terrible attack,
And probing into records of the past,
Through some enchanted hour,
To show the white and black,
And what did not — and what deserved to last!

Poet and Scholar, 'tis in vain
We summon thee from those dim halls

Where only death is absolute and holds unquestioned reign.
Even Shakespeare must go downward in his dust —
And lie with all the rest of us in rust —
And mould and gloom and mildewed tomb
(Mildewed or May-dewed evermore a tomb),
Yet hoping still above the skies
To have his humble place among the just.

And so "Hic Jacet," — that is all
That can be said, or writ, or sung
Of him who held in such a thrall
With his melodious gift of pen and tongue,
Both nations — old and young.

Honor 's a hasty word to speak,
But now I say it solemnly and slow,
To the One Englishman most like the Greek
Who wrote "The Clouds" two thousand years ago.

Adsum.

I.

The Angel came by night,
  (Such angels still come down !)
And like a winter cloud
  Passed over London town,
Along its lonesome streets
  Where Want had ceased to weep,
Until it reached a house
  Where a great man lay asleep ;
The man of all his time
  Who knew the most of men, —
The soundest head and heart,
  The sharpest, kindest pen.
It paused beside his bed,
  And whispered in his ear.
He never turned his head,
  But answered, "I am here."

II.

Into the night they went.
  At morning, side by side,
They gained the sacred Place
  Where the greatest Dead abide :
Where grand old Homer sits
  In godlike state benign :
Where broods in endless thought
  The awful Florentine.
Where sweet Cervantes walks,
  A smile on his grave face :
Where gossips quaint Montaigne,
  The wisest of his race :
Where Goethe looks through all
  With that calm eye of his :
Where — little seen but Light —
  The only Shakespeare is !
When the new Spirit came,
  They asked him, drawing near,
" Art thou become like us ? "
  He answered, " I am here."

CHARLES DICKENS.

DICKENS'S EARLIEST WRITINGS.

CONCERNING Dickens's earliest printed writings, Mr. James Grant, the well-known journalist and author, has supplied us with an account which differs much from what has been elsewhere said upon this part of our author's career. "It is everywhere stated," says Mr. Grant, "that the earliest productions from his pen made their appearance in the columns of the 'Morning Chronicle,' and that Mr. John Black, then editor of that journal, was the first to discover and duly to appreciate the genius of Mr. Dickens. The fact was not so. It is true that he wrote 'Sketches' afterwards in the 'Morning Chronicle,' but he did not begin them in that journal. Mr. Dickens first became connected with the 'Morning Chronicle,' as a reporter in the gallery of the House of Commons. This was in 1835–36; but Mr. Dickens had been previously engaged, while in his nineteenth year, as a reporter for a publication entitled the 'Mirror of Parliament,' in which capacity he occupied the very highest rank among the eighty or ninety reporters for the press then in Parliament. While in the gallery of the House of Commons, he was exceedingly reserved in his manners. Though interchanging the usual courtesies of life with all with whom he came into contact in the discharge of his professional duties, the only gentleman at that time in the gallery of the House of Commons with whom he formed a close personal intimacy was Mr. Thomas Beard, then a reporter for the

'Morning Herald,' and now connected with the newspaper press generally, as furnishing the court intelligence in the morning journals. The friendship thus formed between Mr. Dickens and Mr. Beard so far back as the year 1832 was, I believe, continued till the death of Mr. Dickens.

"It was about the year 1833–34, before Mr. Dickens's connection with the 'Morning Chronicle,' and before Mr. Black, then editor of that journal, had ever met with him, that he commenced his literary career as an amateur writer. He made his *début* in the latter end of 1834 or beginning of 1835, in the 'Old Monthly Magazine,' then conducted by Captain Holland, an intimate friend of mine. The 'Old Monthly Magazine' had been started more than a quarter of a century before by Sir Richard Philips, and was for many years a periodical of large circulation and high literary reputation — a fact which might be inferred from another fact, namely, that the 'New Monthly Magazine,' started by Mr. Colburn, under the editorial auspices of Mr. Thomas Campbell, author of 'The Pleasures of Hope,' appropriated the larger portion of its title. The 'Old Monthly Magazine' was published at half a crown, being the same price as 'Blackwood,' 'Fraser,' and 'Bentley's' magazines are at the present day.

"It was, as I have said, in this monthly periodical — not in the columns of the 'Morning Chronicle' — that Mr. Dickens first appeared in the realms of literature. He sent, in the first instance, his contributions to that periodical anonymously. These consisted of sketches, chiefly of a humorous character, and were simply signed 'Boz.' For a long time they did not attract any special attention, but were generally spoken of in newspaper notices of the magazine as 'clever,' 'graphic,' and so forth.

"Early in 1836 the editorship of the 'Monthly Magazine' — the adjective 'Old' having been by this time dropped — came into my hands; and in making the necessary arrangements for its transfer from Captain Holland — then, I should have mentioned, proprietor as well as editor — I expressed my great admiration of the series of 'Sketches by Boz,' which had appeared in the 'Monthly,' and said I should like to make an arrangement with the writer for a continuance of them under my editorship. With that view I asked him the name of the author. It will sound strange in most ears when I state, that a name which has for so many years filled the whole civilized world with its fame was not remembered by Captain Holland. But he added, after expressing his regret that he could not at the moment recollect the real name of 'Boz,' that he had received a letter from him a few days previously, and that if I would meet him at the same time and place next day, he would bring me that letter, because it related to the 'Sketches' of the writer in the 'Monthly Magazine.' As Captain Holland knew I was at the time a parliamentary reporter on the 'Morning Chronicle,' then a journal of high literary reputation, and of great political influence, he supplemented his remark by saying that 'Boz' was a parliamentary reporter; on which I observed that I must, in that case, know him, at least by sight, as I was acquainted, in that respect, more or less, with all the reporters in the gallery of the House of Commons.

"Captain Holland and I met, according to appointment, on the following day, when he brought me the letter to which he had referred. I then found that the name of the author of 'Sketches by Boz' was Charles Dickens. The letter was written in the most moderate terms. It was simply to the effect that as he (Mr. Dickens) had hitherto given all his contributions — those signed 'Boz' — gratuitously, he would be glad if Captain Holland thought his 'Sketches' to be worthy of any small remuneration, as otherwise he would be obliged to discontinue them, because he was going very soon to get married, and therefore would be subjected to more expenses than he was while living alone, which he was during the time, in Furnival's Inn.

"It was not quite clear from Mr. Dickens's letter to Captain Holland, whether he meant he would be glad to receive any small consideration for the series of 'Sketches,' about a dozen in number, which he had furnished to the 'Monthly Magazine' without making any charge, or whether he only expected to be paid for those he might afterwards send. Neither do I know whether Captain Holland furnished him with any pecuniary expression of his admiration of the 'Sketches by Boz' which had appeared in the 'Monthly.' But immediately on receiving Mr. Dickens's letter, I wrote to him, saying that the editorship of the 'Monthly Magazine' had come into my hands, and that, greatly admiring his 'Sketches' under the signature of 'Boz,' I should be glad if we could come to any arrangement for a continuance of them. I concluded my note by expressing a hope that he would, at his earliest convenience, let me know on what terms per sheet he would be willing to furnish me with similar sketches every month for an indefinite period.

"By return of post I received a letter from Mr. Dickens, to the effect that he had just entered into an arrangement with Messrs. Chapman & Hall to write a monthly serial. He did not name the work, but I found in a few weeks it was none other than the 'Pickwick Papers.' He added, that as this serial would occupy much of his spare time from his duties as a reporter, he could not undertake to furnish me with the proposed sketches for less than eight guineas per sheet, which was at the rate of half a guinea per page.

"I wrote to him in reply that the price was not too much, but that I could not get the proprietor to give the amount, because when the 'Monthly Magazine' came into his hands it was not in the same flourishing state as it once had been. I was myself, at this time, getting ten guineas a sheet from Captain Marryat for writing for his 'Metropolitan Magazine,' which was started by Thomas Campbell and Tom Moore, in opposition to the 'New Monthly Magazine,' and at the rate of twenty guineas per sheet for my contributions to the 'Penny Cyclopædia.'

"Only imagine," concludes Mr. Grant, with pardonable fervor, "Mr. Dickens offering to furnish me with a continuation, for any length of time which I might have named, of his 'Sketches by Boz' for eight guineas a sheet, whereas in little more than six months from that date he could — so great in the interval had his popularity become — have got 100 guineas per sheet of sixteen pages from any of the leading periodicals of the day!"

Dr. Charles Mackay writes: "John Black, of the 'Morning Chronicle,' was always keen to discover young genius, and to help it onward in the struggle of life. He very early discovered the talents of Dickens — not only as a reporter, but as a writer." Dr. Mackay was sub-editor of the 'Morning Chronicle' when Dickens was a reporter. He continues: "I have often heard Black speak of him, and predict his future fame. When Dickens had become famous, Black exerted all his influence with Sir John Easthope, principal proprietor of the 'Chronicle,' to have Dickens engaged as a writer of leading articles. He (Black) had his wish, and Dickens wrote several articles; but he did not seem to take kindly to such work, and did not long continue at it."

And Mr. Gruneisen writes: "I believe I must add my name to the remaining list of editorial workers who became acquainted with Charles Dickens when he was in the Gallery. I hope my memory is not deceiving me when I claim for Vincent Dowling, once a reporter, and for years the respected editor of 'Bell's Life in London,' the credit of having been the first to discover the genius for sketching characters of Dickens. 'J. G.' may remember that the proprietary of the 'Morning Chronicle,' the 'Observer,' and 'Bell's Life' was in the hands, if I remember rightly, exclusively of Mr. Perry, and the publication of the several papers was at the Strand office. I have a distinct recollection that Dr. Black's notice of Dickens was based on writings which had been in print prior to his joining the reporting staff of the 'Morning Chronicle.' Dr. Black was always very emphatic in his prognostications of the brilliant future of Charles Dickens. In 1835 the famed novelist was spoken of among his colleagues as a man of mark. The 'Boz' sketches, if not the rage of the general public, had attracted the attention of the literary circles of the day.

"Respecting the marvelous facility of Dickens as a reporter, many versions of his note-taking of a speech of the late Lord Derby (when Lord Stanley) have been current, and I had a correspondence with Dickens on the subject only some months since, he promising to give me the accurate record of his stenographic feat when he met me. This promise he fulfilled the last time, alas! I ever saw him alive, at the anniversary dinner of the Newsvenders' Benevolent Institution, when he took the chair in Freemasons' Hall — the last banquet at which he presided. It was in consequence of a reporter having broken down for the 'Mirror of Parliament' that the late Lord Derby, after complimenting Dickens for his report in the 'Chronicle,' dictated to him his speech — the 'Mirror,' as you are aware, giving in those days *verbatim* reports."

When Charles Dickens first become acquainted with Mr. Vincent Dowling, editor of "Bell's Life" — or "Sleepless Life," as he facetiously termed it, from its Latin heading, "*Nunquam Dormio*" ("wide awake") — he would generally stop at Old Tom Goodwin's oyster and refreshment rooms, opposite the office, in the Strand. On one occasion, Mr. Dowling, not knowing who had called, desired that the gentleman would leave his name, to be sent over to the office, whereupon young Dickens wrote: —

CHARLES DICKENS,
Resurrectionist,
In search of a Subject.

Some recent cases of body-snatching had then made the matter a general topic for public discussion, and Goodwin pasted up the strange address-card for the amusement of the medical students who patronized his oysters. It was still upon his wall when "Pickwick" had made Dickens famous, and the old man was never tired of pointing it out to those whom he was pleased to call his "bivalve demolishers!"

We may just mention that it was Dowling who rushed down from the reporters' gallery and seized Bellingham, after his assassination of Spencer Perceval.

POPULARITY OF "PICKWICK."

Mr. James Grant has favored us with some personal recollections of the fortune which attended the first publication of "Pickwick": —

"In connection with the rapidity of Mr. Dickens's rise, and the heights to which he soared in the regions of literature, I may mention a few facts which have not before found their way into print. The terms on which he concluded an arrangement with Messrs. Chapman & Hall for the publication of the 'Pickwick Papers' were fifteen guineas for each number, the number consisting of two sheets, or thirty-two pages. That was a rather smaller sum than that at which he offered, just at the same time, to contribute to the 'Monthly Magazine,' then under my editorship.

"For the first five months of its existence Mr. Dickens's first serial, the 'Pickwick Papers,' was a signal failure, and notwithstanding the fact that Mr. Charles Tilt, at that time a publisher of considerable eminence, made extraordinary exertions, out of friendship for Messrs. Chapman & Hall, to insure its success. He sent out, on what is called sale or return, to all parts of the provinces, no fewer than fifteen hundred copies of each of the first five numbers. This gave the 'Pickwick Papers' a very extensive publicity, yet Mr. Tilt's only result was an average sale of about fifty copies of each of the five parts. A certain number of copies sold, of course, through other channels, but commercially the publication was a decided failure. Two months before this Mr. Seymour, the artist, died suddenly, but left sketches for two parts more, and the question was then debated by the publishers whether they ought not to discontinue the publication of the serial. But just while the matter was under their consideration, Sam Weller, who had been introduced in the previous number, began to attract great attention, and to call forth much admiration. The press was all but unanimous in praising 'Samivel' as an entirely original character, whom none but a great genius could have created ; and all of a sudden, in consequence of 'Samivel's' popularity, the 'Pickwick Papers' rose to an unheard-of popularity. The back numbers of the work were ordered to a large extent, and of course all idea of discontinuing it was abandoned.

"No one can read these interesting incidents without being struck with the fact that the future literary career of Mr. Dickens should have been for a brief season placed in circumstances of so much risk of proving a failure ; for there can be no doubt that, had the publication of his serial been discontinued at this particular period, there was little or no probability that other publishers would have undertaken the risk of any other literary venture of his. And he might consequently have lived and died, great as his gifts and genius were, without being known in the world of literature. How true it is that there is a tide in the affairs of men !

"By the time the 'Pickwick Papers' had reached their twelfth number, that being half of the numbers of which it was originally intended the work should consist, Messrs. Chapman & Hall were so gratified with the signal success to which it had now attained, that they sent Mr. Dickens a check for £500, as a practical expression of their satisfaction with the sale. The work continued steadily to increase in circulation until its completion, when the sale had all but reached 40,000 copies. In the interval between the twelfth and concluding number, Messrs. Chapman & Hall sent Mr. Dickens several checks, amounting in all to £3,000, in addition to the fifteen guineas per number which they had engaged at the beginning to give him. It was understood at the time that Messrs. Chapman & Hall made a clear profit of nearly £20,000 by the sale of the 'Pickwick Papers,' after paying Mr. Dickens in round numbers £3,500.

"Probably," concludes Mr. Grant, "there are few instances on record in the annals of literature in which an author rose so rapidly to popularity and attained so great a height in it as Mr. Dickens. His popularity was all the more remarkable because it was reached while yet a mere youth. He was incomparably the most popular author of his day before he had attained his twenty-sixth year; and what is even more extraordinary still, he retained the distinction of being the most brilliant author of the age until the very hour of his death — a period of no less than thirty-five years."

Since the illustrious author's decease even the book-binders who had the charge of "Pickwick" have been claiming the honor of stitching the sheets together, and giving their recollections to the newspapers. It having been stated in the "Daily Telegraph" newspaper that "it was a question between Messrs. Chapman & Hall and their binder, Mr. Bone," "whether a greater or less number than seven hundred copies should be stitched in wrappers; instead of hundreds, it soon became necessary to provide for the sale of thousands; and the green covers of 'Pickwick' were seen all over the country," a Mr. Joseph Aked, of Green Street, Leicester Square, on the following day sent this correction to the same journal:

"SIR, — In your sketch of the Life and Death of Mr. Charles Dickens, in yesterday's 'Telegraph,' you state that the first order given to the binder for Part I. of the 'Pickwick' was seven hundred copies, and it was a question between Messrs. Chapman & Hall, and Mr. Bone, the binder, whether a greater or less number than seven hundred should be stitched in wrapper.

"The first order for Part I. of the 'Pickwick' was for four hundred copies only, and the order was given to myself to execute (not to Mr. Bone) by Messrs. Chapman & Hall, the publishers, who in those days did not consult the binder about the number of copies they would require. Also the first number, stitched and put in the green cover, was done by myself, my work-people having left off work for the day.

"Before the completion of the work the sale amounted to nearly 40,000, the orders being given to myself and to Mr. Bone."

Readers of "Pickwick" found the style so fresh and novel, so totally unlike the forced fun and unreal laughter of the other light reading of their time, that the smallest scrap from any portion of the work was deemed worthy of frequent quotation — a gem in itself. We have seen a little book — now very rare, and not to be found in the British Museum — of which thousands and thousands of copies must have been sold by Mr. Park, of Long Lane, and Mr. Catnach, of Seven Dials, bearing the title of "Beauties of Pickwick."

The famed Pickwick cigar — the "Penny Pickwick" of our childhood — is too well known to need any comment. It was a "brand" originally made by a manufacturer in Leman Street, Minories, and sold in boxes and papers decorated with Mr. Pickwick, hat off, bowing to you in the politest manner, and offering for your notice a long scroll, setting forth the excellence of the cigar — a small cheroot, and containing about one half of the tobacco used in a cigar of this kind sold at 2*d.* At the present day "Pickwicks" are patronized almost entirely by cab-drivers.

Then there were "Pickwick" hats, with narrow brims curved up at the sides, as in the figure of the immortal possessor of that name; "Pickwick" canes, with tassels; and "Pickwick" coats, with brass and horn buttons, and the cloth invariably dark green or dark plum. The name "Pickwick" is said to have been taken from the hamlet or cluster of houses which formed the last resting-stage for coaches going to Bath, which town, it will be remembered, was the scene of Sam Weller's chaffing of "Blazes," the red-breeched footman.

A writer, whose name we have forgotten, remarked that "Pickwick" was made up of "two pounds of Smollett, three ounces of Sterne, a handful of Hook, a dash of the grammatical Pierce Egan — incidents at pleasure, served with an *original sauce piquante.*" And Lady Chatterton, in one of her works, remarked: "Mr. Davy, who accompanied Colonel Chesney up the Euphrates, has recently been in the service of Mohammed Ali Pacha. 'Pickwick' happening to reach Davy while he was at Damascus, he read a part of it to the Pacha, who was so delighted with it, that Davy was on one occasion summoned to him in the middle of the night, to finish the reading of some part in which they had been interrupted. Mr. Davy read in Egypt upon another occasion, some passages from these unrivaled papers to a blind Englishman, who was in such ecstasy with what he had heard, that he exclaimed he was almost thankful he could not see he was in a foreign country, for that, while he listened, he felt completely as though he were again in England."

"Pickwick" Dramatized.

Moncrieff, the famous author of "Tom and Jerry," and a hundred farces and light comedies, dramatized "Pickwick" long before it was finished, for the Strand Theatre, where it was performed under the title of "Sam Weller; or the Pickwickians;" Mr. W. J. Hammond sustaining the character of Sam Weller. The termination of the drama was very different to that given in the book itself, as will be readily seen. The adapter caused Mrs. Bardell to be tried and found guilty of attempted bigamy, her husband being Alfred Jingle. Messrs. Dodson & Fogg, the Freeman Court sharks, were sent to Newgate for conspiracy, and only released upon payment of the sum of £300 or thereabouts, which Mr. Pickwick, on receiving, very generously handed to Jingle to start afresh in the world — the curtain falling with a herald entering and announcing the accession of Queen Victoria, which occurred about this time!

Another version was acted with indifferent success, at the Adelphi, Yates representing Mr. Pickwick, and John Reeve Sam Weller. In February, 1838, Mr. G. W. M. Reynolds started a monthly "Pickwick Abroad; or, A Tour in France," illustrated by Alfred Crowquill. As a curiosity, it deserves to be read, if only to see the immense difference existing between the two books.

The First Hint of "Pickwick."

A great deal has been said as to the origin of "Pickwick," and in the chapter devoted to a consideration of this favorite work the present writer has stated from whence the name, at least, was taken. He did not, however, for the moment remember a conversation upon the subject which he had with a friend not long since, which conversation was shortly followed by a letter from him upon this same topic. The letter runs thus: —

"When I stated to you that Dickens took his ideal of novel-writing from the works of Mr. Pierce Egan, I had nothing but internal evidence to go upon. When he began to write, the most popular fictions were the descriptions of 'Life in London' connected with the names of 'Tom' and 'Jerry.' The grand object of Dickens, as a novelist, has been to depict not so much human life as human life in London, and this he has done after a fashion which he learned from the 'Life in London' of Mr. Pierce Egan. If you remember that once famous book, you will call to mind how he takes his heroes — the everlasting Tom and Jerry — now to a fencing-saloon, now to a dancing-house, now to a chop-house, now to a spunging-house. The object is not to evolve the characters of Tom and Jerry, but to introduce them in new scene after new scene. And so you will find with Dickens. He invents new characters, but he never invents them without at the same time inventing new situations and surroundings of London life. Other novelists would not object to invent new characters appearing in the same position of life as the characters in some preceding novel, and trusting for novelty to the newness of the surroundings and the situation. Dickens insists upon putting the new characters into a new and unexpected trade — doll-making, perhaps, or news-vending — and he has always in view some new phase of London life which he is far more anxious to exhibit than the characters without which it is impossible to bring the phase into prominence. If you look to his writings, or if you talk to him, you will find that his first thought is to find out something new about London life — some new custom or trade or mode of living — and his second thought is to imagine the people engaged in that custom or trade or mode of living. Now this is Pierce Egan's style — and Dickens, with rare genius, and with large sympathies, has followed in grooves which the once celebrated Pierce laid down. Pierce Egan had no wit, and his conversations are not worth mentioning. Dickens riots in wit, and what Pierce would have shown in a description, Dickens makes out in a conversation. But the objects of the two men to magnify London life, and to show it in all its phases, were the same."

Upon examining Pierce Egan's "Finish" — a sequel to his "Life in London" — we certainly find the characters are somewhat similar to those in "Pickwick." In other matters, too, a parallel may be drawn — thus, the Bench instead of the Fleet, and the archery match instead of the shooting party. But the most curious coincidence is that the "Fat Knight" — the counterpart of Mr. Pickwick — is first met by Corinthian Tom at the village of *Pickwick!*

Dickens a Dramatist.

During the publication of "The Pickwick Papers" St. James's Theatre was opened, September 29, 1836, with a burletta entitled "The Strange Gentleman," written by "Boz;" Pritt Harley acted the *Strange Gentleman;* and "Boz," himself, on one occasion took a part. The piece ran until December, when it was withdrawn for an operatic burletta, "The Village Coquettes," by the same author, the music by John Hullah. The parts were sustained by Messrs. Harley (as Martin Stokes), Braham (as Squire Norton), Bennett (as George Edmunds), and John Parry; Mesdames Smith, Rainsforth (as Lucy Benson), and others. It met with a marked reception; and Braham, for a long time after, at different concerts, sang "The Child and the Old Man sat alone," invariably getting encored most enthusiastically. Three other songs in the burletta were great favorites, namely, "Love is not a Feeling to pass away," "Autumn Leaves," and "There 's a Charm in Spring." The book of the words was published by Mr. Bentley, and dedicated to J. Pritt Harley in the following terms: —

"My dramatic bantlings are no sooner born than you father them. You have made my Strange Gentleman exclusively your own; you have adopted Martin Stokes with equal readiness."

The author, "Boz," excuses himself for appearing before the public as the composer of an operatic burletta in the following words: —

"'Either the Honorable Gentleman is in the right, or he is not,' is a phrase in very common use within the walls of Parliament. This drama may have a plot, or it may not; and the songs may be poetry, or they may not; and the whole affair from beginning to end, may be great nonsense, or it may not; just as the honorable gentleman or lady who reads it may happen to think. So, retaining his own private and particular opinion upon the subject (an opinion which he formed upwards of a year ago, when he wrote the piece), the author leaves every gentleman or lady to form his or hers, as he or she may think proper, without saying one word to influence or conciliate them.

"All he wishes to say is this — that he hopes Mr. Braham, and all the performers who assisted in the representation of this Opera, will accept his warmest thanks for the interest they evinced in it from its very first rehearsal, and for their zealous efforts in his behalf — efforts which have crowned it with a degree of success far exceeding his most sanguine anticipations, and of which no form of words could speak his acknowledgment.

"It is needless to add, that the *libretto* of an Opera must be to a certain extent, a mere vehicle for the music; and that it is scarcely fair or reasonable to judge it by those strict rules of criticism which would be justly applicable to a five-act tragedy or a finished comedy."

"Oliver Twist."

Mr. Sheldon M'Kenzie, in the American "Round Table," relates this anecdote of "Oliver Twist:"

"In London I was intimate with the brothers Cruikshank, Robert and George, but more particularly with the latter. Having called upon him one day at his house (it then was in Mydleton Terrace, Pentonville), I had to wait while he was finishing an etching, for which a printer's boy was waiting. To while away the time, I gladly complied with his suggestion that I should look over a portfolio crowded with etchings, proofs, and drawings, which lay upon the sofa. Among these, carelessly tied together in a wrap of brown paper, was a series of some twenty-five or thirty drawings, very carefully finished, through most of which were carried the well known portraits of Fagin, Bill Sykes and his dog, Nancy, the Artful Dodger, and Master Charles Bates — all well known to the readers of 'Oliver Twist.' There was no mistake about it; and when Cruikshank turned round, his work finished, I said as much. He told me that it had long been in his mind to show the life of a London thief by a series of drawings engraved by himself, in which, without a single line of letter-press, the story would be strikingly and clearly told. 'Dickens,' he continued, 'dropped in here one day, just as you have done, and, while waiting until I could speak with him, took up that identical portfolio, and ferreted out that bundle of drawings. When he came to that one which represents Fagin in the condemned cell, he studied it for half an hour, and told me that he was tempted to change the whole plot of his story; not to carry Oliver Twist through adventures in the country, but to take him up into the thieves' den in London, show what their life was, and bring Oliver through it without sin or shame. I consented to let him write up to as many of the designs as he thought would suit his purpose; and that was the way in which Fagin, Sykes, and Nancy were created. My drawings suggested them, rather than individuality suggesting my drawings.'"

Poetical Epistle from Father Prout.

Just before the last installment of "Oliver Twist" was published, there appeared in "Bentley's Miscellany" this

"POETICAL EPISTLE FROM FATHER PROUT TO BOZ.

I.

" A Rhyme! a rhyme! from a distant clime — from the gulf of the Genoese;
O'er the rugged scalps of the Julian Alps, dear Boz! I send you these,
To light the *Wick* your candlestick holds up, or, should you list,
To usher in the yarn you spin concerning Oliver Twist.

II.

" Immense applause you 've gained, O Boz! through Continental Europe;
You'll make Pickwick œcumenick;[1] of fame you have a sure hope:
For here your books are found, gadzooks! in greater *luxe* than any
That have issued yet, ho' press'd or wet, from the types of GALIGNANI.

III.

" But neither, when you sport your pen, O potent mirth-compeller!
Winning our hearts 'in monthly parts,' can Pickwick or Sam Weller
Cause us to weep with pathos deep, or shake with laugh spasmodical,
As when you drain your copious vein for Bentley's periodical.

IV.

" Folks all enjoy your Parish Boy — so truly you depict him:
But I, alack! while thus you track your stinted Poor-law's victim,
Must think of some poor nearer home — poor who, unheeded, perish,
By squires despoiled, by 'patriots' gulled — I mean the starving Irish.

V.

" Yet there 's no dearth of Irish mirth, which, to a mind of feeling,
Seemeth to be the Helot's glee before the Spartan reeling:
Such gloomy thought o'ercometh not the glow of England's humor,
Thrice happy isle! long may the smile of genuine joy illume her!

VI.

" Write on, young sage! still o'er the page pour forth the flood of fancy;
Wax still more droll, wave o'er the soul Wit's wand of necromancy.
Behold! e'en now around your brow th' immortal laurel thickens;
Yea, SWIFT or STERNE might gladly learn a thing or two from DICKENS.

VII.

" A rhyme! a rhyme! from a distant clime — a song from the sunny South!
A goodly theme, so Boz but deem the measure not uncouth.

[1] Ειδωλον της γης οικουμενης.

Would, for thy sake, that 'PROUT' could make his bow in fashion finer,
'*Partant*' (from thee) 'pour la Syrie,' for Greece and Asia Minor.

"GENOA, 14*th December*, 1837."

DICKENS AND IRVING.

Professor Felton, alluding to the death of Washington Irving, in a speech, in the latter part of the year 1859, gave this interesting reminiscence of the friendship existing between Dickens and Irving: —

"The time when I saw the most of Mr. Irving was in the winter of 1842, during the visit of Mr. Charles Dickens in New York. I had known this already distinguished writer in Boston and Cambridge, and, while passing some weeks with my dear and lamented friend, Albert Sumner, I renewed my acquaintance with Mr. Dickens, often meeting him in the brilliant literary society which then made New York a most agreeable resort. Halleck, Bryant, Washington Irving, Davis, and others scarce less attractive by their genius, wit, and social graces, constituted a circle not to be surpassed anywhere in the world. I passed much of the time with Mr. Irving and Mr. Dickens, and it was delightful to witness the cordial intercourse of the young man, in the flush and glory of his youthful genius, and his elder compeer, then in the assured possession of immortal renown. Dickens said, in his frank, hearty manner, that from his childhood he had known the works of Irving; and that, before he thought of coming to this country, he had received a letter from him, expressing the delight he felt in reading the story of 'Little Nell;' and from that day they had shaken hands *autographically* across the Atlantic."

After Professor Felton's reminiscences, it may not be uninteresting to quote the following extract from a letter written by Washington Irving to his niece (Mrs. Storrow), under date May 25, 1841, in which he mentions a letter he had just received from Dickens, in reply to one from himself: —

"And now comes the third letter from that glorious fellow,

Dickens (Boz), in reply to the one I wrote, expressing my heartfelt delight with his writings, and my yearnings towards himself. See how completely we sympathize in feeling: —

"'There is no man in the world,' replies Dickens, 'who could have given me the heartfelt pleasure you have by your kind note of the 13th of last month. There is no living writer, and there are very few among the dead, whose approbation I should feel so proud to earn; and, with everything you have written upon my shelves, and in my thoughts, and in my heart of hearts, I may honestly and truly say so. If you could know how earnestly I write this, you would be glad to read it — as I hope you will be, faintly guessing at the warmth of the hand I autographically hold out to you over the broad Atlantic.

"'I wish I could find in your welcome letter some hint of an intention to visit England. I can't. I have held it at arm's length, and taken a bird's-eye view of it, after reading it a great many times; but there is no greater encouragement in it, this way, than on a microscopic inspection. I should love to go with you — as I have gone, God knows how often — into Little Britain, and Eastcheap, and Green Arbor Court, and Westminster Abbey. I should like to travel with you, outside the last of the coaches, down to Bracebridge Hall. It would make my heart glad to compare notes with you about that shabby gentleman in the oil-cloth hat and red nose, who sat in the nine-cornered back parlor of the Mason's Arms; and about Robert Preston, and the tallow-chandler's widow, whose sitting-room is second nature to me; and about all those delightful places and people that I used to talk about and dream of in the daytime, when a very small and not-over-particularly-taken-care-of boy. I have a good deal to say, too, about that dashing Alonzo de Ojeda, that you can't help being fonder of than you ought to be; and much to hear concerning Moorish legend, and poor unhappy Boabdil. Diedrich Knickerbocker I have worn to death in my pocket, and yet I should show you his mutilated carcass with a joy past all expression.

"'I have been so accustomed to associate you with my pleasantest and happiest thoughts, and with my leisure hours, that I rush at once into full confidence with you, and fall, as it were naturally, and by the very laws of gravity, into your open arms. Questions come thronging to my pen as to the lips of people who meet after long hoping to do so. I don't know what to say first, or what to leave unsaid, and am constantly disposed to break off and tell you again how glad I am this moment has arrived.

" 'My dear Washington Irving, I cannot thank you enough for your cordial and generous praise, or tell you what deep and lasting gratification it has given me. I hope to have many letters from you, and to exchange a frequent correspondence. I send this to say so. After the first two or three, I shall settle down into a connected style, and become gradually rational.

" 'You know what the feeling is, after having written a letter, sealed it, and sent it off. I shall picture you reading this, and answering it, before it has lain one night in the post-office. Ten to one that before the fastest packet could reach New York I shall be writing again.

" 'Do you suppose the post-office clerks care to receive letters? I have my doubts. They get into a dreadful habit of indifference. A postman, I imagine, is quite callous. Conceive his delivering one to himself, without being startled by a preliminary double knock!' "

Irving, writing again to Mrs. Storrow, 29th of October following, says: —

"What do you think? Dickens is actually *coming to America.* He has engaged passage for himself and his wife in the steam-packet for Boston, for the 4th of January next. He says: 'I look forward to shaking hands with you, with an interest I cannot (and I would not if I could) describe. You *can* imagine, I dare say, something of the feelings with which I look forward to being in America. I can hardly believe I am coming."

But to return to Professor Felton and his recollections of Irving and Dickens. He continues: —

"Great and varied as was the genius of Mr. Irving, there was one thing he shrank with a comical terror from attempting, and that was a *dinner speech*. A great dinner, however, was to be given to Mr. Dickens in New York, as one had already been given in Boston; and it was evident to all that no man like Washington Irving could be thought of to preside. With all his dread of making a speech, he was obliged to obey the universal call, and to accept the painful preëminence. I saw him daily during the interval of preparation, either at the lodgings of Dickens, or at dinner, or at evening parties. I hope I showed no want of sympathy with his forebodings, but I could not help being amused with his tragi-comical distress which the thought of that approaching dinner had caused him. His pleasant humor mingled with the real dread, and played with the whimsical horrors of his own position with an irresistible drollery. Whenever it was alluded to, his invariable answer was, 'I shall certainly break down!' — uttered in a half-melancholy tone, the ludicrous effect of which it is impossible to describe. He was haunted, as if by a nightmare; and I could only compare his dismay to that of Mr. Pickwick, who was so alarmed at the prospect of leading about that 'dreadful horse' all day. At length the long-expected evening arrived. A company of the most eminent persons, from all the professions and every walk of life, were assembled, and Mr. Irving took the chair. I had gladly accepted an invitation, making it, however, a condition that I should not be called upon to speak — a thing I then dreaded quite as much as Mr. Irving himself. The direful compulsions of life have since helped me to overcome, in some measure, the postprandial fright. Under the circumstances — an invited guest, with no impending speech — I sat calmly and watched with interest the imposing scene. I had the honor to be placed next but one to Mr. Irving, and the great pleasure of sharing in his conversation. He had brought the manuscript of his speech, and laid it under his plate. 'I shall certainly break down,' he repeated over and over again. At last the moment arrived. Mr. Irving rose, and was received with deafening and long-continued applause, which by no means lessened his apprehension. He began in his pleasant voice; got through two or three sentences pretty easily, but in the next hesitated; and, after one or two attempts to go on, gave it up, with a graceful allusion to the tournament, and the troop of knights all armed and eager for the fray; and ended with the toast, 'Charles Dickens, the guest of the nation.' 'There!' said he, as he resumed his seat under a repetition of the applause which had saluted his rising — 'there! I told you I should break down, and I 've done it.'

"There certainly never was a shorter after-dinner speech; and I doubt if there ever was a more successful one. The manuscript seemed to be a dozen or twenty pages long, but the printed speech was not as many lines.

"Mr. Irving often spoke with a good-humored envy of the felicity with which Dickens always acquitted himself on such occasions."

Immediately after dinner, Irving and Dickens started off together to Washington, to spend a few days, and there took leave of one another. Irving at this time having just received his appointment as Minister to Spain, Dickens wrote to him: "We passed through — literally passed through — this place again to-day. I did not come to see you, for I really had not the heart to say good-by again, and I felt more than I can tell you when we shook hands last Wednesday. You will not be at Baltimore, I fear? I thought at the time, that you only said you might be there, to make our parting the gayer.

"Wherever you go, God bless you! What pleasure I have had in seeing and talking with you, I will not attempt to say. I shall never forget it as long as I live. What would I give if we could have a quiet walk together! Spain is a lazy place, and its climate an indolent one. But if you have ever leisure under its sunny skies to think of a man who loves you, and holds communion with your spirit oftener, perhaps, than any other person alive — leisure from listlessness, I mean — and will write to me in London, you will give me an inexpressible amount of pleasure."

Dickens as an Actor

Dickens's extreme fondness for theatricals had tempted him, as far back as the year 1836, when "Pickwick" was publishing, to take a part in "The Strange Gentleman," at St. James's Theatre. The amateur actor was not successful on this occasion, and we believe no further attempt — except drawing-room performances — was made until the autumn of 1845, when he made another appearance on the stage at the St. James's Theatre, on the 19th of September, the play selected being Ben Jonson's "Every Man in his Humor;" the various parts of the amateur performance being taken by literary and artistic celebrities. The triumph achieved was immense. They were induced to repeat the performance for a Charity, at the same theatre, on the 15th of November following, the only alteration being the substitution of a Mr. Eaton for Mr. A'Beckett as William. The play-bill itself is a curiosity:

A Strictly Private Amateur Performance.

At the St. James's Theatre

(By favor of Mr. Mitchell). Will be performed Ben. Jonson's Comedy of

EVERY MAN IN HIS HUMOR.

Characters:

Knowell	Henry Mayhew.
Edward Knowell	Frederick Dickens.
Brainworm	Mark Lemon.
George Downright	Dudley Costello.
Wellbred	George Cattermole.
Kitely	John Forster.
Captain Bobadil	Charles Dickens.
Master Stephen	Douglas Jerrold.
Master Mathew	John Leech
Thomas Cash	Augustus Dickens.
Oliver Cob	Percival Leigh.
Justice Clement	Frank Stone.
Roger Formal	Mr. Evans.
William	W. Eaton.
James	W. B. Jerrold.
Dame Kitely	Miss Fortesque.
Mistress Bridget	Miss Hinton.
Tib	Miss Bew.

To conclude with a Farce, in One Act called

TWO O'CLOCK IN THE MORNING.

CHARACTERS:

Mr. Snobbington . . . . MR. CHARLES DICKENS.
The Stranger . . . . MR. MARK LEMON.

Previous to the Play the Overture to "William Tell." Previous to the Farce, the Overture to "La Gazza Ladra."

His Royal Highness Prince Albert has been pleased to express his intention to honor the performance with his presence.

Ben Jonson as an acting dramatist, has almost disappeared from the stage he so long adorned, and probably, no performance of his best comedy was ever more successful than the above. Dickens made such an admirable Captain Bobadil, that Leslie, the Royal Academician, took a most characteristic portrait of him in that character. The moment selected is when the Captain shouts out —

'A gentleman! odds so, I am not within."

Act i., Scene 3.

DICKENS AS A JOURNALIST.

The idea was well taken up. Money was freely spent by the various shareholders, and many advertisements told the public that a newspaper, which should supply everything in the first style of newspaper talent, would be published at the price of twopence-halfpenny. The name chosen was the "Daily News," and Mr. Dickens was widely advertised as "the head of the literary department." Expectation was raised to a high pitch by this announcement; and in 1846, on the 21st of January, the first number appeared. The new journal, however, did not prove so successful as was expected. The staffs of other papers had been long organized, their expenses — of course immense — were well and judiciously controlled, and the arrangements complete. All these things were new to the "Daily News," and the expenses entered into did not render it possible, with the circulation it had then reached, to sell the paper at the original price; and it was shortly after raised to threepence, and finally to the same price as the "Times."

Very recently, and only a few days after the death of the great novelist, the paper here alluded to gave this account of his connection with the journal: —

"Some of our readers may not be aware that the 'Pictures from Italy,' which are now included in all editions of Charles Dickens's works, were originally contributed to this newspaper, and that its early numbers were brought out under his editorship. In the first number of this journal, in the 'Daily News' of January 21, 1846, appeared No. 1 of 'Travelling Letters, written on the Road, by Charles Dickens.' In the 'Daily News' of February 14 of the same year, Mr. Dickens wrote the following verses — which will be new to many — elicited by a speech at one of the night meetings of the wives of the agricultural laborers in Wiltshire, held to petition for free-trade: —

THE HYMN OF THE WILTSHIRE LABORERS.

"Don't you all think that we have a great need to cry to our God to put it in the hearts of our greaseous Queen and her members of Parlerment to grant us free bread!" — LUCY SIMPKINS, *at Brim Hill.*

O God, who by Thy Prophet's hand
  Didst smite the rocky brake,
Whence water came at Thy command,
  Thy people's thirst to slake:
Strike, now, upon this granite wall,
  Stern, obdurate, and high;
And let some drops of pity fall
  For us who starve and die!

The God, who took a little child
  And set him in the midst,
And promised him his mercy mild,
  As, by Thy Son, Thou didst:
Look down upon our children dear,
  So gaunt, so cold, so spare,
And let their images appear
  Where Lords and Gentry are!

O God, teach them to feel how we,
  When our poor infants droop,
Are weakened in our trust in Thee,
  And how our spirits stoop:

For, in Thy rest, so bright and fair,
  All tears and sorrows sleep;
And their young looks, so full of care,
  Would make Thine angels weep!

The God, who with His finger drew
  The Judgment coming on,
Write for these men, what must ensue,
  Ere many years be gone!
O God, whose bow is in the sky,
  Let them not brave and dare,
Until they look (too late) on high
  And see an Arrow there!

O God, remind them, in the bread
  They break upon the knee,
These sacred words may yet be read,
  "In memory of Me!"
O God, remind them of His sweet
  Compassion for the poor,
And how He gave them Bread to eat,
  And went from door to door.

CHARLES DICKENS.

"There is the true ring in these lines. They have the note which Dickens sounded consistently through life of right against might; the note which found expression in the Anti-Corn Law agitation, in the protests against workhouse enormities, in the raid against those eccentricities in legislation which are anomalies to the rich and bitter hardships to the poor. Let the reader remark how consistently the weekly periodicals which Mr. Dickens has guided have taken this side, and how the many pens employed on them have taken this side whenever political or social subjects have been discussed, and he will understand that the author was not a mere jester and story-teller, but a true philanthropist and reformer."

Dickens's friends very soon saw that he had taken a false step. The duties of a daily political paper were not suitable to him, and before many months he relinquished the editorship, and retired from participation in the "Daily News"—but not, it is understood, without a considerable loss in money. His place was then filled by Mr. John Forster, the able editor of the "Examiner," and friend — and at that time the champion — of Mr. Macready.

DICKENS AND THACKERAY.

On the 1st of February, 1847, Mr. Thackeray had issued the first monthly portion of "Vanity Fair," in the yellow wrapper which served to distinguish it from Mr. Dickens's stories, and, after some twelve months had passed, critics began to speak of the work in terms of approbation. The "Edinburgh Review," criticising it in January, 1848, says: "The great charm of this work is its entire freedom from mannerism and affectation both in style and sentiment. . . . . His pathos (though not so deep as Mr. Dickens's) is exquisite; the more so, perhaps, because he seems to struggle against it, and to be half ashamed of being caught in the melting mood; but the attempt to be caustic, satirical, ironical, or philosophical on such occasions is uniformly vain; and again and again have we found reason to admire how an originally fine and kind nature remains essentially free from worldliness, and, in the highest pride of intellect, pays homage to the heart."

From this time forward a friendly rivalry ensued between the two representatives of the two schools of English fiction. We say "rivalry," but it never could have existed from Dickens's side; for, when "Vanity Fair" was at its best, finding six thousand purchasers a month, Dickens was taking the shillings from thirty to forty thousand readers; but the gossips of society have always asserted that there *was* a rivalry, and made comparisons so very frequently between the two great men, that we incidentally allude to it here. More than once has Thackeray said to the present writer (or words very similar): "Ah! they talk to me of popularity, with a sale of little more than one half of 10,000! Why, look at that lucky fellow Dickens, with Heaven knows how many readers, and certainly not less than 30,000 buyers!" But the fact is easily explained — only cultivated readers enjoy Thackeray, whereas both cultivated and uncultivated read Dickens with delight.

Julian Young on Dickens and Thackeray.

Last night I happened casually to mention to Miss Coutts and Mrs. Brown that I had never seen Charles Dickens. Although Miss Coutts had a large party to entertain, with that amiable consideration for her friends which belongs to her, she stole into an adjoining room and dispatched a messenger to him with a note inviting him to lunch next day. Before we had retired to bed an answer had been received to say he would gladly come.

I am delighted to have eaten, drunk, and chatted with "Boz." I have so often found the Brobdignagians of my fancy dwindle into Lilliputians when I have been admitted to familiar intercourse with them, that, considering my unqualified admiration of "Boz's" writings, and the magnitude of my expectations, it is something to say that I am not in the least disappointed with him. I longed to tell him of the lifelong obligations he has laid me under; for there was a period in my life when sickness and sorrow, and their attendant handmaid anxiety, were constant inmates in my home, and in those sad days we used to look out for the post-bag which was to bring us the last number of "Nickleby," or "Chuzzlewit," or "Dombey," with all the eagerness with which an invalid listens for the doctor's footstep on the stair. No drug, no stimulant, ever wrought the wondrous effects that the sight of the green covers of each number did on our poor patient. At their advent, grief and pain would flee away; and, in their stead, pleasant tears, and "laughter, holding both his sides," would take their place. How we used to dread coming to the close of a number. What devices we had recourse to for spinning it out. How, like greedy children smacking their lips with the keen sense of enjoyment over some dainty, would we linger over every racy morsel of humor, roll it over our tongues, and repeat it to each other for the sake of protracting our intellectual feast as long as possible.

I hate to hear invidious comparisons made between the merits of Dickens and of Thackeray. Each has his excellencies, and neither trenches on the domain of the other. For though they are both students of human nature, they approach her from different sides. Thackeray writes in pure and idiomatic English; and he has a deep insight into the foibles of his kind. But, though personally he has made many staunch friends, and all who know him love him well, yet he certainly does not take as genial or as generous a view of men and women as Dickens. He sees men and manners with the jaundiced eye of a pessimist; whereas his great competitor sees "good in everything," and has a heart boiling over with good-will to all mankind. None so poor but he can do him reverence; none so depraved in whom he cannot detect some redeeming quality. Thackeray has an intimate knowledge of the hollowness, artificiality, and waywardness of fashionable life; and, from out the depths of his own experience, constructs imaginary lay figures, which he considers as typical representatives of a class. But Dickens's portraits, however antic they may seem, are yet drawn from real flesh and blood. Thackeray's picture gallery is composed of recollections of men and women he has met with in promiscuous society. Dickens's portraits are studies from the life of those whom he has not met with in Rotten Row, or rubbed against in the drawing-room, but whom he has fallen in with in the by-ways of the world, and who have attracted his observation by their individuality. The characters in Dickens's writings which have been most severely criticised as exaggerated or distorted, are actual transcripts of *bonâ fide* originals. Why, who that knew her, could fail to recognize the original of Mrs. Leo Hunter? In younger days I was at one or two of her parties in Portland Place. Who, that is familiar with Manchester, does not know the Cheeryble brothers? Who, that is old enough to remember a certain inn in Holborn in coaching days, can forget the original of Sam Weller? The original of Mrs. Gamp is not so generally known, but I know well the ladies who first introduced her to Dickens's notice.

Dickens, of course, writes for his livelihood; but it is not exclusively for profit, or even for fame: he generally has a moral purpose in view. He never panders to popular prejudices, but boldly rebukes vice in whatever rank of life he finds it; and takes a profound, and yet a practical, interest in the cause of the ignorant, the oppressed, and the debased.

While I write, I am reminded of an anecdote which shows in a very strong light the extraordinary sway he exercises over the hearts even of those "unused to the melting mood." Mrs. Henry Siddons, a neighbor and intimate friend of the late Lord Jeffery, who had free license to enter his house at all hours unannounced, and come and go as she listed, opened his library door one day very gently to look if he was there, and saw enough at a glance to convince her that her visit was ill-timed. The hard critic of "The Edinburgh" was sitting in his chair, with his head on the table, in deep grief. As Mrs. Siddons was delicately retiring, in the hope that her entrance had been unnoticed, Jeffery raised his head, and kindly beckoned her back. Perceiving that his cheek was flushed and his eyes suffused with tears, she apologized for her intrusion, and begged permission to withdraw. When he found that she was seriously intending to leave him, he rose from his chair, took her by both hands, and led her to a seat.

Lord Jeffery (*loq.*). "Don't go, my dear friend. I shall be right again in another minute."

Mrs. H. Siddons. "I had no idea that you had had any bad news or cause for grief, or I would not have come. Is any one dead?"

Lord Jeffery. "Yes, indeed. I'm a great goose to have given way so; but I could not help it. You'll be sorry to hear that little Nelly, Boz's little Nelly, is dead."

The fact was, Jeffery had just received the last number then out of "The Old Curiosity Shop," and had been thoroughly overcome by its pathos.

Dickens began his career when a youth of nineteen, under his uncle, John Henry Barrow, who started "The Mirror of Parliament," in opposition to "Hansard." Hansard always compiled his reports from the morning newspapers, whereas Barrow engaged a special staff of able reporters, sending each important oration in proof to its speaker for correction. When Stanley fulminated his Philippic against O'Connell, it fell to young Dickens's turn to report the last third of it. The proof of the whole speech was forwarded to Mr. Stanley. He returned it to Barrow, with the remark, that the first two thirds were so badly reported as to be unintelligible; but that, if the gentleman who had so admirably reported the last third of his speech could be sent to him, he would speak the rest of it to him alone. Accordingly, at an hour appointed, young Dickens made his appearance at Mr. Stanley's, note-book in hand. It was with evident hesitation that the servant ushered him into the library, the tables of which were covered with newspapers. Presently the master of the house appeared, eyed the youth suspiciously, and said, "I beg pardon, but I had hoped to see the gentleman who had reported part of my speech," etc. "*I* am that gentleman," retorted Dickens, turning red in the face, and feeling his dignity somewhat offended. "Oh, indeed," replied Mr. Stanley, pushing about the papers, and turning his back to conceal an involuntary smile. It was not long before Sir James Graham stepped in, and then Stanley began his speech. At first he stood still, addressing one of the window curtains as "Mr. Speaker." Then he walked up and down the room, gesticulating and declaiming with all the fire and force he had shown in the House of Commons. Graham, with the newspaper before him followed, and occasionally checked him, when he had forgotten some trifling point, or had transposed one proposition in the place of another.

When the entire speech had been fully reported, Stanley returned the revise with Dickens's corrected edition of the parts of the speech which had been bungled, with a note to Barrow highly complimentary to the stripling reporter, and with a shadowy prediction of a great career for him in the future.

Dickens had totally forgotten this incident, until, many years after, he was invited to dine with Lord Derby for the first time. Having been shown with the other guests before dinner into the library, he felt a strange consciousness of having been in it before, which he could not account for. He was in a state of bewilderment about it all dinner-time; for he could not recall the circumstance which brought the reporting adventure to his mind. But, at all events, something did, and he reminded his host of it. Lord Derby was delighted to recognize in his new friend his boy-reporter, and told the story to a select few, who, with Dickens, had stayed after the rest of the company had departed.

"Not so Bad as we Seem."

In June, 1851, a project — which, it is said, Mr. Dickens had long had in contemplation — was brought forward by Sir Edward Bulwer Lytton, namely, the founding of a Guild of Literature and Art; in reality, a provident fund and benefit society for unfortunate literary men and artists. From it the proper persons would receive continual or occasional relief, as the case might be; but the leading feature was the "Provident Fund," to be composed of moneys deposited by the authors themselves, when they were in a position to be able to lay by something. Dickens and Sir Edward Bulwer Lytton (since a peer) were the most active promoters. The precise plan of the "Guild" was discussed at Lord Lytton's seat, at Knebworth, the November previously. There had been three amateur performances, by Dickens and others, of "Every Man in his Humor," for the gratification of his lordship and his neighboring friends, when it was arranged that his lordship should write a comedy, and Dickens and Mark Lemon a farce. The comedy was entitled "Not so Bad as we Seem," and the farce bore the name of "Mrs. Nightingale's Diary." The first performance took place at Devonshire House, before the Queen, the Prince Consort, and the court circles; and afterwards at the Hanover Square Rooms, and at many of the large provincial towns (Bath, Bristol, etc.). At Devonshire House, not the least incident occurred to shade what a late Drury Lane manager might, in his own Titanic way, have called "the blaze of triumph." From the first moment that the scheme was made known to her Majesty and Prince Albert, both the Queen and the Prince manifested the liveliest interest in its success. The Duke of Devonshire, with a munificence that made the name of his Grace a proverb for liberality, dedicated his mansion to the cause of Literature and Art, and his house was for many days in possession of the amateurs.

The play began at half-past nine, Her Majesty, Prince Albert, and the royal family occupying a box erected for the occasion. The seats were filled by the most illustrious for rank and genius. There was the Duchess of Sutherland; there was the "Iron Duke," in his best temper; there was Macaulay, Chevalier Bunsen, Van der Weyer — themselves authors; in fact, all the highest representatives of the rank, beauty, and genius of England, and her foreign ambassadors.

The list of the performers, and the parts taken by them, is a curiosity in its way: —

MEN.

The Duke of Middlesex,	Peers attached to the son of James II., commonly called the First Pretender,	Mr. Frank Stone.
The Earl of Loftus,		Mr. Dudley Costello.
Lord Wilmot, a young man at the head of the *mode* more than a century ago, son to Lord Loftus,		Mr. Charles Dickens.
Mr. Shadowly Softhead, a young gentleman from the city, friend and double to Lord Wilmot,		Mr. Douglas Jerrold.
Mr. Hardman, a rising member of Parliament, and adherent to Sir Robert Walpole,		Mr. John Forster.
Sir Geoffrey Thornside, a gentleman of good family and estate,		Mr. Mark Lemon.
Mr. Goodenough Easy, in business, highly respectable, and a friend to Sir Geoffrey,		Mr. E. W. Topham.
Lord le Trimmer,	Frequenters of Will's Coffee-House,	Mr. Peter Cunningham.
Sir Thomas Timid,		Mr. Westland Marston.
Colonel Flint,		Mr. R. H. Horne.
Mr. Jacob Tonson, a bookseller,		Mr. Charles Knight.
Smart, valet to Lord Wilmot,		Mr. Wilkie Collins.
Hodge, servant to Sir Geoffrey Thornside,		Mr. John Tenniel.
Paddy O'Sullivan, Mr. Fallen's landlord,		Mr. Robert Bell.
Mr. David Fallen, Grub Street, author and pamphleteer,		Mr. Augustus Egg, A.R.A.

Lord Strongbow, Sir John Bruin, Coffee-House Loungers, Drawers, Newsmen, Watchmen, etc., etc.

WOMEN.

Lucy, daughter to Sir Geoffrey Thornside, ... Mrs. COMPTON.
Barbara, daughter to Mr. Easy, ... Miss ELLEN CHAPLIN.
The Silent Lady of Deadman's Lane.

The royal party paid the deepest attention to the progress of the play, Her Majesty frequently leading the applause. And when the curtain fell upon the three hours' triumph, Her Majesty rose in her box, and, by the most cordial demonstration of approval, "commanded" (for such may be the word) the reappearance of all the actors, again to receive the royal approval of their efforts. Nor did the Queen and Prince merely bestow applause. Her Majesty took seventeen places for herself, visitors, and suite; and, further, as a joint contribution of herself and the Prince, headed the list of subscriptions with £150, making the sum total of £225. It is said that the receipts of the night exceeded £1,000. Another representation at Devonshire House took place on the following Tuesday, the admission being £2. The farce written for the occasion, called "Mrs. Nightingale's Diary," was performed, and Charles Dickens and Mark Lemon sustained the principal characters. A critic at the time remarked: "Both these gentlemen are admirable actors. It is by no means amateur playing with them. Dickens seizes the strong points of a character, bringing them out as effectively upon the stage as his pen undyingly marks them upon paper. Lemon has all the ease of a finished performer, with a capital relish for comedy and broad farce."

For the representations in the provinces a portable theatre was constructed, Messrs. Clarkson Stanfield, David Roberts, Grieve, and others, painting the scenes, etc., which are said to have been very beautiful. The funds raised were unfortunately, by a flaw in the act of Parliament, unintentionally tied up for a number of years; but on Saturday, July 29, 1865, the surviving members of the Fund proceeded to the neighborhood of Stevenage, near the magnificent seat of the President, Lord Lytton, to inspect three houses built in the Gothic style on the ground given by him for that purpose. An enterprising publican in the vicinity had just previously opened his establishment, which bore the very appropriate sign of "Our Mutual Friend" — Mr. Dickens's then latest work — and caused considerable merriment.

Dickens and Leigh Hunt.

One of the characters in "Bleak House," Harold Skimpole, an incarnation of a canting and hypocritical scoundrel, whom one longs to kick, was fastened upon as the impersonation of that kind and genial writer, the late Leigh Hunt. Those who had the good fortune to know him personally indignantly refuted the calumny, and, like other unfounded rumors, the matter died out, until, after his death, the idea was again bruited forth.

Mr. Thornton Hunt (his eldest son), in preparing a new edition of his father's famous "Autobiography," prefixed an introductory chapter, in which the following passages occur: —

"His animation, his sympathy with what was gay and pleasurable, his avowed doctrine of cultivating cheerfulness, were manifest on the surface, and could be appreciated by those who knew him in society, most probably even exaggerated as salient traits, on which he himself insisted *with a sort of gay and ostentatious willfulness.*

"The anxiety to recognize the right of others, the tendency to 'refine,' which was noted by an early school companion, and the propensity to elaborate every thought, made him, along with the direct argument by which he sustained his own conviction, recognize and almost admit all that might be said on the opposite side.

"It is most desirable that his qualities should be known as they were; for such deficiencies as he had are the honest explanation of his mistakes; while, as the reader may see from his writing and his conduct, they are not, as the faults of which he was accused would be, incompatible with the noblest faculties both of head and heart. To know Leigh Hunt as he was, was to hold him in reverence and love."

Dickens immediately, in a number of "All the Year Round," under the head of "Leigh Hunt — a Remonstrance," made this statement: —

"Four or five years ago, the writer of these lines was much pained by accidentally encountering a printed statement, 'that Mr. Leigh Hunt was the original of Harold Skimpole in "Bleak House."' The writer of these lines is the author of that book. The statement came from America. It is no disrespect to that country, in which the writer has, perhaps, as many friends and as true an interest as any man that lives, good-humoredly to state the fact that he has now and then been the subject of paragraphs in transatlantic newspapers more surprisingly destitute of all foundation in truth than the wildest delusions of the wildest lunatics. For reasons born of this experience, he let the thing go by.

"But since Mr. Leigh Hunt's death the statement has been revived in England. The delicacy and generosity evinced in its revival are for the rather late consideration of its revivers. The fact is this: Exactly those graces and charms of manner which are remembered in the words we have quoted were remembered by the author of the work of fiction in question when he drew the character in question. Above all other things, that 'sort of gay and ostentatious willfulness' in the humoring of a subject, which had many times delighted him, and impressed him as being unspeakably whimsical and attractive, was the airy quality he wanted for the man he invented. Partly for this reason, and partly (he has since often grieved to think) for the pleasure it afforded him to find that delightful manner reproducing itself under his hand, he yielded to the temptation of too often making the character *speak* like his old friend. He no more thought, God forgive him! that the admired original would ever be charged with the imaginary vices of the fictitious creature than he has himself ever thought of charging the blood of Desdemona and Othello on the innocent Academy model who sat for Iago's leg in the picture. Even as to the mere occasional manner, he meant to be so cautious and conscientious that he privately referred the proof-sheets of the first number of that book to two intimate literary friends of Leigh Hunt (both still living), and altered the whole of that part of the text on their discovering too strong a resemblance to his 'way.'

"He cannot see the son lay this wreath on the father's tomb, and leave him to the possibility of ever thinking that the present words might have righted the father's memory and were left unwritten. He cannot know that his own son may have to explain his father when folly or malice can wound his heart no more, and leave this task undone."

Mr. Thornton Hunt, alluding to his father's incapacity to understand figures, frankly admitted, "His so-called improvidence resulted partly from actual disappointment in professional undertakings, partly from a real incapacity to understand any objects when they were reduced to figures, and partly from a readiness of self-sacrifice, which was the less to be guessed by any one who knew him, since he seldom alluded to it, and never, except in the vaguest and most unintelligible terms, hinted at its real nature or extent."

Very recently, and since the decease of the great novelist, a similar statement about Skimpole and Leigh Hunt, made in the columns of a daily journal, was thus replied to by Mr. Edmund Ollier, an old friend of the deceased essayist: "Dickens himself corrected the misapprehension in a paper in 'All the Year Round,' towards the close of 1859, after Hunt's death; and during Hunt's life, and after the publication of 'Bleak House,' he wrote a most genial paper about him in 'Household Words.' It is also within my knowledge that he expressed to Leigh Hunt personally his regret at the Skimpole mistake."

Leigh Hunt himself, in confessing his inability at school to master the multiplication-table, naïvely adds, "Nor do I know it to this day!" And again: "I equally disliked Dr. Franklin, author of 'Poor Richard's Almanac,' a heap, as it appeared to me, of 'scoundrel maxims.'[1] I think I now appreciate Dr. Franklin as I ought; but, although I can see the utility of such publications as his almanac for a rising commercial state, and hold it useful as a memorandum to uncalculating persons like myself, who happen to live in an old one, I think there is no necessity for it in commercial nations long established, and that it has no business in others who do not found their happiness in that sort of power. Franklin, with all his abilities, is but at the head of those who think that man lives 'by bread alone.'"

And again, in his "Journal," a few years ago, that gentleman, after narrating several agreeable hardships inflicted upon him, says: "A little before this, a friend in a manufacturing town was informed that I was a terrible speculator in the money markets! I who was never in a market of any kind but to buy an apple or a flower, and who could not dabble in money business if I would, from sheer ignorance of their language!"

Gad's Hill Place.

Though not born at Rochester, Mr. Dickens spent some portion of his boyhood there; and was wont to tell how his father the late Mr. John Dickens, in the course of a country ramble, pointed out to him as a child the house at Gad's Hill Place, saying, "There, my boy; if you work and mind your book, you will, perhaps, one day live in a house like that." This speech sunk deep, and in after years, and in the course of his many long pedestrian rambles through the lanes and roads of the pleasant Kentish country, Mr. Dickens came to regard this Gad's Hill House lovingly, and to wish himself its possessor. This seemed an impossibility. The property was so held that there was no likelihood of its ever coming into the market; and so Gad's Hill came to be alluded to jocularly, as

[1] Thomson's phrase in his *Castle of Indolence*, speaking of a miserly money-getter:—

"'A penny savèd is a penny got;'
Firm to this scoundrel maxim keepeth he,
Nor of its rigor will he bate a jot,
Till he hath quench'd his fire and banished his pot."

representing a fancy which was pleasant enough in dream-land, but would never be realized.

Meanwhile the years rolled on, and Gad's Hill became almost forgotten. Then a further lapse of time, and Mr. Dickens felt a strong wish to settle in the country, and determined to let Tavistock House. About this time, and by the strangest coincidences, his intimate friend and close ally, Mr. W. H. Wills, chanced to sit next to a lady at a London dinner-party, who remarked, in the course of conversation, that a house and grounds had come into her possession of which she wanted to dispose. The reader will guess the rest. The house was in Kent, was not far from Rochester, had this and that distinguishing feature which made it like Gad's Hill and like no other place ; and the upshot of Mr. Wills's dinner-table chitchat with a lady whom he had never met before was, that Charles Dickens realized the dream of his youth, and became the possessor of Gad's Hill. The purchase was made in the spring of 1856.

In the "Uncommercial Traveller," under the head of "Travelling Abroad," No. VII., Dickens makes this mention of it : —

"So smooth was the old high-road, and so fresh were the horses, and so fast went I, that it was midway between Gravesend and Rochester, and the widening river was bearing the ships, white-sailed, or black-smoked, out to sea, when I noticed by the way-side a very queer small boy.

"'Hallo !' said I to the very queer small boy, 'where do you live ?'

"'At Chatham,' says he.

"'What do you do there ?' says I.

"'I go to school,' says he.

"I took him up in a moment, and we went on.

"Presently the very queer small boy says, 'This is Gad's Hill we are coming to, where Falstaff went out to rob those travellers and ran away.'

"'You know something about Falstaff, eh ?' said I.

"'All about him,' said the very queer small boy.

"'I am old (I am nine) and I read all sorts of books. But *do* let us stop at the top of the hill and look at the house there, if you please!'

"'You admire that house?' said I.

"'Bless you, sir!' said the very queer small boy, 'when I was not more than half as old as nine, it used to be a treat for me to be brought to look at it. And now I am nine, I come by myself to look at it. And ever since I can recollect, my father, seeing me so fond of it, has often said to me, "If you were to be very persevering and were to work hard, you might some day come to live in it." Though that's impossible!' said the very queer small boy, drawing a low breath, and now staring at the house out of window with all his might.

"I was rather amazed to be told this by the very queer small boy, for that house happens to be *my* house, and I have reason to believe that what he said was true."

Birds of a Feather.

Mr. Crabb Robinson has preserved in his diary some playful lines by Southey; but his editor has omitted to add a circumstance which would have increased their interest. They were written in the album of Mrs. S. C. Hall, and the opposite page contained the autographs of Joseph Bonaparte and Daniel O'Connell, a circumstance which suggested what the Laureate wrote: —

> "Birds of a feather flock together,
> But *vide* the opposite page;
> And thence you may gather I 'm not of a feather
> With some of the birds in this cage."
> Robert Southey, *22d October*, 1836.

Some years afterwards, Charles Dickens, good-humoredly referring to Southey's change of opinion, wrote in the album, immediately under Southey's lines, the following: —

> "Now, if I don't make
> The completest mistake
> That ever put man in a rage,
> This bird of two weathers
> Has moulted his feathers,
> And left them in some other cage." — Boz.

When these last lines first appeared in the "Art Journal," a friend of Southey's, resenting Boz's remark, retaliated by "good-humoredly referring" to the change of style between "Pickwick" and "Our Mutual Friend," and wrote in the margin of the periodical: —

"Put his *first* work and *last* work together,
And learn from the groans of all men,
That if he 's not alter'd his feather,
He 's certainly alter'd his pen."

Dickens as a Smasher.

A story is told that on one pedestrian occasion he was taken for a "smasher." He had retired to rest at Gad's Hill, but found he could not sleep, when he determined to turn out, dress, and walk up to London — some thirty miles. He reached the suburbs in the gray morning, and applied at an "early" coffee-house for some refreshment tendering for the same a sovereign, the smallest coin he happened to have about him.

"It's a bad 'un," said the man, biting at it, and trying to twist it in all directions, "and I shall give you in charge." Sure enough the coin did have a suspicious look. Mr. Dickens had carried some substance in his pocket which had oxydized it. Seeing that matters looked awkward, he at once said, "But I am Charles Dickens!"

"Come, that won't do; any man could say he was 'Charles Dickens.' How do I know?" The man had been victimized only the week previously, and at length, at Mr. Dickens's suggestion, it was arranged that they should go to a chemist, to have the coin tested with *aquafortis*. In due course, when the shops opened, a chemist was found, who immediately recognized the great novelist — notwithstanding his dusty appearance — and the coffee-house keeper was satisfactorily convinced that he had not been entertaining a "smasher."

Dickens and the Queen.

Only since the death of Mr. Dickens is it that the high respect in which Her Majesty has always held the great novelist and his writings has become generally known, but for many years past our Queen has taken the liveliest interest in his literary labors, and has frequently expressed a desire for an interview with him. And here it may not be uninteresting to mention a circumstance in illustration of Her Majesty's regard for her late distinguished subject which came under the writer's personal notice. Six years ago, just before the library of Mr. Thackeray was sold off at Palace Green, Kensington, a catalogue of the books was sent to Her Majesty—in all probability by her request. She desired some memorial of the great man, and preferred to make her own selection by purchase rather than ask the family for any memento by way of gift. There were books with odd drawings from Thackeray's pen and pencil; there were others crammed with MS. notes, but there was one lot thus described in the catalogue:

Dickens (C.) A Christmas Carol, in prose, 1843:
Presentation Copy.
INSCRIBED
"*W. M. Thackeray, from Charles Dickens (whom he made very happy once a long way from home).*"

Her Majesty expressed the strongest desire to possess this, and sent an *unlimited commission* to buy it. The original published price of the book was 5*s*. It became Her Majesty's property for £25 10*s*., and was at once taken to the palace.

The personal interview Her Majesty had long expressed a desire to have with Mr. Dickens took place on the 9th April, 1870, when he received her commands to attend her at Buckingham Palace, and accordingly did so, being introduced by his friend, Mr. Arthur Helps, the clerk of the Privy Council.

The interview was a lengthened one, and most satisfactory to both. In the course of it Her Majesty expressed to him her warm interest in, and admiration of his works; and, on parting, presented him with a copy of her own book, "Our

Life in the Highlands," with an autograph inscription, "Victoria R. to Charles Dickens," on the fly-leaf; at the same time making a charmingly modest and graceful remark as to the relative positions occupied in the world of letters by the donor and the recipient of the book.

Soon after his return home, he sent to Her Majesty an edition of his collected works; and when the clerk of the Council recently went to Balmoral, the Queen, knowing the friendship that existed between Mr. Dickens and Mr. Helps, showed the latter where she had placed the gift of the great novelist. This was in her own private library, in order that she might always see the books; and Her Majesty expressed her desire that Mr. Helps should inform the great novelist of this arrangement.

Since our author's decease the journal with which he was formerly connected has said: —

"We were not at liberty at that time to make known that the Queen was then personally occupied with the consideration of some means by which she might, in her public capacity, express her sense of the value of Mr. Dickens's services to his country and to literature. It may now be stated that the Queen was ready to confer any distinction which Mr. Dickens's known views and tastes would permit him to accept, and that after more than one title of honor had been declined, Her Majesty desired that he would, at least, accept a place in her Privy Council."

Three days before this he had attended the levée and been presented to her son H. R. H. the Prince of Wales, introduced by the Earl De Grey and Ripon.

His daughter, Miss Dickens, was presented at court to Her Majesty on the 10th of the following month, introduced by the Countess Russell.

Dickens's Benevolence.

The late Sheridan Knowles, in a letter to a friend, gave an instance of his generosity: "Poor Haydn, the author of the

'Dictionary of Dates' and the 'Book of Dignities' (I believe I am right in the titles), was working, to my knowledge, under the pressure of extreme destitution, aggravated by wretchedly bad health, and a heart slowly breaking through efforts indefatigable, but vain, to support in comfort a wife and a young family. I could not afford him at the moment any material relief, and I wrote to Charles Dickens, stating his miserable case. My letter was no sooner received than it was answered — and how. By a visit to his suffering brother, and not of condolence only, but of assistance — rescue! Charles Dickens offered his purse to poor Haydn, and subsequently brought the case before the Literary Society, and so appealingly as to produce an immediate supply of £60. I need not say another word. I need not remark that such benevolence is not likely to occur solitarily. The fact I communicate I learned from poor Haydn himself. Dickens never breathed a word to me about it."

Methodical Habits.

He did not work by fits and starts, but had regular hours for labor, commencing about ten and ending about two. It is an old saying that easy writing is very difficult reading; Mr. Dickens's works, so easily read, were by no means easily written. He labored at them prodigiously, both in their conception and execution. During the whole time that he had a book in hand, he was much more thoughtful and preoccupied than in his leisure moments.

His hours and days were spent by rule. He rose at a certain time, he retired at another, and though no precisian, it was not often that his arrangements varied. His hours for writing were between breakfast and luncheon, and when there was any work to be done no temptation was sufficiently strong to cause it to be neglected. This order and regularity followed him through the day. His mind was essentially methodical; and in his long walks, in his recreations, in his labor, he was governed by rules laid down for himself by himself, rules well studied beforehand, and rarely departed from. The so-called men of business, the people whose own exclusive devotion to the science of profit and loss makes them regard doubtfully all to whom that same science is not the main object in life, would have been delighted and amazed at this side of Dickens's character.

No writer set before himself more laboriously the task of giving the public the very best. A great artist who once painted his portrait while he was in the act of writing one of the most popular of his stories, relates that he was astonished at the trouble Dickens seemed to take over his work, at the number of forms in which he would write down a thought before he hit out the one which seemed to his fastidious fancy the best, and at the comparative smallness of manuscript each day's sitting seemed to have produced. Those, too, who have seen the original MSS. of his works, many of which he had bound and kept at his residence at Gad's Hill, describe them as full of interlineations and alterations.

Manner of Literary Composition.

A writer in a weekly journal says: "I remember well one evening, spent with him by appointment, not wasted by intrusion, when I found him, according to his own phrase, 'picking up the threads' of 'Martin Chuzzlewit' from the printed sheets of the half volume that lay before him. This accounts for the seeming incompleteness of some of his plots; in others the design was too strong and sure to be influenced by any outer consideration. He was only confirmed and invigorated by the growing applause, and marched on, like a successful general, with each victory made easier by the preceding one. It seemed hardly to come within his nature to compose in solitary fashion, and wait the event of a whole work. No doubt this resulted in part from his character as a journalist; and so did his utter disdain of the shams which it is the express province of journalism to detect and expose.

"His composition, easy as it seems in the reading—indeed, so natural that it would be difficult to substitute any truer word in any place—was, we are told, elaborate and slow. But in his happier days the process was by no means wearisome. It was the love of the idea, that could not let it go till he had nursed it to its utmost growth. In this he resembled many of the greatest humorists, whose enjoyment of their own fancies is evidenced by the impossibility of passing them into print while a single mirth-stirring thought or word could be added to make the picture perfect. The result was invaluable. With the exception only of Shakespeare, among English writers of drama and fiction, no other author than Dickens yields so many sentences on each page of sterling value in themselves; no other author can be read and re-read with such certainty of finding fresh pleasure on every perusal. Nowhere, with the one exception, does so much thought go to finish the production. It is jeweler's work, inlaying and enriching every part."

Blanchard Jerrold on Dickens.

I was passing in review masses of correspondence, betimes, on June 10, 1870, clearing the weeds from the flowers, and tying up the precious papers of a life passed in the thick of the literary activities of my time, when I received a letter: "I should have written to you earlier to-day but from the smart blow of this sudden illness of our dear Charles Dickens, who had engaged to meet me this very afternoon (June 9) at 3 o'clock, little dreaming of what was to put aside the appointment." I rang for the morning papers.

Charles Dickens had passed away from us! Lay before me his letter in which he told me how, on a certain June day, travelling from Gad's Hill to London, a bluff city man had piped over the edge of his morning paper, "Do you see this? Douglas Jerrold is dead!" Dickens was inexpressibly shocked, for he had seen into the heart of his friend; and they had parted only a few days before, with the intention of spending some happy hours in the house by Rochester. "Few of his friends," — I have the words before me in a blurred writing not often written by that firm and willing hand, — "I think, can have had more favorable opportunities of knowing him, in his gentlest and most affectionate aspect, than I have had. He was one of the gentlest and most affectionate of men."

So of Dickens. Who knew him best and closest, saw how little he would ever produce to the outer world, of the bright, chivalrous, engaging, and deep and tender heart that beat within his bosom. The well of kindness was open to mankind, and from it generations will drink; but it was never fathomed. Charles Dickens, as all writers about him have testified, was so graciously as well as lavishly endowed by Nature that every utterance was sunny, every sentiment pure, every emotional opinion instinctively right, — like a woman's. The head that governed the richly-stored heart was wise, prompt, and alert at the same time. He communicated to all he did the delightful sense of ease with power. Prodigal as he was, he seemed ever to reserve more love and tenderness than he gave. His vigor was sustained, as well as brilliant and daring. His mind, so marked in its self-respect and equal poise, was never weak on great occasions, as the judicial mind so often is. There was something feminine in the quality that led him to the right verdict, the appropriate word, the core of the heart of the question in hand. The air about him vibrated with his activity, and his surprising vitality. In a difficulty men felt safe, merely because he was present. Most easily, among all thinkers it has been my fortune to know, was he master of every situation in which he placed himself. Not only because of the latent, conscious power that was in him, and the knightly cheerfulness which became the pure-minded servant of humanity who had used himself to victory; but because he adopted always the old plain advice, and deliberated well before he acted with the vigor which was inseparable from any activity of his.

The art with which Charles Dickens managed men and women was nearly all emotional. As in his books, he drew at will upon the tears of his readers; in his life he helped men with a spontaneous grace and sweetness which are indescribable. The deep, rich, cheery voice; the brave and noble countenance; the hand that had the fire of friendship in its grip, — all played their part in comforting in a moment the creature who had come to Charles Dickens for advice, for help, for sympathy. When he took a cause in hand, or a friend under his wing, people who knew him breathed in a placid sense of security. He had not only the cordial will to be of use wherever his services could be advantageously enlisted, but he could see at a glance the exact thing he might do; and beyond the range of his conviction as to his own power, or the limit of proper asking or advancing, no power on earth could move him the breadth of a hair.

Slow to adopt a cause, Charles Dickens was the first in the battle for it when he had espoused it. He had the qualities of the perfect trooper, as well as the far-seeing captain. I have a letter of his, about Italy, dated 1844, in which, amid hearty gossip, he turns to a cause that was dear to him at the time. "Come and see me in Italy," he says to my father. "Let us smoke a pipe among the vines. I have taken a little house surrounded by them, and no man in the world should be more welcome to it than you;" and from the midst of the vines he turns to the Sanatorium in the New Road, nearly opposite the Devonshire Place in which so many wisely-happy evenings have been passed. "Is your modesty really a confirmed habit, or could you prevail upon yourself, if you are moderately well, to let me call you up for a word or two at the Sanatorium dinner? There are some men — excellent men — connected with that institution who would take the very strongest interest in your doing so, and *do* advise me one of these days, that if I can do it well and unaffectedly, I may." Dickens had steadfastness, endurance, thoroughness, in all he undertook. If he invited a friend to his house, and it was at a distance, he would write the most minute directions, — a way-bill, — and enliven every mile-stone with a point of humor or a happy suggestion of pleasure to come out of the excursion. "Think it over." (This from Switzerland to a dear friend in London.) "I could send you the minutest particulars of the journey. It 's nearly all railroad and steamboat, and the easiest in the world." I have another letter of invitation to Paris, written some three-and-twenty years ago. Amid exquisite touches of humor, and in the glow of his friendship, lie details of the precisest kind, beginning,—"The fifteenth of March is on a Monday. Now you can't cross to Boulogne on a Sunday, unless in summer time. . . . . The railroad from Abbeville hither, finished some time, is announced to open on the 1st of March." There are directions, in the event of the railroad being open, and in the event of its remaining closed, and an offer to secure the proper seat in the *malle poste* at Boulogne. The coming, the visit, the return, the hour of arrival in London, are all mapped out, winding up with "in London on Saturday night the 27th. *Voilà tout*—as *we* say."

In more serious matters, he was a man of order and of righteous doing indeed. Cant is so well aired about the world, and people have come to take a spice of it so much for granted in every public man who holds the cause of his brethren to heart, that they can hardly conceive of the noblest servant that he had not the most infinitessimal particle of it. Writing from the South, when he was about to travel to London with the MS. of "The Christmas Carol," more than a quarter of a century ago, to read it to a few friends in Mr. John Forster's chambers in Lincoln's Inn Fields, he observed of the book, "I have tried to strike a blow upon that part of the brass countenance of wicked Cant, where such compliment is sorely needed at this time; and I trust that the result of my training is at least the exhibition of a strong desire to make it a staggerer. If you should think at the end of the four rounds (there are no more) that the said Cant, in the language of 'Bell's Life,' 'comes up piping,' I shall be very much the better for it." Dickens abhorred a sham with his whole soul. When he published his "Child's History of England," the mass took it for granted that the chapters which were appearing in the columns of "Household Words" were so much copy, and that the writing of it for his own children was only a common, and, to the world, warrantable artistic fiction. Such fiction was not possible to the greatest fiction-writer of our century. I have his words before me on this history, and the ink is yellowing fast:—

"I am writing a little history of England for my boy, which I will send you when it is printed for him, though your boys are too old to profit by it. It is curious that I have tried to impress upon him (writing, I dare say, at the same moment with you) the exact spirit of your paper,[1] for I don't know what I should do if he were to get hold of any Conservative or High Church notions; and the best way of guarding against such horrible result is, I take it, to wring the parrot's neck in his very cradle. O heaven! if you could have been with me at the hospital dinner last Monday. There were men there, — your city aristocracy, — who made such speeches, and expressed such sentiments, as any moderately intelligent dustman would have blushed through his cindery bloom to have thought of. Sleek, slobbering, bow-paunched, over-fed, apoplectic, snorting cattle — and the auditory leaping up in their delight! I never saw such an illustration of the power of purse, or felt so degraded and debased by its contemplation, since I have had eyes and ears. The absurdity of the thing was too horrible to laugh at. It was perfectly overwhelming. But if I could have partaken it with anybody who would have felt it as you would have done, it would have had quite another aspect, or would at least, like a 'classical' mask, have had one funny side to relieve its dismal features.

"Supposing fifty families were to emigrate into the wilds of North America, — yours, mine, and forty-eight others, picked for their concurrence of opinion on all important subjects, and for their resolution to found a colony of common sense, — how soon would that devil, Cant, present itself among them in one shape or other? The day they landed, do you say, or the day after?

"That is a great mistake, almost the only one I know, in the 'Arabian Nights,' where the Princess restores people to their original beauty by sprinkling them with the Golden Water. It is quite clear that she must have made monsters of them by such a christening as that."

There is a manuscript the world knows nothing about this

[1] *The Preacher Parrot.*

day, and yet which has been for many years in existence, and in circulation among those who were native to the author's hearth. "The Life of our Saviour," was written by Charles Dickens to guide the hearts of his children; and if ever a labor of love was done by that most affectionate nature, this was preëminently it. "I wish it were in my power," writes his dear friend, Mr. James T. Fields, "to bring to the knowledge of all who doubt the Christian character of Charles Dickens certain other memorable words of his, written years ago, with reference to Christmas. They are not as familiar as many beautiful things from the same pen on the same subject, for the paper which enshrines them has not as yet been collected among his authorized works. Listen to these loving words, in which the Christian writer has embodied the life of his Saviour: 'Hark! the waits are playing, and they break my childish sleep. What images do I associate with the Christmas music, as I see them set forth on the Christmas tree! known before all others, keeping far apart from all the others, they gather round my little bed. An angel speaking to a group of shepherds in a field; some travellers, with eyes uplifted, following a star; a baby in a manger; a child in a spacious temple, talking with grave men; a solemn figure, with a mild and beautiful face, raising a dead girl by the hand; again, near a city gate, calling back the son of a widow, on his bier, to life; a crowd of people looking through the opened roof of a chamber where he sits, and letting down a sick person on a bed, with ropes; the same in a tempest, walking on the water to a ship; again, on a seashore, teaching a great multitude; again, with a child upon his knee, and other children round; again, restoring sight to the blind, speech to the dumb, hearing to the deaf, health to the sick, strength to the lame, knowledge to the ignorant; again, dying upon a cross, watched by armed soldiers, a thick darkness coming on, the earth beginning to shake, and only one voice heard, "Forgive them, for they know not what they do."'" By the eloquent pages that now will shortly be put within reach of every English and American household, the children of Charles Dickens were taught their first lessons of Christian love and Christian chivalry. With what patience and thoroughness he wrought out his creed in his home can be known only to the happy few who were privileged to live his life, and to study the splendid and unbroken harmonies which dwelt in the life within, as well as in the life without. How far the ripples of his home-spirit rounded into the outer world, will I hope, for the sake of the world, be drawn by the hand to which the solemn duties of biographer shall be presently confided. The circles broadened into far-off places from that vehement central vibration of love, and strangers stretched out their arms to Dickens, and weary men unknown, sought his cheery and valiant temperament as balm and comfort.

When Ada, Lady Lovelace, was dying, and suffering the tortures of a slow, internal disease, she expressed a craving to see Charles Dickens, and talk with him. He went to her, and found a mourning house. The lady was stretched upon a couch, heroically enduring her agony. The appearance of Dickens's earnest, sympathetic face was immediate relief. She asked him whether the attendant had left a basin of ice, and a spoon. *She had.* "Then give me some now and then, and don't notice me when I crush it between my teeth: it soothes my pain, and — we can talk."

The womanly tenderness, the wholeness, with which Dickens would enter into the delicacies of such a situation, will rise instantly to the mind of all who knew him. That he was at the same moment the most careful of nurses, and the most sympathetic and sustaining of comforters, who can doubt?

"Do you ever pray?" the poor lady asked.

"Every morning and every evening," was Dickens's answer, in that rich, sonorous voice which crowds happily can remember; but of which they can best understand all the eloquence, who knew how simple and devout he was when he spoke of sacred things, — of suffering, of wrong, or of misfortune. "He taught the world," said his friend Dean Stanley, over his new-made grave in Westminster Abbey, "great lessons of the eternal value of generosity, of purity, of kindness, and of unselfishness; and by his fruits shall he be known of all men." His engaging manner when he came suddenly in contact with a sick friend, defies description; but from his own narrative of his walk with my father, which he told me made his heart heavy, and was a gloomy task, it is easy for friends to understand the patience, solicitude, and kindly counsel, and designed humor with which he went through with it. My father was very ill; but under Dickens's thoughtful care, he had rallied before they reached the Temple. "We strolled through the Temple," Dickens wrote me, "on our way to a boat, and I have a lively recollection of him stamping about Elm Tree Court, with his hat in one hand, and the other pushing his hair back, laughing in his heartiest manner at a ridiculous remembrance we had in common, which I had presented in some exaggerated light to divert him." Then again, — of the same day, — "The dinner-party was a large one, and I did not sit near him at table. But he and I arranged, before we went in to dinner, that he was only to eat some simple dish that we agreed upon, and was only to drink sherry-and-water." Then, "We exchanged, 'God bless you!' and shook hands."

And — they never met again.

But how full of wise consideration is all this day spent with the invalid friend, in the midst of merriment, even to the ridiculous remembrance "presented in some exaggerated light, to divert him." Mr. Charles Kent has told me how he met Dickens a few weeks before his death, and was observed, at a glance, by that most masterly and piercing observer, to be in low spirits and feeble.[1] Whereupon Dickens, who had ample

[1] Mr. Arthur Helps recently said that, during a walk with Charles Dickens, the great novelist observed nine objects for every one that he, Mr. Helps, observed. The same might be said by most men who have ever walked frequently in company with Mr. Dickens. Besides this, I can vouch for another yet more important and striking fact, viz., that Mr. Dickens scarcely ever looked direct at anything. He walked along without turning his head or staring in front (as some of those horrid, colored, *glaring* photographs represent him), as one should say — "Here I am looking right through you!" He saw everything at a glance, or with "half an eye." It was only on very particular occasions that he looked hard at anything. He had no need. His was one of those gifted visions upon which objects photographed themselves on the retina in rapid succession. The Poet Laureate possesses a vision

momentous business of his own on hand, put it aside, sketched a pleasant day together: a *tête-à-tête* dinner and a walk. In short, to watch the many sides of his unselfishness, and the fund of resources for the good of other people he had at his command, was to be astonished at his extraordinary vitality. How good he was to all who had the slightest claim on him, who shall tell? But that which Hepworth Dixon said over my father's dust may be assuredly repeated by the narrow bed near Macaulay, Sheridan, and Handel. If every one who has received a favor at the hands of Dickens should cast a flower upon his grave, a mountain of roses would lie upon the great man's breast. And, in truth, his grave was filled with flowers.

To plaster a few of the ills which obtrude themselves unpleasantly upon the attention, with checks handed to resounding cheers, is a kind of charity that is strongly spiced with selfishness. The sham of charity-dinner speakers and donors Dickens abhorred, as I have shown. And in like manner, and with like vehemence, he detested slip-shod assistance, or careless, unreflecting giving. The last time I sat with him on a business occasion was at a council meeting of the Guild of Literature and Art. There had been an application from the wife of a literary brother. The wrecked man of letters was suffering from that which would never relax its hold upon him. But it could not be said that his misconduct had not brought on the blow. The firmness and delicacy with which Dickens sketched the case to the council, passing wholly over the cause, to get at once to the imploring fact upon which our hearts could not be closed, left in my mind a delightful sense of his abounding goodness. He spoke of the wife, and her heroic self-abandonment to her husband, through years which would have tried beyond endurance very many wives. He begged that the utmost might be done; and at the same time he remained firmly just. What were the objects of the fund,

of a similar kind, though no doubt more intense, if not so universal. He has no need to fix his eyes upon anything; and, indeed, has been found sometimes to have seen the whole of an exquisite landscape when apparently looking inwardly, as in a waking dream, and lost to all around him.

as laid down in the rules? Did the case come strictly within the limits of our mission? Friendship, sympathy, apart, was it a proper and deserving case? The points were argued with the greatest care; and all the time an acute anxiety was upon the countenance of the chairman. When at length we saw our way to afford the help desired, Dickens's face brightened as he became busy with his minutes and his books, and his secretary, who was at hand; and he remarked cheerily how glad he was we had seen our way to do something.

Another occasion thrusts itself through a crowd of recollections. A very dear friend of mine, and of many others to whom literature is a staff, had died. To say that his family had claims on Charles Dickens is to say that they were promptly acknowledged, and satisfied with the grace and heartiness which double the gift, sweeten the bread, and warm the wine. I asked a connection of our dead friend whether he had seen the poor wife and children.

"Seen them!" he answered. "I was there to-day. They are removed into a charming cottage. They have everything about them; and, just think of this, when I burst into one of the parlors, in my eager survey of the new home, I saw a man in his shirt-sleeves, up some steps, hammering away lustily. He turned. It was Charles Dickens; and he was hanging the pictures for the widow."

Dickens was the soul of truth and manliness, as well as kindness; so that such a service as this came as naturally to him as help from his purse. His friend, Paul Fèval, has said over his grave, "Nothing in him was false, not even his modesty."

There was that boy-element in Charles Dickens which has been so often remarked in men of genius as to appear almost inseparable from the highest gifts of nature. "Why, we played a game of knock'em down only a week or two ago," a friend remarked to me last June, with brimming eyes. "And he showed all the old, astonishing energy and delight in taking aim at Aunt Sally."

My own earliest recollections of Charles Dickens are of his

gayest moods: when the boy in him was exuberant, and leap-frog or rounders were not sports too young for the player who had written "Pickwick," twenty years before. To watch him through an afternoon, by turns light and grave; gracious and loving and familiar to the young, apt and vigorous in council with the old; ready for a frolic upon the lawn — leap-frog, rounders; as ready for a committee-meeting in the library; and then to catch his cheery good-night, and feel the hand that spoke so truly from the heart, — was to see Charles Dickens the man, the friend, the companion, and the counselor, all at once, and to get at something like a just estimate of that which was beautiful in the brilliant and noble Englishman we have lost. The sweet and holy lessons which he presented to humanity out of the humble places in the world could not have been evolved out of a nature less true and sympathetic than his was. It wanted such a man as Dickens was in his life to be such a writer as he was for the world. He drew beauties out of material that to the common eye was vulgar, unpromising stuff. Shallow readers have said of him that he could not draw a gentleman or a lady; and this charge has provoked some remarks from "The Times," which are bold and to the point: —

"We have heard it objected also by gentlemen, that Charles Dickens could never describe 'a lady,' and by ladies that he could never sketch the character of 'a gentleman;' but we have always observed, that when put to the proof, these male and female critics failed lamentably to establish their case. We are not sure that Charles Dickens's gentlemen were all as well dressed as those who resort to Poole's Temple of Fashion, or that his ladies were always attired after the very last fancy of Worth. Dress is no doubt what may be called, in the catechism of gentility, the 'outward and visible sign' of a gentleman, just as the outward fashion of a lady is shown by her dress. But even these are nothing if that 'inward and spiritual grace' which is characteristic of the true gentleman and real lady be wanting; and in that grace, however negligent they may be in their attire, the ladies and gentlemen in Charles Dickens's works are never deficient. We are not denying that the true type of gentle life is to be found in the upper classes. Far from it. We only insist, when we are told that Charles Dickens could not describe either a lady or a gentleman, that there are ladies and gentlemen in all ranks and classes of life, and that the inward delicacy and gentle feeling which we acknowledge as the only true criterion of the class, may be found under the smock-frock of the ploughboy as well as beneath the mantle of an earl."

The "fierce light" which beats not only about a throne, but about all stations in life in these days, has discovered the absolute truth of the creed which animated Dickens, when, working upon his own observation, he drew a gentleman in the rough form of Joe Gargery, and planted a little chivalry in the breast of the convict who was grateful to Pip. In the long gallery of Dickens's portraits of the men and women of his time, — to which I beseech the attention of the young reader, — there are gentlemen and ladies of all degrees. He made no fuss about "Nature's noblemen;" but he painted what he saw, and delighted to find strong elements of that goodness which he loved so passionately, and worshipped so devoutly, in all his rambles and prospectings in the unlikeliest places. That he drew with an impartial hand, is witnessed not only by the hold his creations at once got upon the public mind, but by the whole tenor of his life and work, away from his desk. The conventional gentleman and lady had no picturesque side to attract him; and they could seldom be got into the frame of his subject. He was an artist, and he consequently preferred a green lane and a gypsy camp any and every day to the Ladies' Mile and a lounge in his club. If you want to make your most conventional gentleman look noble in marble to all posterity, you strip the figure Poole has dressed in his inspired moment, and shake out a toga, and think about sandals. The poor and lowly come to the artist's hand ready-made pictures. Besides, the observer's sense of justice is gratified when he finds himself enabled, out of the fund of his own discoveries among the neglected of his fellow-creatures, to rehabilitate the humble and despised. While the tendency of modern party warfare has been grievously to quicken and heat class animosities, the writings of Charles Dickens, which have been spread over every level of society, have been powerful counter-agents, teaching all classes the truth that is the best bond and the safest, viz., that, in the words of "The Times," the gentlemen is to be found "under the smock-frock of the ploughboy as well as beneath the mantle of an earl."

Only Charles Dickens wrought this out many years ago, by patient travels in the midst of the smock-frocks, and by obtaining proof positive that there was occasionally a gentle heart under the corduroy of a costermonger. Dickens's triumph lay in this, that he convinced mankind of the truth and completeness of his diagnosis. None of the genteel classes are on intimate terms of daily intercourse with hostlers; and yet who has not accepted Sam Weller as a part of the breathing population of the empire? Dickens's men and women ought to be included in the census.[1]

[1] *The British Medical Journal* declares: "How true to Nature, even in the most trivial details, almost every character and every incident in the works of the great novelist whose dust has just been laid to rest really were is best known to those whose tastes or whose duties led them to frequent the paths of life from which Dickens delighted to draw. But none, except medical men, can judge of the rare fidelity with which he followed the great Mother through the devious paths of disease and death. In reading *Oliver Twist*, and *Dombey and Son* or *The Chimes*, or even *No Thoroughfare*, the physician often felt tempted to say, 'What a gain it would have been to physic if one so keen to observe and so facile to describe had devoted his powers to the medical art!' It must not be forgotten that his description of 'hectic' (in *Oliver Twist*) has found its way into more than one standard work both in medicine and surgery." The *Law Journal* bears testimony to his truth and force as a painter of lawyers: "He has left us a whole gallery of legal caricatures. We have the wonderful trial of Bardell *v.* Pickwick, introducing the fussy Buzfuz, and that rare phenomenon, a modest junior. In the same book we have the smart Dodson and Fogg, the excellent Mr. Perker, and the solicitor to the Wellers. In *Bleak House* we have the great chancery suit of Jarndyce *v.* Jarndyce with graphic descriptions of the court, of the lawyers engaged in the suit, of the shrewd solicitor of the Dedlock family, and of the poor law-writer. In the *Old Curiosity Shop*, we have Sampson Brass, the masculine Sally Brass, and the mirth-provoking

By this admirable standpoint for his observation of humanity which he had adopted, Dickens had come to regard all men and women so thoroughly and exclusively on account of their moral, intellectual, and spiritual worth, that he was at home with all kinds of society, in the highest and the humblest walks. So that it is easy to picture him standing in a drawing-room at Windsor Castle, one arm just resting upon the sofa, and talking in his quiet earnest manner to the first lady in the land. There would not be the least shadow of nervousness in him; so great was the command which his trained brain and heart had given him, in the presence of humanity of every degree, under every conceivable circumstance, — by the throne, or facing thousands of his countrymen, who loved him, one and all, so well.

> "The best of men
> That e'er wore earth about him was a sufferer;
> A soft, meek, patient, humble, tranquil spirit,
> The first true gentleman that ever breathed."

The "soft, meek, patient, humble, tranquil spirit," how often has Dickens painted! — the Christian gentleman, if not Poole's; the modest, high-souled gentlewoman, a lady, if not Worth's! He inclined to the Biblia Pauperum, and was delighted to catch heavy thumbs turning over the holy pictures. But he turned no sour face upon the well-to-do. Of the foibles and pretenses of these, he was an unsparing critic; but he was as unsparing when he had the vices of the ignorant and the poor to deal with. He was pre-Raphaelite in his allegiance and constancy to nature; but his eye loved the beautiful, and his spirit leaned to all that was valiant, noble, and holy in the human heart. If he took his heroes amid the lower or middle ranks of life, it was because here the picturesque in these won the artist's eye; and if he drew the good that was in the scenes he analyzed, rather than the bad, it was because he delighted in finding it under the most unpromising circumstances, and in showing, to quote a line from my father,

Dick Swiveller. In *Great Expectations* we have that wonderful character, Wemmick, and his well-conceived employer, the Old Bailey attorney. We need not add to the list."

"there is goodness, like wild honey, hived in strange nooks and corners of the world."

But I am not presuming to elaborate a literary estimate of Charles Dickens. The time is not now, if indeed it can ever be, necessary; for the popularity of his prodigious and glorious work has been, is, and will be universal. People tell you that Mrs. Gamp will not do, in French, as Madame Gamp, and that his fiction will not bear transplanting: but the transplanting steadily goes on nevertheless, and every day shows us how far the range of human sympathy stretches, when the name of Dickens wakes it. Papers in any tongue that has a printing-press have echoed the lamentations of our own over him whom Mr. Chorley has called "one of the greatest and most beneficent men of genius England has produced since the days of Shakspeare."

After writing the page on which Dickens as a painter of gentlefolk was handled, I saw the tearful, eloquent record which Mr. Chorley, who knew his subject so well, printed in "The Athenæum." I was delighted to find my view supported by so sound an authority and so intimate a friend. Mr. Chorley says: "It has been said that he could not draw gentlemen and ladies (as footmen understand the designation). This is false. The characters of Sir Leicester Dedlock in 'Bleak House,' that of Mrs. Steerforth in 'David Copperfield,' and fifty indications more, may be cited in disproof. That he found greater pleasure in selecting and marking out figures where the traits were less smoothed, or effaced by the varnish of polite society, than in picturing those of a world where the expression of individual characters becomes less marked, is true. To each man his own field. An essay could be recalled, written to prove that Scott was a miserable creature, because his imagination delighted in the legends and traditions of feudal times, with their Lords and their retainers. And yet Scott gave us the fisher-folk in 'The Antiquary,' and Jeannie Deans. But though, as 'a man of the people,' Dickens loved to draw the people in all their varieties and humor and incomplete ambitions; and though he was by nature and experience a shrewd redresser of abuses, — tracing them back to their primal causes, — he was in no respect the destroyer it was for a while the whim of fools of quality and the faded people who hang on their skirts, to consider him. One who redresses grievances is not, therefore, an overthrower of thrones. The life and work of Dickens expressed a living protest against Disorder, — no matter what the Order."

And in another place Mr. Chorley bears witness to that love of completeness, as well as of order, I have touched upon: "Those who were permitted to know Charles Dickens in the intimacy of his own home cannot, without such emotion as almost incapacitates the heart and hand, recall the charm of his bounteous and genial hospitality. Nothing can be conceived more perfect in tact, more freely equal, whatever the rank of his guests, than was his warm welcome. The frank grasp of his hand, the bright smile on his manly face, the cheery greeting, are things not to be forgotten while life and reason last, by those who were privileged to share them. Thus, his exquisite knowledge and punctuality gave him time, even when most busily at work for himself and others, to care for and to consider the pleasure of all whom he harbored beneath his roof."

Signs of the end, and that he knew the end was at hand, were revealed day by day, immediately after his death; and they are so many marks of the love of order that was a ruling passion in Dickens throughout his life. Death could not catch Charles Dickens unprepared, in any sense. That he had misgivings, warnings, we cannot doubt; and these led him to prepare for the change. Only a few days before his death, he transferred the property of "All the Year Round" to his eldest son, and formally resigned its editorship. On the very day on which he died he was to have met his stanch and affectionate friend and fellow-worker, W. H. Wills, to make a final settlement of accounts. He wrote to his "ever-affectionately" Charles Kent: "To-morrow is a very bad day for me to make a call, as, in addition to my usual office business, I have a mass of accounts to settle; but I hope to be with you at three o'clock. If I can't be, why then I shan't be." — (The letter was written an hour or two before he lay insensible, his light forever quenched, in the dining-room of Gad's Hill Place.) — "You must really get rid of those opal enjoyments. They are too overpowering.

'These violent delights have violent ends.'

I think it was a father of your church who made this wise remark to a young gentleman who got up early (or strayed out late) at Verona?"

The "opal enjoyments" refer to the early sky, and the whole is pleasant banter on the vehement devotion of his friend (the distinguished poet) to his work as editor of "The Sun."

I had met Dickens about the middle of May, at Charing Cross, and had remarked that he had aged very much in appearance. The thought-lines of his face had deepened, and the hair had whitened. Indeed, as he approached me, I thought for a moment I was mistaken, and that it could not be Dickens; for that was not the vigorous, rapid walk, with the stick lightly held in the alert hand, which had always belonged to him. It was he, however; but with a certain solemnity of expression in the face, and a deeper earnestness in the dark eyes. However, when he saw me and shook my hand, the delightful brightness and sunshine swept over the gloom and sadness, and he spoke buoyantly, in the old kind way, not in the least about himself, but about my doings, about Doré, about London as a subject (which I and my friend had just resolved to write upon together), — about all that could interest me, and which occurred to him at the moment. And he wrung my hand again as we parted; and the cast of serious thought settled again upon the handsome face, when he turned, wearily, I thought for him, toward the Abbey.

That within a month he would be resting there forever, buried under flowers cast by loving hands, and that the whole civilized world would be lamenting the loss of the great and good Englishman, I never for one moment dreamed. But I thought sadly of him, I remember, after we had parted. Nor was I alone in this. He was walking with a dear friend of his a few weeks ago, when this one said, speaking of "Edwin Drood," —

"Well, you, or we, are approaching the mystery" —

Dickens, who had been and was at the moment, all vivacity, extinguished his gayety, and fell into a long and silent reverie, from which he never broke during the remainder of the walk. Was he pondering another and a deeper mystery than any his brain could unravel, facile as its mastery was over the hearts and brains of his brethren?

We can never know.

It is certain, however, that the railway accident on the 9th of June, 1865, in which Dickens so nearly lost his life, made an ineradicable impression on him; and that, when he referred to it, he would get up and describe it with extraordinary energy. He closed his last completed work with a reference to it: "I remember with devout thankfulness that I can never be much nearer parting company with my readers forever than I was then, until there shall be written against my life the two words with which I have this day closed this book, — THE END."

Too soon, for the country that loved him and was so proud of him, were those two words written; and they were written on the 9th of June 1870!

SIR ARTHUR HELPS ON DICKENS.

When a great man departs from us, what we desire to know about him is not so much what he did, as what he was.

Volumes of criticism might be written upon the characters which Mr. Dickens has drawn for us, for they are persons with whom we have lived, and, as regards the reality of whose existence, even the most incredulous and unimaginative people refuse to entertain any historic doubts. But though these creatures of his brain tell us much about a man, they do not tell us all that we want to know, or even that which we crave to know most about him.

It is the same with great generals and great statesmen as

with great authors. Their skill in statesmanship or war has had its effect, and is duly chronicled; but, after a time, we are more anxious to know what the general or statesman was like; what manner of man he was; than to read about his military glories or his cruel triumphs.

There will be few households that will not desire some portrait of Mr. Dickens; but, alas, how little can any portrait tell of such a man! His was one of those faces which require to be seen with the light of life. What portrait can do justness to the frankness, kindness, and power of his eyes? They seemed to look through you, and yet only to take notice of what was best in you and most worthy of notice. And then his smile, which was most charming! And then his laughter — not poor, thin, and ambiguous laughter, that is ashamed of itself, that moves one feature only of the face, — but the largest and heartiest kind, irradiating his whole countenance, and compelling you to participate in his immense enjoyment of it.

He was both witty and humorous, a combination rarely met with; and both in making and appreciating fun — which we may perhaps define as a happy product of humor and geniality, upborne by animal spirits — I never met his equal.

It need hardly be said that his powers of observation were almost unrivaled; and therein, though it is a strange observation to make, he used to remind me of those modern magicians whose wondrous skill has been attained by their being taught from their infancy to see more things in less time than any other men. Indeed, I have said to myself, when I have been with him, he sees and observes nine facts for any two that I see and observe.

As is generally the case with imaginative men, I believe that he lived a great deal with the creatures of his imagination, and that they surrounded him at all times. Such men live in two worlds, the actual and imaginative, and he lived intensely in both.

I am confirmed in this opinion by a reply he once made to me. I jestingly remarked to him that I was very superior to him, as I had read my "Pickwick" and my "David Copperfield," whereas he only wrote them. To which he replied, that I did not know the pleasure he had received from what he had written; and added words which I do not recollect, but which impressed me at the time with the conviction that he lived a good deal with the people of his brain, and found them very amusing society.

He was of a commanding and organizing nature; a good man of business, frank, clear, decisive, imperative; a man to confide in and look up to as a leader, in the midst of any great peril.

This brings me to another part of his character which was very remarkable. He was one of the most precise and accurate men in the world; and he grudged no labor in his work. Those who have seen his MSS. well recollect what elaborate notes, and comments, and plans (some adopted, many rejected) went to form the basis of his works. To see those manuscripts would cure anybody of the idle and presumptuous notion that men of genius require no forethought or preparation for their greatest efforts, but that these are dashed by the aid of a mysterious something which is comprehended in the mysterious word "genius." It was one of Mr. Dickens's theories, and I believe a true one, that men differ in hardly anything so much as in their power of attention, and he certainly, whatever he did, attended to it with all his might.

Mr. Dickens was a very good listener, paying the greatest attention to the person who was speaking (that is, if he was saying anything worth attending to), and never interrupting, except perhaps by uttering, as if he approved of what was being said, the words, "surely, surely," which was a favorite expression of his.

He was very refined in his conversation, at least what I call "refined," for he was one of those persons in whose society one is comfortable from the certainty that they will never say anything which can shock other people, or hurt their feelings, be they ever so fastidious or sensitive.

I have hardly spoken enough of his punctilious accuracy.

As a curious instance of this, I may mention that where most men use figures, he would use words: for example, in his letters, writing the day of the month always in full. He had a horror of being misunderstood, and grudged no labor to be "understanded of the people."

His love of order and neatness was almost painful. Unpunctuality made him unhappy. I am afraid, though, some people would hardly have called him punctual, for he was so anxious to be in time that he was invariably before the time. The present writer has this same fault if fault it be, which was once the cause of a droll circumstance that occasioned some amusement to our friends. We were going to a railway station together. I planned to be a quarter of an hour before the time, and he, who had the final ordering of the carriage, and who had not a proper belief in my punctuality, added another quarter of an hour of his own; so that our conjoint punctualities brought us to the station a good half hour before the time. That time, however, that we spent together on that occasion, was well spent by me in listening to him as he discoursed upon the beautiful forms of clouds.

At home, and as a host, he was delightful. I think I have observed that he looked at all things and people dramatically. He assigned to all of us characters; and in his company we could not help playing our parts.

He had the largest toleration. I had not intended to say anything about his works; but I must do so now, as I see that they afford a singular instance of this toleration. Think of this precise, orderly, methodical man depicting so lovingly such a disorderly, fearless, reckless, unmethodical character as that of Dick Swiveller, and growing more enamored of it as he went on depicting! I rather think that in this he was superior to Walter Scott, for in almost all Scott's characters there appears one or the other, or both combined, of Scott's principal characteristics, namely, nobility of nature and shrewdness. Andrew Fairservice is comparatively ignoble; but he is always shrewd. And, in fact, I think it may be maintained that one or other of these characteristics is visible in every one of Scott's characters.

Mr. Dickens's own kindness of nature is visible in most of his characters. He could not well get rid of that, as a general rule, by any force of fiction Still there are a few characters, such as that of Jonas Chuzzlewit, in which he has succeeded in denuding the character of any trait belonging to himself.

We doubt whether there has ever been a writer of fiction who took such a real and loving interest in the actual world about him. Its many sorrows, its terrible injustice, its sufferings, its calamities, went to his heart. Care for the living people about him — for his "neighbor," if I may so express it — sometimes even diminished his power as an artist; a diminution of power for which, considering the cause, we ought to love his memory all the more.

I have sometimes regretted, perhaps unwisely, that he did not take a larger part — or shall I say a more prominent part? — in public affairs. Not for our own sakes, but for his. Like all men who see social evils very strongly and clearly, and also their way to remedies (to be, as they think, swiftly applied), he did not give enough weight, I think, to the inevitable difficulties which must exist in a free State to prevent the rapid and complete adoption of these remedies. "Circumlocution" is everywhere — in the Senate, at the bar, in the field, in ordinary business as well as in official life; and men of Mr. Dickens's temperament, full of ardor for the public good and somewhat despotic in their habits of thought, find it difficult to put up with the tiresome aberrations of a freedom which will not behave itself at once in a proper way, and set to work to provide immediate remedies for that which ought to be remedied. When you come close to any great man, you generally find that he has somewhat of a despotic nature in this respect.

There is a certain characteristic of the highest and best minds; and perhaps it tends, more than almost any other, to produce greatness of character. It is the habit of telling the truth to one's self. The world would be a much more happy place to live in, if its inhabitants would only adopt the habit of telling the truth occasionally to themselves. Now, this habit will not make what is called a consistent character; but it will make, what is far more important, a truthful character. Everybody knows that Mr. Dickens was simple in his ways of living, in his tastes, in his ambition. Probably, in the inevitable imitation of a great man, there will, for some time, be a run upon simplicity of this kind. But there are many persons whom such simplicity does not suit, or become. Now, if Mr. Dickens had professed a love for what is not simple, if he had been devoted to what is grand, and gorgeous, and resounding, we should have known it, because *he* would have known it, and would have been the first person to have told himself of it, and would, to use an official phrase, have "governed himself accordingly." That exquisite sincerity of nature which produces such a result was most manifest in him. He was very dramatic in his imagination, and brought all that he saw and felt into a magic circle of dramatic creation. But he never dramatized himself to himself. Of course, Shakespeare perceived the full meaning aad depth of this great quality which I have endeavored to portray as belonging preëminently to Mr. Dickens. We feel that Shakespeare must have done so, when he says —

> "To thine own self be true,
> And it must follow, as the night the day,
> Thou canst not then be false to any man."

Mr. Dickens loved the poor. He understood them. He was wise enough to see how very needful recreation is for them; and I shall never forget the delight with which he described to me, giving it with all those details that were with him pure touches of art, an entertainment that he had provided for the neighboring poor in his own fields; and how he rejoiced in their orderliness and good behavior.

He ardently desired, and confidently looked forward to, a time when there would be more intimate union between the different classes in the State — a union embracing alike the highest and the lowest.

It always seemed to me that he had a power of narration which was beyond anything even which his books drew forth. How he would narrate to you, sitting on a gate or on a fallen tree, some rustic story of the people he had known in his neighborhood! It was the very perfection of narrative. Not a word was thrown away, not an adjective misused; and I think all those who have had the good fortune to hear him recount one of these stories will agree with me, that it was a triumph, — an unconscious triumph of art.

He was one of those men who almost invariably speak well of others behind their backs; one of the truest friends, and very little given to reveal any injury that concerned himself alone. In that respect he often reminded me of Lord Palmerston, though he was not equal to that statesman in supreme serenity of temper. There was, however, a considerable resemblance between these two remarkable men in several points. They had both a certain hearty bluffness of manner. There was a sea-going way about them, as of a captain on his quarter-deck. They were both tremendous walkers, and took interest in every form of labor, rustic, urban, or commercial. Then, too, they made the most and best of everything that came before them: stood up sturdily for their own way of thinking, and valued greatly their own peculiar experiences.

Mr. Dickens delighted to praise; and there were few persons who appreciated more fully than he did the works of his contemporaries.

His criticisms on the literary works of others were given in that frank, friendly, helpful way which makes criticism most effective. I knew a brother author of his who received such criticisms from him very lately, and profited by it. Mr. Dickens, seeing that the said author was much perplexed in finding a good title for a work which he was preparing, took the greatest interest in aiding his friend; and during the last few weeks of his life, amidst all his own labors, would write sometimes more than one letter a day to make fresh suggestions about this troublesome, but most important thing, this title of a work. These are small traits to mention; but they are very significant.

Everybody has heard of Mr. Dickens's preëminence as an

actor, but perhaps it is not generally known what an admirable speaker he was. The last speech, I believe, that he ever made was at the Academy dinner; and I think it would be admitted by every one, including those who also made excellent speeches on that occasion, that Mr. Dickens's was the speech of the evening. He was herein greatly aided by nature, having that presence conveying the idea of courage and honesty, which gives much effect to public speaking, and also possessing a sweet, deep-toned, audible voice, that had exceeding pathos in it. Moreover, he had most expressive hands — not beautiful, according to the ordinary notions of beauty, but nervous and powerful hands. He did not indulge in gesticulation; but the slight movement of these expressive hands helped wonderfully in giving additional force and meaning to what he said, as all those who have been present at his readings will testify. Indeed, when he read, or when he spoke, the whole man read or spoke.

It was Mirabeau, who had the happy thought of combining the names of well-known persons in history or fiction, in order to describe some great contemporary; and who, most graphically, gave the compound name of Cromwell-Grandison to Lafayette. Now, if we were to try to make a similar compound name for Charles Dickens, whose names should we chose? That hackneyed quotation — may it remain hackneyed to the end of time! —

"A man 's a man for a' that,"

gives the key-note of Burns's character: and, as all that the quotation signifies, there is a profound resemblance between Robert Burns and Charles Dickens. Then, there is Le Sage. There is much likeness, without the faintest imitation on the part of the later author, between "Gil Blas" and some of Mr. Dickens's works. Then there is Cervantes. At first there may be thought to be very little similarity between these two great masters of tears and laughter. But in one material point there is the closest resemblance. They were such tender-hearted men that they could not be satisfied with making the characters they drew, remarkable for what is merely ludicrous or ridiculous. And, infallibly, as they went on writing, they wove in worth and goodness with all that is most comic. Unfortunately, the names that I have suggested will not combine prettily, but this endeavor to find such a compound name may serve to convey some of Mr. Dickens's principal characteristics, as shown in his writings.

I have done my best to describe Mr. Dickens such as he appeared to me, and certainly I have not uttered one word of flattery. But who can describe a great man — or indeed any man? We map down his separate qualities; but the subtle combination of them made by Nature eludes our description; and, after all, we fail, as I have failed now, in bringing before the reader the full sweetness, lovingness, and tenderness, wit and worth and sagacity, of such a man as Charles Dickens, whose death is not merely a private grief — unspeakably irreparable — to his family and his many friends, but a public sorrow which all nations unite in deploring.

Reminiscences of Dickens.

Even the trivialities connected with a great man are interesting, and the *mildest* anecdotes of a hero's private life are full of flavor to those who know him only on the pedestal of his public career. It is not my intention to enter into any of the vexed questions regarding his domestic unhappiness, but to merely give a true detail of my impressions of him during the period of the few months in which I was in daily intercourse with Charles Dickens and his family. These reminiscences of him, though disinterred from the memories of nearly twenty-nine years ago, may still afford amusement to others, as they do to me in recalling them. So vivid is my first impression of our great author that I can see him now "in my mind's eye" as clearly depicted as if days, and not years, had intervened since I was presented to him at the house of a relative of mine. I was first introduced to his wife in the sanctuary of the bedroom, where I was arranging my hair before the glass. I thought her a pretty little woman, with the heavy-lidded large blue eyes so much admired by men. The nose was a little *retroussé*, the forehead good, mouth small, round, and red-lipped, with a pleasant smiling expression, notwithstanding the sleepy look of the slow-moving eyes. The weakest part of the face was the chin, which melted too suddenly into the throat. She took kindly notice of me, and I went down with a fluttering heart to be introduced to "Boz."

The *first* ideas that flashed through me were, "What a fine characteristic face! What *marvelous* eyes! And what horrid taste in dress!"

He wore his hair long, in "admired disorder," and it suited the picturesque style of his head; but he had on a surtout with a very wide collar, very much thrown back, showing a vast expanse of waistcoat, drab trousers, and drab boots with patent leather toes, and the whole effect (apart from his fine head) gave evidence of a *loud* taste in costume, and was not proper for evening dress.

Of course, I listened eagerly during dinner to catch the pearls and other precious things that fell from his lips, and watched, in reverent admiration, every flash of his clear gray eyes, for I was enthusiastic, and in my teens. He did not speak much, and his utterance was low-toned and rapid, with a certain thickness, as if the tongue were too large for the mouth. I found afterwards that this was a family characteristic; and he had a habit of sucking his tongue when thinking, and at the same time running his fingers through his hair till it stood out in most leonine fashion. When writing, if his ideas got entangled, he would work away with his left hand, dragging viciously at certain locks until the subject became satisfactorily "evolved out of his inner consciousness."

Before uttering an amusing speech I noticed a most humorous scintillation gleaming in his eyes, accompanied by a comic elevation of one eyebrow; but he did not strike me as possessing the sarcastic, searching expression that I expected. I discovered afterwards, that without appearing to notice what was going on around, nothing escaped him; and at the times when his eyes had a far-off look, wide-opened and almost stony in their fixity, he was in reality making mental notes of his surroundings.

How many times have I been betrayed into committing myself in thoughtless discourse, duped by his abstracted air! How often have I indulged in sundry foolish acts, and given utterance to much silly *persiflage* and ill-digested reasoning among our circle, in the full confidence of his being in the seventh heaven of rapt reverie, to find him suddenly rising up, shaking his mane like a lion from his slumbers, and, with a face radiant with mischief and fun, recapitulating all my girlish "slip-slop," twisting and turning it into the most unexpectedly distorted shapes, and tacking on to it a running commentary of witty criticisms.

He never thought himself too great a genius to enter into our games, but he somehow always contrived to transfuse such a tone of cleverness and depth into them that they became "keen encounters of our wits," and we were all put on our mettle to play *up* to the subtle spirit with which the master-mind impregnated the most sterile matter. How proud I used to feel whenever I had said a better thing than usual to get an approving smile or word from our *maestro!* The first time he thus noticed me is marked with a white stone in my memory. A number of us were playing the simple game of "How, when, and where do you like it?" The word given was "scull," and the object is to puzzle the querist by the several meanings given to the word. Frederick Dickens was the questioner, and I gave, in reply to "How I liked it?" "With the accompaniment of a fine organ." 2d. "When?" "When youth is at the helm and pleasure at the prow." 3d. "Where?" "Where wanders the hoary Thames along his silver winding way."

Dickens rose and came over to me, saying laughingly, "Of course, little goose, your answers betrayed the word to the most simple comprehension, but they were good answers and apt quotations nevertheless, and I think it would add to the interest of the game if we all sharpened our wits, and tried to give a poetical tone to it by good quotations as answers." After this time we had to read up to keep pace with the fund of quaint sayings he introduced into this pastime.

Another game was nothing but a series of leading questions, which we called "Animal, mineral, or vegetable." The first time we played it, Mr. Dickens was obliged to give up, after exhausting himself in questioning. He had arrived at the facts that the article in question was vegetable, mentioned in mythological history, and belonging to a queen, and that the destiny was pathetic. After a display of his classic lore in attaining this much he gave it up, and was good-naturedly indignant at finding the subject over which he had wasted so much time and erudition was one of the tarts mentioned in the rhymes —

> "The Queen of Hearts she made some tarts,
> Upon a summer's day;
> The Knave of Hearts he stole the tarts,
> And took them *quite* away."

We promised in future to abstain from such unworthy subjects; but on another occasion he pulled my hair in pretended wrath, because I puzzled him with "The wax with which Ulysses stuffed the ears of his crew to prevent them hearing the songs of the sirens."

Sometimes we played vingt-et-un, and he was as playfully eager, as full of noisy glee, as the veriest schoolboy. One evening his friend Mr. M—— made his appearance in a preposterously long stock which he evidently thought was perfectly *chic.* Dickens eyed it for some time with a perplexed and thoughtful demeanor.

"Hollo, Charley!" said Mr. M., "what are you staring at my stock for?"

Dickens threw into his countenance an exaggerated expression of relief from a harassing doubt, and cried —

"Stock? Oh, I'm glad to know it is meant for a stock; it was so painful to think you might have intended it for a waistcoat."

A great deal of amusement was excited by Mrs. Charles

Dickens perpetrating the most absurd puns, which she did with a charming expression of innocence and deprecation of her husband's wrath; while he tore his hair and writhed as if convulsed with agony. He used to pretend to be utterly disgusted, although he could neither resist laughter at the puns nor at the pretty comic *moue* she made (with eyes turned up till little of the whites were visible) after launching forth one of these absurdities.

Every autumn it was Mr. Dickens's custom to take his family to Broadstairs, and shortly after I became acquainted with him the usual flitting took place. He begged my friends Mr. and Mrs. S—— to take a house there also, and offered to look for one for them. This they agreed to, and a few days after he wrote the following note to Mr. M——: —

"DEVONSHIRE TERRACE, *Thursday, 19th August.*

"MY DEAR M——, — The only intelligence we can get about the houses on the Terrace at Broadstairs is, that there are two to let or nearly to let, one (certainly empty at this moment) a little to the left of our old house, supposing you were looking out of the window upon the blue, the fresh, and ever free; the other a little more to the left still, and commonly called or known by the name of Barfield's Cottage.

"This Barfield's Cottage will be vacant (we are told) upon the twenty-first. But the devil of it is that at this season of the year they won't keep the houses even a week for you, and consequently Barfield's Cottage is meat for our masters. The other house must be either the one which S—— looked at, or one close to and exactly like it.

"If he wants to get up a picture of this last-named tenement in his mind, ask him if he don't remember going with Kate and me and the man from the library to look at a house, and stealing in at the kitchen-door past the water-butt and coal-cellar. That house was next the library on the side nearest London — the library being between it and ours. I am not sure that this particular house is the same, but it must be either the next door to it, or the next door but one. The terms I don't know, but they are *certainly not more* than five guineas per week, I should say.

. . . . . .

"In short, nothing can be done without going down in person, for the place is very full indeed, and the people wildly rapacious and rearing up on their hind legs for money. The day to go down upon is *a Monday*, for there is a chance of some family having gone out on that morning, it being a great departure day. If you put all this into your partner's pipe, tell him that I wish, for his sake and my own too, I could fill it with more substantial matter."

Shortly after this my friends took the house, and I accompanied them as a visitor, to my intense delight, for I hoped to be privileged to daily enjoyment of the presence of this man of genius. And now began a time which I look back to as almost the brightest in my life, as far as enjoyment went. Every day was spent by our family and the Dickens's together, either doing the usual seaside recreations, or at each other's houses. In the familiarity which such friendly association engenders we got up ridiculous relations to each other. He pretended to be engaged in a semi-sentimental, semi-jocular, and wholly nonsensical flirtation with me as well as with Milly T——, one of my friends, a charming woman of a certain age, and we on our side acted mutual jealousy towards each other; and Mrs. Charles Dickens entered into the fun with great gusto and good-humor. My friend Milly he called his "charmer," "the beloved of his soul," and I was his "fair enslaver" and his "queen." We generally addressed each other in the old English style of euphuism, and he would ask us to dance in such bombastic nonsense as —

"Wilt tread a measure with me, sweet lady? Fain would I thread the mazes of this saraband with thee."

"Aye, fair sir, that I will right gladly; in good sooth I 'll never say thee nay."

I need not say that the stately and courtly gravity with which we "trod our measure" was truly edifying, and the spectators were convulsed at the wonderful "Turvey-drop" deportment of Mr. Dickens, and the Malvolio-like conceit he contrived to call into his countenance.

"I think I could act a pompous ass to perfection!" he exclaimed, after one of these dances. "Let us get up some charades, and test our histrionic powers."

After some discussion we fixed on the word "Pompadour," and he took the part of Louis XIV. Milly was a Comtesse de Soubise, and I as Madame Pompadour was supposed to be jealous of her with good cause. The first syllable represented the stiff etiquette and tiresome observances of the court of the Grand Monarque, and was acted entirely in pantomimic action. The second syllable (converted into *adore*) was a love scene, in which Louis did a deal of inflated bombast in the ancient French style of love-making to the rival comtesse. The whole was completed by the wily mistress obtaining by stratagem a *lettre de cachet* from the king, and consigning the rival to the Bastile, while the triumph of Pompadour was complete. This was all acted on the spur of the moment, without any costume but such drapery and finery as could be obtained readily and twisted into use. Mr. Dickens was very grandiose, although he figured in a lady's broad-brimmed hat, pinned up on one side, and a rather draggled feather stuck nearly on end, which which would keep turning round the wrong way.

We rarely heard Dickens attempt punning, for which he professed profound contempt, but on one occasion he was accused of irreverence in making one. A game of whist was going on, and one of the ladies who was not playing (I think it was his mother, but am not positive) fell into a slight nap in the background. At the last trick of the game, one of the party banged down the King of Trumps in such loud glee as to awaken this lady, who started up with a scared look of bewilderment. Dickens turned round laughingly, and said, "Don't be alarmed, but you look awfully like one of the defunct on the day of judgment!" "Why? "Because you were awakened by the sound of the *last trump*."

One night a gentleman visitor insisted on singing "By the

sad sea waves," which he did vilely, and he wound up his performance by a most unexpected and misplaced embellishment, called in music "a turn." Dickens was perfectly excruciated during this trying ordeal, but managed to preserve a decorous attention and solemnity of visage till this sound met his ears, when he turned upon me a look of utter astonishment. "Whatever did he mean by that extraneous effort of melody?" I whispered. "Oh, that 's quite in rule — according to the proverb — 'When things are at *their worst* they always take *a turn*,'" answered he with imperturbable gravity. I unfortunately exploded into a giggle, and greatly offended the singer.

About this time there was a rumor flying about that Dickens had gone insane, at which he was much annoyed. We were all walking on the beach one day accompanied by a gentleman, a Mr. F——, a sculptor, who had only come down on a visit to Mr. Dickens the day before. This gentleman was, to use the mildest term, very eccentric, and did the most unaccountable things in moments of impulse. He was several yards in front of us, and was behaving in a very flighty manner. Some strangers passed him, and as they neared us stood to look after him. "Ah," said one, with a lugubrious look and a Lord-Burleigh shake of the head, "you see it 's quite true! Poor Boz! What a pity to see such a wreck!" Dickens scowled at them, and then called out, "Hollo, F——, I wish you'd moderate your insane gambolings! There are fools among the British public who might mistake you for me."

These representatives of the British public slunk away, followed by the glowing anger of Dickens's eyes, which seemed to shrivel them into nothingness. Dickens walked on with inflated nostrils and compressed lips for a few moments, and then burst out laughing. "I am afraid I was rather down on those poor beggars," said he, "but I don't like that ambling ass to be taken for me."

Next day he was sitting with us, when Mr. M—— ran in with consternation in every feature, calling out, "Charley! for God's sake come and put a stop to this! There 's F—— has walked out of the sea, without a rag on him, right among the people on the beach. You never saw such a scatter in your life!"

Dickens jammed his hat on his head with a muttered "D——d fool!" and tore down-stairs with M——; he came back in about half an hour, and Mr. S—— asked him jokingly how he had disposed of the naked truth?

"I never dreamt in childhood's hour," said Dickens, commencing poetically and then sinking suddenly into prose, "that I should ever turn myself into a preambulating screen; but the magnanimous way in which I have sacrificed my self-esteem in bobbing and sidling about with my coat-tails spread out to shield this rampant Achilles from the chaste eyes of the fair *sect* and the innocent babbies, deserves the thanks of the nation! I told him *that* was not the place for '*poses-plastiques;*' but he was so enthusiastically intent on doing the antique that I could only frantically, and I may say heroically, interpose my devoted body between him and the spectators." This was all nonsense, as he told us afterwards that he found F—— had returned into the water as fast as he got out, and he had no occasion to be a screen.

Why is it that by the sea one loses an immense deal of decency? Is it that the contemplation of the "vasty deep" enlarges and expands the ideas so much that they roam out into space, and become lost in its immensity? Nobody seemed profoundly shocked at this affair, which was treated quite jocularly.

A few days after this Milly accompanied me to bathe, though she did not enter the water herself. After I had got out and was dressing, we heard a splash from the next machine, succeeded by spluttering and panting, interspersed with expletives and one or two "D——ns" at the coldness of the water. We emerged from our car, and, on crossing the plank which united a long row of machines, the first object that met our eyes was Dickens disporting in the waves within six yards of us, but with only his head and shoulders visible.

"What! my charmers?" he called out, with chattering

teeth. "Behold a man who has taken a fatal plunge in the briny, and wishes himself well out of it. A crab is attempting to seize my great toe, so I 'm off. Ta ta till we meet again at Philippi," and off he went swimmingly.

Like all poetical natures he delighted in gazing at the sea. He would remain for hours as if entranced; with a rapt, immovable, sphinx-like calm on his face, and that far-off look in his magnificent eyes, totally forgetful of everything, and abstracted from us all. We always respected his isolation, and carefully kept aloof.

I drew a sketch of him during one of these meditative moods, and showed it to a Miss F—— who was staying with them. This young lady had testified a good deal of petty jealousy at the notice which Dickens took of me, and I have no doubt wished to make a little mischief between us, as she told him privately that evening that I had been *caricaturing* him. I was surprised to find him looking stony and stand-off when I met him again, and, greatly hurt, I went to Mrs. Charles Dickens (who was always kind and good-natured), and asked her what I had done to offend him.

"Well," she answered gently, "Charles is annoyed at your having drawn a caricature of him. Miss F—— told him she had seen a horrid caricature you had made of him."

I hastily took the sketch from between the leaves of the book I was carrying, and handed it to her without a word.

"Why, this is very like him," she cried in pleased surprise. "This is not a caricature, but a very nice sketch. Will you give it to me? I should like Charles to see it, and he will soon be convinced that Miss F—— was mistaken. Thank you, dear," and she kissed me kindly. "Don't let the tears come into your eyes about such nonsense; it will be all right, I promise you."

She went off with it; and the same evening I saw him again, with no cloud on his brow and as pleasant as ever.

"Mr. Dickens," I said, with tears in my voice (as the French say), "how could you think I would presume to caricature you? That odious girl put that into your head because she can't bear you to be amiable to any one but herself. Horrid, red-haired thing! I can't think why you like her!"

"My enslaver," he replied, with the odd twinkle of the eye, "I always loved gingerbread, even after childhood's hours had vanished into the dim past, and her tresses awaken fond memories of my lollipop days; but I don't like her ginger as I do your gold," and he pulled my long yellow curls playfully as he passed on.

The next night we were all assembled on the little pier or jetty which ran out into the sea, with an upright spar fixed at the extreme end. At the beginning was a railed-off space with seats, which he called the family pew. Mr. Dickens was in high spirits, and enjoyed the darkness of the evening, because he escaped the curious eyes of the Broadstairs population. We had a quadrille all to ourselves, the music being Frederick Dickens's whistling, and Mr. Dickens's accompaniment on his pocket-comb. We then strolled farther down to watch by the fading light the tide come rippling in. The night grew darker, starless, and moonless; the only light being a lingering, lurid gleam, which touched the crest of the waves with a phosphorescent glimmer. Dickens seemed suddenly to be possessed with the demon of mischief; he threw his arm around me and ran me down the inclined plane to the end of the jetty till we reached the tall post. He put his other arm round this, and exclaimed in theatrical tones that he intended to hold me there till "the sad sea waves" should submerge us.

"Think of the sensation we shall create! Think of the road to celebrity which you are about to tread! No, not exactly to *tread*, but to flounder into!"

Here I implored him to let me go, and struggled hard to release myself.

"Let your mind dwell on the column in the "Times" wherein will be vividly described the pathetic fate of the lovely E. P., drowned by Dickens in a fit of dementia! Don't struggle, poor little bird; you are powerless in the claws of such a kite as this child!"

By this time the gleam of light had faded out, and the water close to us looked uncomfortably black. The tide was coming up rapidly and surged over my feet. I gave a loud shriek and tried to bring him back to common sense by reminding him that "My dress, my best dress, my *only* silk dress, would be ruined." Even this climax did not soften him; he still went on with his serio-comic nonsense, shaking with laughter all the time, and panting with his struggles to hold me.

"Mrs. Dickens!" a frantic shriek this time, for now the waves rushed up to my knees; "help me! make Mr. Dickens let me go — the waves are up to my knees!"

"Charles!" cried Mrs. Dickens, echoing my wild scream, "how can you be so silly? You will both be carried off by the tide" (tragically, but immediately sinking from pathos to bathos), "and you'll spoil the poor girl's silk dress!"

"Dress!" cried Dickens, with withering scorn. "Talk not to me of *dress!* When the pall of night is enshrouding us in Cimmerian darkness, when we already stand on the brink of the great mystery, shall our thoughts be of fleshly vanities? Am I not immolating a brand-new pair of patent leathers still unpaid for? Perish such low-born thoughts! In this hour of abandonment to the voice of destiny shall we be held back by the puerilities of silken raiment? Shall leather or prunella (whatever that may be) stop the bolt of Fate?" with a sudden parenthetical sinking from bombast to familiar accents, and back again.

At this point I succeeded in wresting myself free, and scampered to my friends, almost crying with vexation, my *only* silk dress clinging clammily round me, and streaming with salt water. My chaperone, Mrs. S——, received me with unjust severity, evidently thinking I could have got away if I had chosen.

"Run home at once," she said majestically, "and take off your wet things. I am surprised at you!"

During this wrestling match between us, I cannot describe the ridiculous effect produced by his "mouthing" in the Ercles vein, with now and then a quick descent into comicality — the contrast between the stiltified language, and the gasping struggles caused by my efforts to get free, his suppressed chuckles at my dismay, my wild appeals, and the expostulations of his wife and the rest, who stood by, like the chorus in a Greek play, powerless to help.

I went off, escorted by Frederick Dickens, after hearing Mrs. Charles say—

"It was too bad of you, Charles; remember poor E. cannot afford to have her dress destroyed. Of course you 'll give her another?"

"Never!" was the reply. "I have sacrificed her finery and my boots to the infernal gods. Kismet! It is finished! Eureka! etc., etc.; and now I go to tug myself black in the face getting off my pedal covers."

Dickens was rather reckless in his fun sometimes, and my wardrobe suffered woefully in consequence. There was a sort of promontory stretching out into the sea, where, in rough weather, the waves used to rush up several feet, and come splashing down like a shower-bath. On two occasions, when I had thoughtlessly ventured near this spot, he seized me and ran me, *nolens volens*, right under the cataract, to the irretrievable ruin of two bonnets of frail fabric, and my slender purse was taxed to the utmost to replace them.

It was arranged that we should make an excursion to Pegwell Bay, and lunch at the small hotel on prawns and bottled porter; and on a lovely morning two open carriages stood at our door ready to receive us. Mrs. Dickens and two of her lady visitors had walked to our house, and we were only waiting for Mr. Dickens and some gentlemen friends. Presently he came in in high glee, flourishing a yard of ballads, which he had just bought from a beggar in the street.

"Look here! fair dames and damosels," he cried exultingly. "All for one penny! invested by yours truly for the delectation of the company. One song alone is worth a Jew's eye—quite new and original—the subject being the interesting announcement about our Gracious Queen. It is in the vulgar tongue, but you are all so familar with 'Nix my Dolly,' and other songs of that kind, that I dare say you will not be shocked."

He commenced to give us a specimen, but after hearing one verse there arose a cry of universal execration. The song was founded on the official notice that a prince or princess might shortly be expected, and was sung to the tune of "The King of the Cannibal Islands." He pretended to be vexed at us "shutting him up," said there "was nothing wrong in it; he had written a great deal worse himself," and when we were going to enter the carriages he said—

"Now, look here, I give due notice to all and sundry, that I mean to sing that song and a good many of the others during the ride, so those ladies who think them vulgar can go in the other carriage. I am not going to invest my hard-earned penny for nothing."

I was quite certain that Charles Dickens was the last man in the world to shock the modesty of any female, and too much of a gentleman to do anything that was annoying to us, but I thought it was as well to go in the other carriage, and so he had no ladies with him but his wife and Mrs. S——. I was not sorry on the whole to be where I was, as I heard for the next half hour small portions of those songs wafted on the breeze to us whenever our vehicle approached near them, and the bursts of laughter from ladies and gentlemen, and the mischievous twinkle in Dickens's eye, proved that he was in such a madcap mood that it was as well there were none but married people with him, the subject being what it was, of a "Gampish" nature.

He was not always full of spirits or even-tempered: indeed, I was somewhat puzzled by the variability of his moods. After indulging in the greatest fun and familiarity over-night, we would sometimes meet him walking alone, when he would look at us with lack-lustre eye, and pass on with a hurried "How d'ye do?"

One day he strolled by our window where Milly and I were standing on the balcony. He turned back, "struck" an attitude (in actor's phrase); with one hand on his heart, and the other upraised, he began mouthing—

"'’T is my lady, ’t is my love. Oh would I were a glove upon that hand, that I might kiss that cheek.'"

"Which of us do you intend to be the Juliet to your Romeo?" asked Milly.

"Whichever you choose, my little dears," he said nonchalantly, and, touching his hat, sauntered on.

The next morning he came by again, and found us as before, but he only returned a sulky "How do?" and walked by. Of course we knew he was in the midst of some brain-spinning, and wanted to be alone. I got to understand his face so well that when I saw the preoccupied look I used to pretend not to see him at all, so as to spare him even the trouble of recognizing me, and I found he was all the better pleased.

One night we all went to the Tivoli Gardens, a place in the style of Vauxhall on a small scale. There was a covered portion set apart for dancing, and we saw some very respectable people footing it with great enjoyment. We had a consultation whether it would be very *infra dig.* if the young ones of our party had a private quadrille among themselves, and, as no one knew us, we decided to enjoy ourselves too. Mr. Dickens, meanwhile, walked about, not venturing into the glare of the lights, as his face was too well known for him to preserve his incognito. There was a girl dancing near us, who had long plaited tails of hair down her back, sandaled shoes, and frilled drawers, to whom, by universal acclamation, we affixed the name of Morleena Kenwigs. Dickens was amused at the resemblance, and was making a laughing remark on her, when a man came close to him and stared knowingly and rather offensively in his face. Dickens moved away, but this bore followed him, glowering with all his eyes, and with ears on full cock to catch every stray word. At last Dickens lost patience, and turning suddenly, confronted him with —

"Pray, sir, are you a native of this place?"

"N — no, sir," stammered the individual.

"Oh, I beg your pardon!" returned Dickens, with elaborate politeness. "I fancied I could detect *broad-stares* on your very face."

I need not say that the unhappy wight vanished into the shades of evening.

One morning at his own house Dickens was talking on art to a gentleman present, and they discussed the statue of Venus, which Byron raves about in his "Pilgrimage." Dickens objected to the expressions used by Byron, "Dazzled and drunk with beauty," "The heart *reels* with its fullness," etc., as being an unpoetical metaphor, and said it must have been written tipsily, under the influence of that beverage (gin-and-water) which sometimes inspired this great poet. I defended the verse, and Dickens rose up, pushed his hands through his flowing locks so as to give them their most weird look, turned down his shirt-collar, slapped his brow, and exclaimed, in the Bombastes Furioso style —

"Stand back! I am suddenly seized with the divine afflatus. Don't disturb me till I have given birth to my grand conceptions."

He took out his pencil, and finding there was no paper in the room, he stalked with grotesquely melo-dramatic air to the window, and wrote on the white shutter. Frederick Dickens copied the writing afterwards for me, and it was as follows: —

LINES, AFTER BYRON, TO E. P——.

"O, maiden, of the amber-dropping hair,
May I, Byronically, thy praises utter?
Drunk with *thy* beauty, tell me, may I dare
To sing thy pæans *borne upon a shutter?*"

We were strolling one day on the sands, and stood to watch the gambols of his children at play with the little Macreadys. They had built a mimic fort, and young Macready was defending it against a storming party headed by Charley Dickens. The besieged Castellan threw himself into an attitude of defiance, with head erect, and his sand-spade held as a trenchant blade. Mr. Dickens burst into one of his hearty laughs, and pointing to the boy, exclaimed — "'Lay on, Macduff! and dashed be he who first cries, Hold, enough!' Did you ever see such a miniature of his pater in Macbeth? 'It's a wise child that knows his own father,' but there's no mistake about the parentage here."

"I suppose he naturally imitates his father after seeing him act."

"No, that can't be, because Macready carefully prevents his children knowing that he is an actor. I don't think they have ever entered a theatre."

"Is he ashamed of his profession?"

"No. But he wisely thinks that they may misunderstand his position. It is because he takes such an elevated view of his art that he fears it being misrepresented to them. He thinks, and rightly too, that there is no small merit in being able to interpret properly the conceptions of a great mind; and he who gives breathing and moving life, who embodies with reality, and stamps with individuality, the poet's aërial creations, must be himself endowed with some of this majestic light by reflection. He fears that servants, or such-like, may speak of acting to his children in such a way as to impress on their small minds a low idea of a profession which he believes to be so full of dignity and moving power when nobly 'acted' up to. I hope the time is past when actors were ranked as vagabonds and authors as Grub-street hacks, cringing in servile submission to truculent publishers, or dangling in search of a dinner in the ante-room of some addle-headed nobleman. If books enlighten the understanding, so likewise the stage has its purpose, next to the pulpit, to elevate and refine by placing more palpably and forcibly before us the grandeur of human passions."

"I know one instance among many in which the stage produced an effect which no homily or sermon ever had been capable of doing to the individual I speak of. He accompanied me to see Charles Kean in the drama of 'Faust,' in which he acted Mephistopheles so artistically. There was one scene where a riotous mob of graceless German students (under the influence of lager-beer, I presume) are heard in the distance roaring their songs of wassail. Mephisto. listened with a sardonic grin of approval on his demoniac phiz, and said gloatingly words something like these: 'Go on, my fine fellows, sing and shout, and drink, in your delightful exuberance of animal spirits. It refreshes me to hear you. Go on, *for you are all fast coming my way!'* My friend, who was a young 'sawbones,' told me a thrill of horror ran through him, and he was struck by a conviction of the consequences of sinful indulgence such as he had never felt before. He was quite sober and thoughtful for some little time after."

Dickens listened with his usual attention and searching fixity of eye, and then said, smilingly —

"I 'm afraid *that* youth was open to conviction only through his skin. Nothing but fire and brimstone (minus the treacle) would keep *him* in order. Where the spiritual nature is low one is obliged to threaten the rod-in-pickle."

My father was a Scottish author of considerable reputation, and had died suddenly at the age of forty-two of apoplexy, when I was only twelve years old. I lent Mrs. Dickens some volumes of his writings about this time, and she expressed to me how delighted she was in their perusal. In my presence she asked Mr. Dickens to read them. He looked his distaste at the idea, and when she pressed him "just to read one tale, such a beautifully written one, and very short," he turned and walked off abruptly, muttering — "I hate Scotch stories, and everything else Scotch." I thought this was very unkind to his wife as well as to me, as she was Scotch too. She colored up, but laughed it off.

There were times when we gave Mr. Dickens "a wide berth," and Milly and I have often run round corners to get out of his way, when we thought he was in one of these moods, which we could tell by one glance at his face. His eyes were always like "danger lamps," and warned people to clear the line for fear of collision. We felt we had to do with a genius, and in the throes and agonies of bringing forth his conceptions, we did not expect him to submit to be interrupted by triflers like ourselves: at these times I confess I was horribly afraid of him. I told him so, to his great amusement.

"Why, there 's nothing formidable about *me!*"

"Is n't there?" I answered. "You look like a forest lion

with a shaggy mane at these seasons ; and I always think of the words —

> ' He roared so loud, and looked so wondrous grim,
> His very shadow dared not follow him.' "

He laughed aloud, and said, " What! do you play shadow to my lion ? Nay, then, as Bottom the weaver says, ' I must aggravate my voice, I will roar you as gently as any suckling dove.' " After this I did not feel quite so frightened of him, though I got out of his way all the same.

On another day Milly and I were on the shore in time to see him clambering down some rocks with his brother Fred. They came towards us laughing, and Dickens, pointing to the knees of his trousers said, " Look at this fresh sacrifice I have laid on your altar ! These good pants nearly destroyed by climbing up that precipitous cliff to carve your name in gigantic letters upon a spot where the tide never reaches, so that you may go down to posterity with your name built upon a rock ! "

" Did you likewise carve ' Charles Dickens *fecit ?* ' " asked I.

" No, I did not."

" Then you might as well have scratched my name on the shifting sands, for all the fame I shall ever attain."

They both walked on laughingly, but I never arrived at the truth whether it was Mr. Dickens or his brother Fred who did the carving. Certainly, there was my name in letters a foot long on the very face of the rock. Fred and I went to look at it a year afterwards, and found it still existing.

At last came the sad day when we must leave them, to return to our " local habitations " in smoky London, and I parted with Mr. and Mrs. Dickens with tears of regret. " Never mind, dear," she said in her sweet caressing way, " we shall all meet again in London."

Alas ! we never met again in the same kindly way. Everything was changed.

When the Dickenses came home we went to luncheon there, and I remarked how preoccupied he looked, how changed in manner. Mrs. S——, who knew him better than I did, was quite prepared to find him different in London from what he was in Broadstairs, but I was very disappointed. I seldom saw him after this, as he was always full of engagements, but Mrs. Dickens I often met at my friend's house. I went one evening intending to spend it with them, and found Mrs. S—— and Milly dressing to go to a small charade party at the Dickenses. Milly immediately proposed to take me with them, but Mrs. S—— said, looking puzzled and uncertain, that she feared Mr. Dickens might think it a liberty! "If it was anybody else but Charles Dickens I should not hesitate an instant, but he is so odd! One never knows how he might take such a thing. Although I am his daughter's godmother, and we are such friends, I cannot do it."

Mrs. S—— mentioned to Mrs. Dickens how greatly it would be to my advantage (being a young artist struggling into notice, and helping to support my mother and sister) if Mr. Dickens would sit to me for his likeness. With that ready good-heartedness which I always found in her, she immediately offered to sit first herself as an inducement to him, which she kindly did. She wished it kept secret from Mr. Dickens, as she proposed to give it to him as a birthday gift, I believe. The portrait was nearly completed, and all who saw it thought it an excellent likeness; it was arranged that I should bring it myself in case he might suggest any alteration. Accordingly I went to Devonshire Terrace in a cab with my picture, but found Mr. and Mrs. Dickens were out, but were momentarily expected. I was shown into the dining-room, and requested by the domestic to wait, as Mrs. Dickens expected me. The cloth was laid, either for dinner or luncheon. I waited for an hour, and at last I heard the carriage draw up to the door. Mrs. Dickens came to me with her usual kiss, and "so sorry for keeping you waiting." It was raining fast, and her thin boots were wet with only walking from the carriage, so she took them off there and then, and fancying I was in a state of suspense, she would not wait for her slippers, but went straight into the library to Mr. Dickens with the portrait in her hand. Notwithstanding the closed door, and that

I sat far from it at the fire, I could hear the tones of their voices. Mrs. Dickens's expostulatory, Mr. Dickens's imperatively; at last she returned, looking flurried, but trying to put the best face on the matter. She made apologies for him, "That he was not very well, and tired. She hoped I would excuse him not being able to see me."

I faltered out, "Does he not like the portrait?"

"He has not had time to look at it properly. Of course he will think it like. You must n't mind, dear, but to tell the truth he is a little grumpy just now, but it will be all right presently. You know a man is always cross when he has been kept without his dinner. Won't you stay?" she added, hesitatingly, and in such a tone that I knew she was *afraid* I might.

I don't know what I answered. I was thoroughly cut up, and wanted to have a "good cry." I broke from her even while she was kissing me, and telling me she would write and let me know how he liked it; she slid into my hand a folded piece of green paper, which I knew was a check, and which I purposely dropped as I passed into the hall. She came after me looking very vexed, and put it in my reticule, saying, "For my sake!" Glad to get out of the house I did not stay to discuss the point, but almost ran into the rain. Round the corner I found an empty cab, and in it I cried to my heart's content all the way home. I never crossed his threshold again.

Whether it was really that Mr. Dickens was hungry and cross, or whether he was annoyed with Mrs. Dickens for having her portrait done without his knowledge; or whether it was because he did not like the picture, I never could discover. "He was so odd," was the only explanation I ever received from the several "mutual" friends to whom I mentioned the affair. Old Mrs. Dickens liked the picture so much that she begged to have it (I was told), and so it ended. It was some salve to my *amour propre* that I had, in the same spring, a portrait of the Speaker Shaw Lefevre's daughter in the Academy, hung "on the line," and favorably noticed by several of the papers; and that it was considered a "speaking" likeness.

It is not just or satisfactory to depict only one side of any man's character, and Dickens was no faultless monster. A portrait is incomplete if painted (as Queen Elizabeth, of glorious and despotic memory, insisted on being done) without its proper proportion of shadows. To describe Dickens as always amiable, always just, and always in the right, would be simply false and untrue to nature. It is right to soften as much as possible all the hard edges (as artists do their work with a brush called a "sweetener"), and to throw a shade over the shortcomings of a *truly great man*, touching his weaknesses with a tender and delicate hand, but speaking of his acts as impartially as possible; more especially when he is gone from us into that unknown region where we may be sure all is truth or nothing. After great inward discussion, I feel that I ought to shake off all moral cowardice, and speak of Mr. Dickens as he was to *me*, "nothing extenuate, nor aught set down in malice;" it is only justice to the living to be truthful to the dead. I must entreat my readers to absolve me of any wish to obtrude my small identity in the slightest degree. It is no egotism which makes the pronoun "I" so often repeated in these pages, but the impossibility to detail Dickens's words or acts without also telling what led to them.

The next occasion on which I met Mr. Dickens was at a large ball, of nearly 200 persons, given by a gentleman connected with me by marriage. He came accompanied by Mrs. Dickens, his two brothers, Frederick and Alfred, and Mr. Maclise, the great painter, since dead. Mr. Dickens looked very handsome, and seemed to enjoy himself immensely; but he never danced once with me, and was only coldly polite, which did not increase my enjoyment. He proposed the health of cur host at supper, in a short speech, but with such rapid utterance and in so low a tone that I scarcely caught the whole sense of his words.

The only time I ever felt cross with Mrs. Dickens was on

this evening, I was engaged to dance with Mr. Maclise, and he was coming forward to claim me when she interposed and asked him to dance with her. He told her he was engaged to me, but she would take no refusal, and they whirled off together. Frederick said, "What a shame!" and asked me to try and put up with him instead. Both he and his brother Alfred were very attentive to me, and I danced with each repeatedly. Fred told me he thought Charles was acting "very capriciously," and seemed sorry for me, as I took it to heart; but he was "*odd sometimes.*" The evening concluded with "Sir Roger de Coverley," danced in two long *double* rows. It was a sight to see Maclise at one end and Dickens at the other rushing forward alternately, both with long locks flying free. At one part I had to meet and perform the figure with Mr. Dickens, and he unbent a little, giving me something of the old smile, and whirling me round with something of the old familiar style; but, alas! it was only like a ghost of the happy past, and I could have burst out crying. I had been so proud of the notice of so great a man, I had so sunned myself in his smiles, that it was like an untimely frost, come to "nip my buds from blowing."

Next year I was married, after a long engagement, and shortly afterwards went to Broadstairs with my husband. I had not expected to see the Dickenses there, as it was late in the season, and I was sure they would have returned. Fred, who was a great friend of my husband, soon found us out, and we were constantly together; but I kept aloof from his brother, and only spoke to him on one occasion during our stay, which was when we went, accompanied by Fred, to the Tivoli Gardens, and Mr. Dickens and his party were there. If I remember rightly, Miss Hogarth danced with my husband and I with Fred, in a few quadrilles made up with their set. Mrs. Dickens was as kind as ever, and "Boz" danced with her and her sister alternately, with as much enjoyment of the fun as any of us.

After this I never saw him but twice again; once at a concert where the lady who afterwards became Fred's wife performed on the piano. He was with his wife and Maclise, and favored me with his usual "How d'ye do?" *en passant.* The last time I ever saw him was a few years ago, when he gave a reading of the "Christmas Carol," and he was indeed marvelously changed. Lined in face, and with grizzled beard, but with even more power than ever in expression, the nostril still, like that of the war-horse, dilated and sensitive. I was astonished at the wonderful difference in his voice and utterance, which was now sonorous and emphatic. His long career of reading and acting had completely cured the thickness which I before remarked, and his declamation was no longer hurried.

A great deal has been said about his hearty willingness to help young struggling people, and his kindly feeling for governesses. All I can say is he never helped me, though he had it in his power to do so to a great extent. There was an excellent lady, a friend of Mrs. S——, whom he often met at her house, who supported her step-mother by her salary as a governess, and whom he knew to be a marvel of self-denial, but he never took any notice of her more than politeness required, though she was enthusiastically enraptured with him, and a little extra kindness would have been the sweetest drop in the tasteless cup of her daily avocations. In 1846, when I had been married about four years, a young lady, only seventeen years of age, of very uncommon ability as an artist, implored me to get Mr. Dickens to look at some very clever outline illustrations she had made of his "Chimes" and the "Cricket on the Hearth," hoping to excite his interest in her. I yielded to her solicitations, but knowing how "odd" Mr. Dickens was, I wrote a letter to Mrs. Dickens requesting her to use her influence with him, and I gave such an account of this young lady's praiseworthy endeavors to earn a livelihood as would, I think, have interested most people. I received this reply from Mrs. Dickens: —

"MY DEAR MRS. C., — Many thanks for your obliging note, and interesting account of your young friend.

"Mr. Dickens is so very much occupied just now that he has not as yet been able to look over the drawings, but I have no doubt he will do so very shortly. I trust that yourself and baby are quite well, and that you have good accounts from your husband.

"I saw our mutual friends, Mrs. S—— and Miss J——, yesterday.

"Excuse this hasty scrawl, and believe me,

"My dear Mrs. C——,

"Very sincerely yours,

"CATHERINE DICKENS.

"1 DEVONSHIRE TERRACE, 30*th April*, 1846."

My poor little artist was dreadfully disappointed by merely receiving a polite note, thanking her for the sight of her very talented outlines, and that was all. I introduced her shortly after this to my good friend J. Sidney Cooper, R. A., the eminent cattle-painter, and he invited her to his house to meet people of note and influence, and treated her with such true kindness that she never ceased to thank me. To prove that he must have infinitely benefited her, I have a letter from her sister, written long after, in which she says they had had no chance of getting on till I "used my fairy wand and conjured up that bright circle at Mr. Cooper's for her; so that, you see, treat the matter as you will, it comes back to *you* at last; Minnie owes her highest encouragement, and both of us some of our best friends, to your active kindness."

The other members of Mr. Dickens's family whom I knew continued always on the same terms, and a few years ago Fred came, accompanied by his father-in-law, and stayed some days with us. After that he came with Mrs. S——, and remained with us a week, and he would never admit that his brother felt unkindly towards me, though he could not explain his strange conduct.

The last I ever had to do with Mr. Dickens was when I wrote to ask the favor of a few lines from him in support of an appeal I was about to make to a statesman high in office on behalf of the aged and necessitous widow of an author of repute formerly; but he declined in a few curt sentences, on the grounds that I had been "absurdly misinformed" as to his having any influence in such quarter.

OBITUARY POEMS.

Charles Dickens.

Born February 7, 1812; Died June 9, 1870.

While his life's lamp seemed clearest, most intense,
A light of wit and love to great and small,
By the dark angel he is summoned hence,
To solve the mightiest mystery of all.

Hearing that he has passed beyond the veil,
Before the Judge who metes to men their dues,
Men's cheeks, through English-speaking lands, turn pale,
Far as the speaking wires can bear the news —

Blanched at this sudden snapping of a life
That seemed of all our lives to hold a share:
So were our memories with his fancies rife,
So much of *his* thought *our* thoughts seemed to share.

Charles Dickens dead! It is as if a light
In every English home were quenched to-day;
As if a face all knew had passed from sight,
A hand all loved to press had turned to clay.

Question who will his power, its range, its height,
His wisdom, insight, — this at least we know,
All in his love's warmth and his humor's light
Rejoiced and reveled, — old, young, high or low, —

Learnéd, unlearnéd, from the boy at school
To the judge on the bench, none read but owned
The large heart o'er which the large brain held rule,
The fancy by whose side clear sense sat throned,

The observation that made all its own,
  The shaping faculty that breathed life's breath
In types, all felt they knew and still had known,
  Like-life, except that they are safe from death.

Since Shakespeare's, where the pen that so hath lent
  Substance to airy nothings of the brain,
His fancies seem with men's experience blent,
  Till to take each for other we are fain?

And who that ever wielded such a power
  Used it so purely, to such Christian end,
Used it to quicken the millennial hour,
  When rich to poor shall be as man to friend?

Who can say how much of that love's pure leaven
  That leavens now the lump of this our world,
With influence as of a present Heaven,
  Like light athwart chaotic darkness hurled,

May be traced up to springs by him unsealed,
  To clods by him stirred round affection's roots,
To hearts erst hard, but by his fires annealed
  To softness whereof Love's works are the fruit?

Mourn, England, for another great one gone
  To join the great ones who have gone before —
And put a universal mourning on,
  Where'er sea breaks on English-speaking shore.

His works survive him, and his works' work too —
  Of love and kindness and good-will to men,
Hate of the wrong, and reverence of the true,
  And war on all that shuns truth's eagle-ken.

Earth's two chief nations mourners at his tomb:
  Their memories for his monument: their love

For his reward. Such is his glorious doom
  Whom mortal praise or blame no more shall move!

DICKENS AT GAD'S HILL.

One summer day — ah, saddest eighth of June!
  My brooding heart, my very soul descries
Around a châlet, in a grove at noon,
  Dream-children from the flowering earth arise.

So hushed (like death!) the calm, sequestered scene,
  One notes with eye, not ear, the fitful breeze,
Through sunlight branches, flickering gold and green,
  About yon Swiss roof nestling 'mid the trees.

Like fitful wanderers seen returning home,
  Like magnets trembling truthful to the north,
To this one spot of all the world they roam,
  Again they throng round him who called them forth.

No shadowy semblance theirs of human life,
  Ideal shapes of visionary birth:
They breathe, they move with vital force more rife
  Than fleeting, fleshly forms that people earth.

The Angel-Child, the Guardian Guide of age,
  With soul as pure as all the tears we shed
When swimming eyes first read on blotted page,
"Dear, gentle, patient, noble Nell was dead."

The fading boy, the blossom nipped in bud,
  Whose infant grace had oft the quaintest air,
Who questioned voices in the ocean flood,
  Whose looks of love were sad as tones of prayer,

Till passed, like sigh in sleep, his parting breath,
  And o'er the couch where lay the gentle Paul,
Naught stirred above the "old, old fashion, Death,"
  Naught save "the golden ripple on the wall."

The sweet Child-wife, the darling of a heart
  Whose tenderest chords that solemn eve were riven,
When Dora's doom was told with speechless art—
" That mute appeal, that finger raised to heaven ! "

The little cripple with the active crutch,
  At thought of whom the mother's eyes grew dim,
Sighing, as fell the black work from her touch,
  It was " the color — Ah, poor Tiny Tim ! "

The stripling frail, who, dying with a kiss,
  A child at heart, a man but to the sight !
Poor Rick ! began the world again, — not this,
  Ah no, " not this, — the world that sets this right."

And orphan Johnny, his lost home afar,
  An infant waif on awful billows hurled,
No mother clinging to it, floats, frail spar,
" O'er that dark sea that rolls round all the world."

Around the sunlight châlet, where, within,
  Dreams the great Dreamer 'neath the shadowing trees,
From flowering earth, fresh dews of love to win,
  Dream-children rise in lovely forms like these.

No spectral shades for glimpses of the moon,
  But radiant shapes in calm of summer-day,
They come unbidden to his haunts at noon,
  Down the bright path they went — to point the way.

These haunts the aptest symbols of a life
  That loved the pleasaunce winter ne'er bereaves
Of verdure, in those grand old cedars rife
  Crowned with a lasting glory of Green Leaves.

And yonder, basking in the golden air,
  Luring his thoughts where 'er his thoughts may roam,

Cinctured by blossoms in a garden fair,
  The dear familiar roof-beams of his home.

Between that home and this secluded haunt
  Flows the broad highway, symbol here again
That alien to his hearth no tread of want
  Or toil was held, or ever passed in vain.

O Friend! O Brother! dearer to my heart
  Than even thy loving friendship could discern,
Thy thoughts, thy dreams were of our lives a part,
  Thy genius love, not merely fame, could earn.

Affection, admiration, honor, praise,
  Innocent laughter and ennobling tears,
Are thine by right, not through mere length of days,
  A loftier life, in never-ending years.

Dickens in Camp.

Above the pines the moon was slowly drifting,
    The river sang below;
The dim Sierras, far beyond, uplifting
    Their minarets of snow.

The roaring camp-fire, with rude humor, painted
    The ruddy tints of health
On haggard face and form that drooped and fainted
    In the fierce race for wealth;

Till one arose, and from his pack's scant treasure
    A hoarded volume drew,
And cards were dropped from hands of listless leisure
    To hear the tale anew.

And then, while round them shadows gathered faster,
    And as the firelight fell,
He read aloud the book wherein the Master
    Had writ of "Little Nell."

Perhaps 't was boyish fancy, — for the reader
Was youngest of them all, —
But, as he read, from clustering pine and cedar
A silence seemed to fall :

The pine-trees, gathering closer in the shadows,
Listened in every spray,
While the whole camp, with "Nell" on English meadows,
Wandered and lost their way.

And so in mountain solitudes ; — o'ertaken
As by some spell divine —
Their cares dropped from them like the needles shaken
From out the sturdy pine.

Lost is that camp, and wasted all its fire :
And he who wrought the spell ? —
Ah, towering pine and stately Kentish spire,
Ye have one tale to tell !

Lost is that camp ! But let its fragrant story
Blend with the heart that thrills
With hop-vines' incense all the pensive glory
That fills the Kentish hills.

And on that grave where English oak and holly
And laurel wreaths entwine,
Deem it not all a too presumptous folly, —
This spray of Western pine !

At Gad's Hill.

Gadshill is famous. What of old
To the world's poet made it dear,
Whether what country gossips told,
Or stolen hours of cheer
Spent there with men of kindred mind ;
Less, yet the largest of mankind,

We know not, and we need not care :
  Enough that Shakespeare loved the place :
And settled in possession there
  The merriest of his race, —
Falstaff, whose thirsty spirit still
Haunts all the taverns at Gad's Hill !

Could Shakespeare, with prophetic eyes,
  Who were to follow him have seen,
And be, if not so great and wise,
  As what man since hath been ?
Yet wise and great in smaller ways
The lords of life of coming days,

He would have chosen out of all
  Dickens, as knowing, loving men,
And let on him the mantle fall
  That was to vanish then !
Long lost, late found, now lost once more —
Ah, who that mantle shall restore ?

Sacred to all but Shakespeare's shade,
  And to his ghosts of crownless kings
Abandoned, wretched queens betrayed,
  And high, heroic things,
Is Stratford : let no mortal dare
Disturb its hushed and reverent air !

But Gad's Hill, whither Falstaff went
  From Eastcheap (glad to hasten back),
Though plundered, still on plunder bent,
  Puffed out with lies and sack, —
What spot of English earth so fit
For one with more than Falstaff's wit ?

Nay, Shakespeare's self was not his peer
  In that humane and happy art
To wake at once the smile and tear,
  And captive hold the heart!
Make room, then Shakespeare, this is he
Hath taken the throne of mirth from thee.

The world of kings and queens is thine,
  Thou hast the soldier's, scholar's ear:
England and Rome, Greece, "Troy divine,"—
  Hamlet, Othello, Lear:
Small elves that dance on yellow sands,
And all the spells of fairy lands!

This common, work-day world of ours;
  Our little lives of joy and care;
Green lanes, where children gather flowers;
  And London's murky air;
Thieves, paupers, women of the town,
And the black Thames in which they drown;—

These were the things that Dickens knew:
  Before his sight like dreams they passed.
If saddened, he was gladdened, too,
  For sorrow should not last:
Happy must be his heart and mind
Whose task it is to help his kind!

Healthy his nature was, above
  All shallow griefs and sympathies:
What others hated he could love,
  And what they loved despise.
His mirth was harder to be borne
Than Thackeray's sadness, Byron's scorn.

He taught the virtues, first and last;
  He taught us manhood more and more;
The simple courage that stands fast,
  The patience of the poor:
Love for all creatures, great and small,
And trust in Something over all!

This gave him more than royal sway,
  The benefactor of his race,
He would have wiped with smiles away
  The tears from every face!
They drop to-day from many an eye:
He draws them, but he cannot dry.

The hand is still that held his pen,
  His eyes are shut, but not in sleep;
Weeping around his bed are men
  Who do not often weep!
Laughter no more the house shall fill,
For Death is master at Gad's Hill!

INDEX.

CRITICAL NOTICES.

From the Christian Union.

"To all lovers of literary anecdote, and of gossip whose whispers are the murmurs of fame, the book will prove a refreshment in many a tired mood."

From the Boston Post.

"No more refreshing volume could be carried into the country or to the sea-shore, to fill in the niches of time which intervene between the pleasures of the summer holidays."

From the N. Y. World.

"We undertake to say that no one will feel the fatigue even of a long day's journey, if, in a Pullman car, he will undertake to satisfy himself with a 'Bric-a-Brac.'"

From the Congregationalist.

"It is of handy size, and with the pleasant tint of its paper, agreeable face of its type, and cover of odd device, has a generally 'natty' look which will make friends for it at once."

From the N. Y. Daily Times.

"One of the most compact, fresh, and entertaining volumes of literary and artistic *ana* that has lately been offered a public always eager for this precise variety of entertainment . . . . The editor has used his material with such admirable tact and skill that the reader glides insensibly from one paragraph into another, now amused, now instructed, but never wearied."

From the Boston Journal.

"A pleasanter volume than this, it has not been our fortune to happen upon for a long time. It is thoroughly delightful in style and manner, as it is unique in method."

From the N. Y. Evening Post.

"Mr. Stoddard's work appears to be done well-nigh perfectly. There is not a dull page in the book."

From the Worcester Gazette.

"We commend the book to the summer tourist who can be content with anything better than a novel, and will condescend to be amused."

From the Providence Press.

"The new 'Bric-a-Brac Series;' something unique and beautiful, both in design and execution . . . . If this first volume is a fair specimen of his judgment and skill, the series will prove first-class and popular, among lovers of pure literature."

From the Springfield Union.

"If we do not allow ourselves the luxury of quotation, it is because of a veritable *embarras de richesse* with such a collection of titbits to pick from. The get-up of the Bric-a-Brac Series is something quite unique and gorgeous."

From the Philadelphia Age.

"These reminiscences are highly interesting, as they not only give an insight into the every-day life of the individuals themselves (Chorley, Planché, and Young), but teem with anecdotes of the distinguished men and women with whom they associated or came in contact."

From the Buffalo Courier.

"Judging from the volume before us, none of these will be disappointed, for it is in reality a feast calculated to pique the dullest literary appetite, and spread in the daintiest possible way to boot. . . . . 'Infinite riches in a little room,' is the motto Mr. Stoddard has taken, and its spirit is faithfully kept in the sample of the series now given to the public."

www.ingramcontent.com/pod-product-compliance
Lightning Source LLC
LaVergne TN
LVHW020217110826
845151LV00003B/746

* 9 7 8 1 4 2 5 5 3 3 7 5 5 *